# "As Ever, Gene"

George Jean Nathan and Eugene O'Neill, Sea Island, Georgia, 1936. *(Courtesy of Cornell University Library.)*

# "*As Ever, Gene*"

The Letters of Eugene O'Neill to George Jean Nathan

*Transcribed and edited,*
*with introductory essays by*
Nancy L. Roberts and Arthur W. Roberts

Rutherford ● Madison ● Teaneck
Fairleigh Dickinson University Press
London and Toronto: Associated University Presses

Associated University Presses
440 Forsgate Drive
Cranbury, NJ 08512

Associated University Presses
25 Sicilian Avenue
London WC1A 2QH, England

Associated University Presses
2133 Royal Windsor Drive
Unit 1
Mississauga, Ontario
Canada L5J 1K5

The paper used in this publication meets the requirements
of the American National Standard for Permanence of Paper
for Printed Library Materials Z39.48-1984.

**Library of Congress Cataloging-in-Publication Data**

O'Neill, Eugene, 1888–1953.
  "As ever, Gene".

  Includes bibliographical references and index.
    1. O'Neill, Eugene, 1888–1953—Correspondence.
  2. Nathan, George Jean, 1882–1958—Correspondence.
  3. Dramatists, American—20th century—Correspondence.
  I. Nathan, George Jean, 1882–1958.   II. Roberts,
  Nancy L., 1954–   .   III. Roberts, Arthur W., 1926–
  IV. Title.
  PS3529.N5Z495   1987     812'.52 [B]       86-45800
  ISBN 0-8386-3303-X (alk. paper)

Printed in the United States of America

For Dodd Demas and Doris Pellettier Roberts

# CONTENTS

# FOREWORD

It is ironic in many respects that O'Neill should have come to national acclaim when he did. The United States in the early twentieth century was heady with growth and greatness as a world power. There was faith—some said self-deception—that the nation could solve any problem with old-fashioned common sense and self-sufficiency. As an age of optimism nurtured by a sense of grand national destiny in which sectional and ethnic differences would dissolve, the time hardly seemed right for a depressive like O'Neill whose characters often struggled with despair and futility of Nietzschean proportions.

But during his rise as the premier American playwright, O'Neill enjoyed critical and financial success unprecedented in the American theater. Unless one accepts a "great person" view of literary history, one must look to more than his artistic merit or development to explain this paradox—especially since he had yet to write his best plays.

Part of the answer lies in changes affecting the American marketplace for the arts. Primarily, the creation of a popularized American culture was a virtual precondition of O'Neill's success. Several factors certainly influenced the development of popularized culture in the late nineteenth century just before O'Neill began to write. These included a growing consciousness of what it meant to be "American," publishing practices, and the emergence of professional critics.

According to late nineteenth-century European and American littérateurs, America had not developed a strong native literature owing to its more than two centuries' preoccupation with westward settlement and expansion. The production of high art required men and women of leisure, so the theory went, and America's frenetic growth was a maelstrom that swallowed time and creative energy that otherwise might have flowed into artistic pursuits.

In contrast to the reigning theory about American literature, author Hamlin Garland argued that the experience of westward expansion actually was, and should be, the prime source of American identity and the sum and substance of a native literature. As historian Richard Hofstadter has pointed out, Garland's view was the literary equivalent of Frederick Jackson Turner's frontier thesis—that Americans became truly American in the experience of the West. In a sense, Garland simply ratified a trend in American literature that had been going on for better than a generation from Cooper to Twain. However, his pronouncement offered evidence of an increasing literary consciousness that Americans had a unique perspective to offer.

But the full development of a native American literature was stifled to some extent by the practice of publishing houses that supposed the American marketplace for arts and literature was composed primarily of women. Perhaps deferring to romanticized notions about feminine sensibilities, many municipal and self-appointed censors stood ready to suppress works of art that transgressed parochial but vague moral boundaries.

Furthermore, American publishing houses discouraged native writers by refusing to honor international copyrights. That had been national policy since the 1830s, with the result that American publishers shamelessly stole foreign (mainly British) works, paying no royalties to their authors. There was little pressure to sign royalty contracts with Americans when British and European works could be had only for the cost of publishing. However, in 1891, under pressure from American writers and newspapers, Congress for the first time ratified international copyright agreements.

But the U.S. market for arts had started to change by the early twentieth century. Lionel Trilling has observed that by the time O'Neill had begun to write, the art-patronizing public had swelled to include the "literate" as well as "intellectual" middle class. This expanding market fostered competition for audiences and set loose an interplay of influences forming public taste about what was good and bad in art.

One of these important influences was the emergence of full-time professional critics such as George Jean Nathan. Inclined by his European training and temperament to despise the naïve conceits that passed for American drama, Nathan also revolted against the "unholy alliance" of newspaper editors, critics, and Broadway producers who paid for favorable reviews to tighten their hold on public taste. Nathan and his colleague, Henry L. Mencken, were determined to change the taste of the literate middle class— by far the majority—which heretofore preferred simple, melodramatic tales running the gamut from Belasco to Zangwill. As they joined battle for the aesthetic hearts and minds of Americans, they were influenced partly by their predecessors of the "Bohemian" school of criticism—James Huneker, Percival Pollard, and Vance Thompson—who fired the first rounds in the 1890s.

Although considering himself a virtual critical anarchist ("All criticism is, to a lesser or greater degree, a convincing and indisputable lie"), Nathan argued that his training, background and erudition gave him a superior claim to influence public taste over those who produced or favorably reviewed "piffle for the proletariat." Like Mencken, Nathan contended that the average playgoer had neither the time nor the inclination to learn enough about drama fully to benefit from it. The critic functioned as a mediator of the aesthetic experience "to provoke a reaction" between playgoer and play. Nathan also believed that native American art flourished in an atmosphere of controversy. Critical ax-swinging as a personal manner thus fit nicely with his acknowledged goal of shattering reigning theatrical idols and enshrining O'Neill and others whom he considered superior.

Nathan and like-minded critics were looking for an American drama to call their own, and O'Neill appeared to be one of their best gambles. But while Nathan was highly conscious if bemused by this battle over public taste, so too was O'Neill, as several of his letters to the critic indicate. The playwright bubbled with grand plans to turn conventional American theater upon its head, particularly in the early years of his career. Nathan provided a willing ear and pen to accomplish a common objective: to change the focus of American dramatic taste and criticism from players and performances to plays and playwrights. The relationship between O'Neill and Nathan, which began as a symbiosis of aesthetic purpose, became friendship.

O'Neill had little control over the conditions of popularized American culture that first propelled him to notoriety. Despite Nathan's and other critics' efforts, O'Neill's public acclaim declined under a younger generation of critics, beginning in the 1930s. It is ironic that simultaneously his best work appeared: those plays that continue to tell truths about the human condition beyond the time, place, and circumstances of their creation. These later plays and the restoration of O'Neill's reputation give hope that there *is* artistic life after popular culture.

The letters herein, to which I was introduced in 1973 by Nathan's widow, Julie Haydon Nathan, who inspired this project, are a fascinating revelation of the magnificent and the mundane in O'Neill's growth as a dramatic artist. Unfortunately, Nathan's letters have not survived, but we have his many published observations about O'Neill to provide counterpoint. O'Neill's letters show him refining his dramatic skills, working through artistic quandaries, emotionally and physically rising and falling, encountering the stress of fame, fortune, and public expectations, and facing the difficulties of domestic life. They give the kind of insight one would wish to have about all important dramatists—Shakespeare, for instance. We are fortunate to have them about O'Neill.

John R. Finnegan, Jr.
School of Journalism and Mass Communication
University of Minnesota
Minneapolis

# PREFACE

Shortly after George Jean Nathan died in 1958, his alma mater, Cornell University, received as bequest many of his personal papers. Among them were three decades of correspondence from Nathan's most celebrated literary discovery, Eugene O'Neill. The 130 letters from the dramatist tell a fascinating story. Again and again, a master artist comments upon his own craftsmanship. Frequently O'Neill discusses the concepts behind various characters, scenes, and even whole works. Occasionally he muses candidly about his plans for future efforts, including the cycle of eleven plays he did not live to finish. In their entirety, O'Neill's letters to Nathan illuminate one of the most significant playwright-critic friendships in modern times.

It is now, alas, a one-sided correspondence, because Nathan's letters to O'Neill long ago disappeared. This has made our task as editors more challenging. And so we are grateful to Julie Haydon Nathan and to Patricia Angelin for sharing biographical information about Nathan that was all but impossible to unearth elsewhere.

We would like to thank the Board of Cornell University Library for graciously and speedily granting permission to publish the letters, as well as photographs from the George Jean Nathan Collection. We acknowledge the permission granted by Yale University to publish the letters.

We owe a considerable debt to John R. Finnegan, Jr., who first suggested this project. At every stage, he has provided inspiration, encouragement, and practical assistance in the truest spirit of scholarly cooperation. We are deeply grateful for his contribution.

We have benefited from the scholarship of many. They include O'Neill biographers Louis Sheaffer, Arthur Gelb, and Barbara Gelb; James M. Highsmith, who painstakingly documented the Cornell collection of O'Neill's letters to Nathan; and Jordan Miller and Roderick Robertson, whose work provided invaluable bibliographical leads. (Complete citations are given in the introductory essay for Part I.)

The staffs of several libraries came to our aid. We thank Donald Eddy, Curator; Lucy B. Burgess, Catherine Herbert, and Jim Tyler of the Department of Rare Books, Cornell University Library, for the cheerful and efficient dispatch with which they handled all our requests for information. We are also indebted to the University of Minnesota's Document Delivery,

Inter-Library Loan, and Reference staffs, particularly Kate Bergquist, Jennifer Lewis, and Nancy Soldatow; to the staff of the State University of New York College at Morrisville Library, especially Mike Gieryic, Phyllis Petersen, and Mary Lou Wasilewski; and to the Colgate University Library staff.

Nancy Roberts acknowledges with gratitude financial assistance from the National Endowment for the Humanities in the form of a Travel to Collections Grant, and from the University of Minnesota in the form of a Faculty Summer Research Fellowship. A Faculty Single-Quarter Leave speeded the completion of this project. I am grateful to all of my University of Minnesota colleagues for their encouragement and support, but especially to the late F. Gerald Kline, former director of the School of Journalism and Mass Communication.

Arthur Roberts gratefully acknowledges assistance in the form of a sabbatical leave granted by the State University of New York College at Morrisville. Among the many colleagues whose encouragement and support eased my work are James Dorland, Tom Glaser, Dennis Sands, and John R. Schiavone.

We have been heartened by the enthusiastic encouragement of our publisher, Thomas Yoseloff. Scholars have long appreciated his efforts to keep the works of Nathan in print.

We are indebted to our colleagues, George Hage of the University of Minnesota, Anne Klejment of the College of St. Thomas, and Renate Simpson of the State University of New York College at Morrisville, for their insightful criticisms of our work. Special thanks to John R. Finnegan, Jr., Jim Godfrey, and Sandy Munro for assistance with photographs.

Finally, we owe the greatest debt of thanks to our spouses, Dodd Demas and Doris Pellettier Roberts.

# EXPLANATION OF EDITORIAL METHOD

In preparing O'Neill's letters for publication, we have chosen to correct his frequent spelling errors. To a lesser degree, insofar as it inhibits easy understanding, we have corrected his faulty punctuation. Since his lack of prowess at both has already been well documented, we thought it permissible to make such corrections in the interest of readability.

Where the date on a letter or the location from which it was written is unclear but conjecturable from internal or other evidence, we have placed it in brackets.

Except where it seemed particularly important, we have not listed for each letter such characteristics as type of stationery (e.g., letterhead), page size, or writing (e.g., handwriting or typewriting). This information has already been carefully documented and published by James M. Highsmith (complete citation given in the introductory essay for Part I). Of the 130 letters, about one-half were handwritten.

Occasionally, Carlotta Monterey O'Neill added handwritten or typed postscripts to her husband's letters. It is impossible to reproduce her distinctive handwritten dashes, but we have tried to communicate their flavor by the use of two-em dashes.

# "As Ever,
## Gene"

PART I

*The Protégé and the Mentor*

# INTRODUCTORY ESSAY

Of all Eugene O'Neill's critic friends, none was so close, none so faithful, and none so essential as George Jean Nathan.[1] The Nobel Prize-winning playwright and the dean of drama critics built a friendship that grew ever closer over thirty years.[2] Its warmth and duration are perhaps surprising, for they differed both in function—one an artist, one a critic—and in temperament. Nathan was a boulevardier and bon vivant, six years O'Neill's senior. Of wealthy French-German parentage, he had enjoyed private schools and liberal studies in Europe. In 1900 he entered Cornell University, where he was a grand success. Slim, dark, with a boyishly round face, he was a star of the fencing team. As editor of both the student newspaper and the humor magazine, he wielded words with the same finesse. A favorite ploy for Nathan was the lampoon, where he could showcase his mordant wit. After his graduation in 1904, family connections opened the way, but Nathan's own brilliance quickly established his formidable reputation as a critic of the drama, his chosen journalistic domain. For half a century, in *Smart Set,* which he founded in 1914 and coedited with H. L. Mencken, and then in the *American Mercury, Vanity Fair, Judge,* and scores of other publications here and abroad, Nathan's criticism would reign over the theater.

By 1907, Nathan had already fashioned himself an ordered life. He took up quarters in the Royalton Hotel, within walking distance of New York's theater district. There he would reside until his death fifty years later. A favorite pastime was dining with friends whose intelligence and sophistication approximated his own. Nathan, who favored London-tailored suits and French cuffs, was the consummate dandy.[3] He was born in 1882 on Valentine's Day, an ironic date, for he reserved some of his most caustic criticism for the institution of marriage. While O'Neill would marry three times, Nathan remained a bachelor until 1955, when he wed the actress Julie Haydon. Through most of his life he remained an avowed agnostic, at peace with himself (although shortly before his death in 1958, he converted to Roman Catholicism). He was "an iconoclast, a gourmet and self-professed hedonist, a superior intellect acutely aware of his own superiority, an American Original who cultivated his originality."[4] Perhaps Nathan's most characteristic expression was a smile of amusement at the foibles of the human race.

In contrast, Eugene Gladstone O'Neill was a man tormented by guilt.[5]

George Jean Nathan. *(Courtesy of Cornell University Library.)*

George Jean Nathan. *(Courtesy of Cornell University Library.)*

He had a mouth that in repose turned downward—suggesting his stark view of the world. Though Nathan would claim O'Neill "can laugh"[6] with the best of them and was "no . . . sourball,"[7] other intimates reported him as pensive, often morose—a private man who sometimes sat brooding even as friends in the same room were holding a revel. The punch line that would call forth an explosion of mirth from Nathan would often elicit only an enigmatic smile from O'Neill.

Somehow the friendship grew until the two became as brothers. In 1933 Nathan could write, "I have eaten, drunk, walked, motored, bicycled, slept, shaved, edited, run, worked, played, even sung with him."[8] And O'Neill, later on, would fondly dream a little of opening a saloon with his friend.[9]

O'Neill's origins were more modest than Nathan's. His father James was an Irish immigrant of little formal education. As a young actor, he had once been favorably compared with Edwin Booth. But the elder O'Neill had squandered his substantial talent in a single melodrama, playing the lucrative but banal role of the Count of Monte Cristo for decades. Ella Quinlan O'Neill, the playwright's mother, was convent-bred and devout. Her sheltered upbringing had little prepared her for the trials of an actor's wife. During Eugene's childhood, the family accompanied James O'Neill as he starred in hundreds of performances around the country. But it was not a happy existence for Eugene, for both parents were preoccupied with their own problems. This rootlessness was not remedied when, like his older brother Jamie, a talented actor who would die an alcoholic, Eugene was shunted off to boarding school at seven.

Separated during the acting season, the family spent summers in New London, Connecticut, a town with lots of tourists and much for a young boy to do. But one terrible night in 1903, the fourteen-year-old Eugene was devastated by a revelation that would haunt him the rest of his life. His mother Ella, stupefied by morphine, tried to drown herself in the nearby Thames River. Jamie told him then that she had suffered from drug addiction ever since Eugene's birth, when the doctor had prescribed morphine for her pains. Horrified by this linking of his very existence with his mother's anguish and attempted suicide, O'Neill would always blame himself for her addiction.

But all was not dark at home. During Ella's normal periods, which sometimes lasted for months, the family atmosphere brightened considerably. The playwright's only comedy, *Ah, Wilderness!* celebrates these glimpses of what family life could be.

As his biographers have shown, O'Neill's childhood experiences left him with a tangled web of feelings toward his family. In adolescence, his reaction took the form of rebellion against his Catholic faith because, despite his prayers, his mother remained an addict. Later he turned to alcohol, flunked out of Princeton, and began to frequent saloons and whorehouses. By the time he was twenty-one he had fathered a son during a brief marriage, gone off hunting gold to Honduras where he contracted malaria, returned, and sailed off again, this time to Argentina.

All the while, his talent was stirring. From his earliest days he had been an avid reader, especially affected by Baudelaire, Nietzsche, Strindberg and Swinburne, and, to a lesser degree, by the American anarchist Benjamin R. Tucker. In his own right he sought to be a poet and he wrote continually. He became destitute in Argentina, labored at the most menial of jobs, worked his way back to New York on a freighter and then, after shipping out to Southampton, returned in 1911 to live in a sleazy room above a saloon in lower Manhattan. Troubled by a love-hate ambivalence toward parents and brother, he would find what resolution he could through his plays, ultimately through the highly autobiographical *Long Day's Journey Into Night*, one of his last.

All his life, Eugene O'Neill tended to see the world in sad hues. Many described him as gentle and shy. But sometimes the weight of his introspection proved too ponderous. Then he was known to go on an occasional rampage, ripping pictures from walls and overturning furniture. By 1912, O'Neill's depression over family estrangement and his failure to find a satisfying direction in life finally sank into despair. One winter night in his flophouse room above Jimmy the Priest's (James J. Condon's saloon at 252 Fulton Street), he turned his destructive impulses upon himself. He swallowed a toxic dose of Veronal, a sedative not unlike the morphine to which his mother had so long been addicted.

He had lapsed into a coma when a friend found and rescued him. The episode was the turning point. After a bout with tuberculosis, from which he quickly recovered, he did a stint as a reporter for the *New London Telegraph*. Then—by his account it was 1913—he decided to be a dramatist. Losing little time, O'Neill completed his formal education with a playwriting course at Harvard, briefly tried screenwriting, and quickly turned onto the path that would lead to unrivaled success, writing for the legitimate stage. Intent upon production, he wrote one-act plays one after another as he honed his skills.

Sometime in 1917, O'Neill and Nathan began exchanging letters (the earliest ones have been long since lost).[10] They met at last in New York in May 1919. Accounts vary as to when and how. According to Nathan, they met at the *Smart Set* offices at Eighth Avenue and Thirty-fourth Street.[11] Relying upon O'Neill's unclear memory much later as their evidence, his biographers Arthur and Barbara Gelb report that the meeting occurred at the Beaux Arts restaurant.[12] O'Neill's account, contained in a letter he wrote from Bermuda to Nathan's biographer Isaac Goldberg (14 June 1926) admitted the playwright couldn't "for the life of me recall much about my first meeting with Nathan. It was with John D. Williams at some restaurant, I believe, and I was three-fourths 'blotto.' I remember thinking how much he looked like an old friend of mine who wrote animal stories at that era for Street and Smith."[13]

Playwright and critic were mutually impressed. O'Neill found Nathan "warm and friendly and human" where he "half-expected an aloof and caustic intelligence completely enveloping and hiding the living being. *Half*-expected,—for his letters to me had given me an inkling."[14] Nathan "found O'Neill to be an extremely shy fellow, but one who nevertheless appeared to have a vast confidence in himself . . . O'Neill is a deep-running personality,—the most ambitious mind I have encountered among American dramatists,—an uncommon talent."[15]

Nathan, the established critic, was in a position to give the promising young playwright a boost. And he had strong motivation to do so, for he was not pleased by the current state of American drama. In the first two decades of the twentieth century, plays followed the successful grooves of the past. Some were overly romantic, many were trite, and most lackluster. In fiction and poetry such masters as Twain, James, and Whitman had shaped a distinctive native tradition. The nation was discovering Melville and Dickinson. But counterparts in the American theater had not materialized. In Europe, drama had been profoundly altered by the imaginative vitality of playwrights such as Ibsen, Hauptmann, Maeterlinck, and Shaw. The best that America could offer seemed to be the shallow melodramas of Augustus Thomas, the superficial satires of Clyde Fitch, and the transient spectaculars of David Belasco.

"In the last half dozen years, I doubt if there have been more than five or six plays out of all the many hundred-odd presented in each season that have merited approach by the critic seriously interested in drama," Nathan charged in 1917. "The rest? Trick melodramas, fussy farces, mob mush, leg shows."[16]

This escapist drama was to be challenged, for Nathan's disgust reflected a growing national mood. The world war had been bloody. One hundred thousand men killed by bayonet, bullet, cannon or poison gas was shocking news. And the most brutal battles seemed to be succeeded only by further slaughter in a crescendo of horror. The savagery and the scale of the war, magnified by twentieth-century technology, made many question human-kind's values, even its fundamental nature. There grew an audience, hitherto undetected, ready to support serious drama. If art is the reflection of a people's vision, the American mirror was turning inward.

While Nathan awaited a new and original voice in American dramaturgy, O'Neill was writing. In 1915 he joined the Provincetown Players on Cape Cod, an amateur group dedicated to experimental theater, whose other novices included Susan Glaspell, George "Jig" Cook, Robert Edmond Jones, and Kenneth Macgowan. *Bound East for Cardiff,* O'Neill's first staged play, was produced for the Provincetowners' second season in July 1916, to great acclaim. By the fall of 1916, *Bound East* was produced in Greenwich Village in the Provincetown Players' new Macdougal Street theater. On 13 November 1916, O'Neill and the Provincetowners got their first notice from a professional critic, Stephen Rathbun of the *New York Evening Sun*, who singled out *Bound East* as the best of the bill. Writing in the *New York Herald Tribune* on 30 January 1917, Heywood Broun praised *Bound East* for its "mood and atmosphere," its "successful approximation" of the sailors' "true talk."[17]

What Nathan thought of *Bound East* and other early O'Neill plays at the time is unrecorded, but many years later he dismissed *Thirst*, an early (1916) work, as "wholly negligible and plainly the work of a novice," and *Before Breakfast* (1916) as "a trifle." But in *Bound East for Cardiff*, he discerned "the first indication of a significant new dramatic talent. A striking performance containing the seed of its author's future mental cast."[18]

Although he was immersed in the Provincetowners' activities, O'Neill in 1917–18 continued to seek out his old Greenwich Village cronies at the "Hell Hole," a shabby bar at the southeast corner of Sixth Avenue and Fourth Street that he later immortalized in *The Iceman Cometh*. They included poet Maxwell Bodenheim, the Irish anarchist Terry Carlin, and Dorothy Day, a journalist for the *Masses* who would later cofound the Catholic Worker movement and its paper of the same name. One night a brooding O'Neill recited all of Francis Thompson's poem, "The Hound of Heaven," to Day. She was fascinated by the applicability of its theme, God's pursuit of the soul, to O'Neill, the solitary Catholic apostate. While the playwright would never resolve his religious skepticism, his loneliness was assuaged for a time when, one night in the Hell Hole, he met Agnes Boulton, a magazine short-story writer. They married on 12 April 1918.

The season of 1917–18 saw four O'Neill "fo'c'sle" plays presented in New York: *In the Zone* (produced by the Washington Square Players), and *The Long Voyage Home*, *Ile*, and *The Rope* (produced by the Provincetown Players). All, especially *In the Zone* and *The Rope*, were praised by the New York critics, who liked the blend of realism and experimental forms. On the basis of O'Neill's early sea plays, Barrett H. Clark pronounced him "our most promising native dramatist" in the spring of 1919.[19]

George Jean Nathan had seen some of the Provincetown Players' productions in 1916–17, but his first true review of an O'Neill drama did not appear until January 1918, when he evaluated *In the Zone* in *Smart Set*. The critic praised O'Neill as "one of the most promising men [to] come in several years the way of the American theatre."[20] "Until Eugene O'Neill came along," Nathan wrote later of the *S.S. Glencairn* cycle (consisting of *The Moon of the Caribbees*, *Bound East for Cardiff*, *In the Zone*, and *The Long Voyage Home*, each of which had been produced separately by the Provincetowners and the Washington Square Players), "the American stage knew the sea only as a large piece of canvas painted blue and agitated from underneath by three or four husky members of the Stagehands' Local." O'Neill, Nathan continued, "made the stage canvas smell less of paint and more of salt; he made the stage sailor smell less of rouge and more of rum and actuality."[21]

As Nathan quickly recognized, O'Neill was a major talent. He emerged foremost among those who, from 1916 to 1924, changed the character and imagination of American drama, giving it a previously unglimpsed depth, vitality, and inventiveness. And since the reception of artistic revolutionaries is rarely assured, the young playwright especially appreciated Nathan's early support. The critic's advocacy resulted in the influential publication of three plays in the brilliant and respected *Smart Set* (*The Long Voyage Home*, October 1917; *Ile*, May 1918; and *The Moon of the Caribbees*, August 1918). Such exposure, his first true recognition, earned the fledgling dramatist a reading audience and boosted his confidence immeasurably. It was Nathan, too, who successfully brought *Beyond the Horizon* to Broadway producer John D. Williams; the critic also evangelized for other early O'Neill plays.

However, the incisive Nathan did not fail to point out where he believed O'Neill went wrong, even in those heady days of first recognition. "His weakness is the weakness of italics and monotony," Nathan wrote in 1920 in *Smart Set*. "He sees life too often as drama. The great dramatist is the dramatist who sees drama as life."[22] Yet in the same article the critic also asserted that "of all the playwrights America has produced in the last dozen years," clearly only one—Eugene O'Neill—rose "above the local crowd." This was to be Nathan's major theme in the early years of O'Neill's career, and such support helped him win serious consideration from producers and a public accustomed to far more conventional dramatic fare. By the early 1920s, O'Neill had been noticed by foreign critics, as well; the Viennese Hugo von Hofmannsthal in 1923 judged such plays as *The Emperor Jones*, *Anna Christie*, and *The Hairy Ape* to be "clear-cut and sharp in outline, solidly constructed from beginning to end."[23]

The playwright's earliest preserved letters to his mentor, starting in 1919, exude a youthful buoyancy. O'Neill always seemed most pleased with a new play immediately after he had finished it, although later, more leisurely reflection sometimes altered his initial appraisals. This may be expected, considering the striking unevenness of his work, not only in this early period but nearly to the close of his career. As O'Neill biographer Louis Sheaffer has noted, O'Neill produced, almost alternately, good plays and bad.[24]

But while the dross of 1919–26 is considerable—for instance, *Exorcism* (1919), which O'Neill later destroyed; *Gold* (1920); *Welded* (1923)—the dramatist also created outstanding, creatively unconventional plays such as

*The Emperor Jones* (1921), the Pulitzer Prize-winning *Anna Christie* (1922), and *Beyond the Horizon*. The latter also won a Pulitzer and launched its author on Broadway in 1920, thus establishing him as a major new talent. Reviewing *Beyond*, critics of the stature of the *New York Times*'s Alexander Woollcott praised its "elements of greatness."[25] As expected, Nathan, who had arranged O'Neill's debut in the pages of *Smart Set*, stepped forward to acclaim his discovery, judging *Beyond* as "a manuscript of uncommon native quality," although he gently criticized the playwright's tendency "at times to underscore a trifle too heavily." The critic concluded that "by all odds he is the most important newcomer the American stage has greeted in many years."[26]

Nathan's endorsement meant even more when other critics were unkind. Not only some reviewers, but the general public expressed outrage at *All God's Chillun Got Wings*, in which O'Neill dared to explore the problems of a white woman married to a black man. When the play was published in the February 1924 *American Mercury*, nearly three months before its presentation by the Provincetown Players, it provoked a bitter assault. National newspaper stories sensationalized the racial aspect of the play, while church organizations and women's groups passed resolutions condemning it as immoral. Many, including the president of the Society for the Prevention of Vice, worried that production of *All God's Chillun* would provoke a breach of the public peace.

Nathan eloquently championed O'Neill in the May 1924 *American Mercury* before the play was even produced, asserting that it offered "absolutely nothing . . . that is in the slightest degree offensive to any human being above the mental level of an apple dumpling. . . . To object . . . because it treats of miscegenation is to object to the drama 'Othello' . . . or to the opera 'L'Africaine,' or to the Kipling story of 'Georgie Porgie.' "[27] Ultimately, *All God's Chillun* saw production in May 1924 as planned. Most critics were lukewarm, some carping; but all the notoriety and doubtless Nathan's words gave the play a long run.

The critic also saw the playwright through the attempted censorship of *Desire Under the Elms* (1924), which treated controversial themes of incest and infanticide. Although he judged it unequal to O'Neill's earlier efforts, Nathan found it "far and away so much better than most of the plays being written by anyone else who hangs around here that one gratefully passes over even its obvious deficiencies."[28]

Eager for recognition, the young O'Neill labored over his plays and their productions, usually becoming so involved with the latter that he had little energy left for anything else. Accordingly, many of his letters to Nathan, written in the heat of playwriting and production, are impersonal, containing much shoptalk and single-minded discussion of O'Neill's art. They illuminate the intensity of the dramatist's mind at work, his singular devotion to the tragic characters with whom he peopled his plays, to the point that he often neglected family and friends.

Although he might be agitated by grave personal problems, O'Neill scarcely revealed them in his early correspondence with Nathan. Nor was Nathan his confidant in person, for their meetings were comparatively infrequent during this time. As his biographers have shown, O'Neill could take years to reveal aspects of himself to another. Thus he required a full year to abandon the rather formal salutation, "My dear Mr. Nathan," in favor of "Dear Mr. Nathan"; and more than a decade to employ "Dear George." Similarly, O'Neill signed his first preserved letter in 1919 as "Very sincerely yours, Eugene G. O'Neill," and not until the following year was it "Sincerely, Eugene O'Neill." A decade more passed before it became "As ever, Gene." The gradual deepening of the bond between the two men can thus be traced.

Certain psychological needs of the playwright probably fostered the relationship. In many ways Nathan was like O'Neill's brother Jamie. Both were acutely intelligent, witty, talented dandies. Both enjoyed alcohol, night life, and the company of women. But they differed in direction and discipline. Jamie was, like his brother Eugene, a troubled man. He dissipated his energies by excess and eventually drank himself to death. Nathan, by contrast, followed a controlled, precise routine. Daily he isolated himself in his rooms at the Royalton and wrote. Later, he enjoyed cocktails, dinner, and, as a critic, went to the theater. Meetings in restaurants in the theater district with close friends characterized his social life. His romantic liaisons were always tasteful and discreet. In short, Nathan, six years older than O'Neill, was a visible reminder of what O'Neill's beloved brother Jamie might have been.

While Nathan for most of his life lived in one place, the Royalton Hotel, O'Neill was a lifelong nomad. The years 1919–26 saw him shuttling among New York, Provincetown, Ridgefield (Connecticut), and Bermuda. He required absolute solitude to write, ideally near the sea, which all his life had an unusually invigorating, almost mystical effect on him. And so the O'Neill family—Agnes Boulton and their children Shane (born 1919) and Oona (born 1925)—moved frequently to accommodate his needs. In 1929 O'Neill divorced Boulton to marry Carlotta Monterey, an actress; at the time the dramatist characteristically never hinted in his letters to Nathan of the domestic turmoil in which he was engulfed. Nor did he call upon him to aid him in this then-illicit romance. If O'Neill looked up to Nathan as an idealized version of Jamie, he wished to present only his best side to the critic. Thus O'Neill asked not Nathan but Kenneth Macgowan to deliver roses to Carlotta in New York.

O'Neill's life in the years 1919–26 continued his already established pattern. Overwhelmed by relentless personal guilt, he went on marathon drinking binges. These were invariably followed by episodes of maudlinism, depression, and endless self-recrimination. By all accounts he was difficult to live with, haunted by a family at least as troubled as any of his characters. In this period, he was immersed in his lifelong struggle to come to grips with his anguish over his parents and brother, each of whom died within a few years of the others—James in 1920, Ella in 1922, and Jamie in 1923. Only in the last two years before his father's death did O'Neill achieve any kind of reconciliation with the retired actor, and he was immensely grateful that the old man lived long enough to see him launched on Broadway.

By 1926, O'Neill's star was shining over the American theater, although it would take him several years more to find his truest voice in plays such as *Mourning Becomes Electra, The Iceman Cometh,* and *Long Day's Journey Into Night.* His first preserved letters to Nathan reveal some of the musings, plans, and dreams that he would later incorporate into such masterworks.

## NOTES

1. Helpful sources covering Nathan's criticism are: Constance Frick, *The Dramatic Criticism of George Jean Nathan* (Ithaca: Cornell University Press, 1943); Charles Angoff, "Introduction" to *The World of George Jean Nathan,* ed. Charles Angoff (New York: Alfred A. Knopf, 1952); and Seymour Rudin, "George Jean Nathan: A Study of His Criticism" (Ph.D. diss., Cornell University, 1953). Aspects of Nathan's criticism are indexed in Arthur S. Ruffino, "A Cumulative Index to the Books of George Jean Nathan" (Ph.D. diss., Southern Illinois University, 1971).

2. Chronicled by Roderick Robertson, "The Friendship of Eugene O'Neill and George Jean Nathan" (Ph.D. diss., University of Wisconsin, 1970).

3. Charles Angoff, "George Jean Nathan: Superlative Dandy," *New Republic* 150 (4 January 1964): 17.

4. Louis Sheaffer, *O'Neill: Son and Playwright* (Boston: Little, Brown and Co, 1968), 453.

5. The most complete collection of O'Neill sources is Jordan Y. Miller, *Eugene O'Neill and the American Critic: A Bibliographical Checklist,* 2d ed., rev. (Hamden, Conn.: Archon Books, 1973).

6. George Jean Nathan, "The Cosmopolite of the Month," *Cosmopolitan* 102 (February 1937): 11.

7. George Jean Nathan, "The Bright Face of Tragedy," *Cosmopolitan* 143 (August 1957): 66.

8. George Jean Nathan, "O'Neill," *Vanity Fair* 41 (October 1933): 54.

9. Arthur Gelb and Barbara Gelb, *O'Neill* (New York: Harper and Brothers, 1962), 870.

10. An excellent introduction to Cornell University's collection of O'Neill's letters to Nathan is James M. Highsmith, "A Description of the Cornell Collection of Eugene O'Neill's Letters to George Jean Nathan," *Modern Drama* 14 (February 1972): 420–25 and "The Cornell Letters: Eugene O'Neill on His Craftsmanship to George Jean Nathan," *Modern Drama* 14 (May 1972): 68–88.

11. Isaac Goldberg, *The Theatre of George Jean Nathan* (New York: Simon and Schuster, 1926), 76.

12. Gelb and Gelb, *O'Neill,* 391.

13. Goldberg, *The Theatre of George Jean Nathan,* 77.

14. Goldberg, *The Theatre of George Jean Nathan,* 77.

15. Goldberg, *The Theatre of George Jean Nathan,* 76–77.

16. George Jean Nathan, *Mr. George Jean Nathan Presents* (New York: Alfred A. Knopf, 1917), 172–73.

17. Heywood Broun, "News of the Theatres," *New York Herald Tribune,* 30 January 1917.

18. George Jean Nathan, "The Theatre: O'Neill: A Critical Summation," *American Mercury* 63 (December 1946): 714.

19. *New York Sun,* 18 May 1919.

20. George Jean Nathan, "The Chewing Gum Drama," *Smart Set* 54 (January 1918): 134.

21. George Jean Nathan, "O'Neill Steams Into Port," *Judge* 87 (29 November 1924): 10, 11.

22. George Jean Nathan, "The American Playwright," *Smart Set* 62 (July 1920): 133.

23. Hugo von Hofmannsthal, "Eugene O'Neill," *The Freeman,* 21 March 1923.

24. Louis Sheaffer, *O'Neill: Son and Artist* (Boston: Little, Brown and Co., 1973), 47.

25. Alexander Woollcott, *New York Times,* 8 February 1920.

26. George Jean Nathan, "The Hooligan at the Gate," *Smart Set* 61 (April 1920): 135.

27. George Jean Nathan, "The Theatre," *American Mercury* 2 (May 1924): 113–14.

28. George Jean Nathan, "The Kahn-game," *Judge* 87 (6 December 1924): 26.

# LETTERS: MAY 1919–DECEMBER 1925

West Point Pleasant, N.J.[1]
May 1st 1919.

My dear Mr. Nathan:

I am sending under separate cover, for Mr. Mencken[2] and yourself, two volumes of my book[3] which has just appeared. I hope you will accept them as small remembrances that I remember how much of gratitude I owe both of you for your encouragement and constructive criticism. I feel that in a great measure the book is already yours since you published three of the plays[4] and had the very first peep at one of the others.

Your name, it appears, does not adorn the jacket in spite of the fact that, when I suggested to Boni and Liveright that they use what recognized critics had said about my work for the cover instead of any self-appointed boost, I carefully placed some words of yours[5] regarding *The Moon of the Caribbees*[6] at the head of the list. All this matter is puerile, of course; but as I value your commendation more than that of all the others put together, it rather makes me peevish.

One of my two new long plays—*Chris. Christophersen*[7]—is typed and now in the hands of the agent. (Yes, Williams'[8] dilatory tactics drove me to an agent—The American Play Company). Williams probably has it by this time since my contract with him gives him first choice on future plays. I intended sending you a copy at once but I find my two carbons need doctoring and so will wait until my next trip to New York—about the middle of the month—when I shall bring it around to the office personally in the hope of finally meeting you.[9]

With sincerest regards to Mr. Mencken and yourself,

Very sincerely yours,
Eugene G. O'Neill.

---

1. The former home of Mrs. O'Neill (Agnes Boulton), within easy commuting distance from New York City.

2. Henry Louis Mencken (1880–1956), who coedited *Smart Set* and the *American Mercury* with Nathan.

3. Refers to *Moon of the Caribbees and Six Other Plays of the Sea* (New York: Boni and

33

Liveright, June 1919), which contained the four *Glencairn* tales *(The Moon of the Caribbees, Bound East for Cardiff, The Long Voyage Home, and In the Zone)*, as well as *Ile, The Rope,* and *Where the Cross Is Made. (Zone, The Rope,* and *Cross* received their first publication in this volume.)

4. *The Long Voyage Home* appeared in *Smart Set* 53 (October 1917): 83–94; *Ile,* in *Smart Set* 55 (May 1918): 89–100; *The Moon of the Caribbees,* in *Smart Set* 55 (August 1918): 73–86. Merely seeking criticism, O'Neill sent the plays to H. L. Mencken, who approvingly passed them on to his *Smart Set* coeditor, Nathan. The critic also liked them and the plays were published, giving O'Neill his most significant recognition to that date.

5. Probably contained in a letter from Nathan to O'Neill (not extant); eventually the critic's comments found their way into Boni and Liveright's 1923 reissue of the book (as part of the new Modern Library series). In his Introduction to the 1923 edition, Nathan wrote: "notably in . . . 'The Moon of the Caribbees,' one detects the first springs of a talent that, rapidly coming to flower in succeeding longer plays, is at the present time surely the finest in the American theatre" (Nathan, Introduction to Eugene O'Neill, *The Moon of the Caribbees and Six Other Plays of the Sea* [New York: Boni and Liveright, The Modern Library, 1923], vii).

6. *The Moon of the Caribbees* was first produced in New York on 20 December 1918, second bill, Playwrights' Theatre; directed by Thomas Mitchell. (It appeared again as part of the four-act composite, *S. S. Glencairn,* produced 3 November 1924.)

7. Copyrighted as *Chris Christopherson,* the play was later renamed *The Ole Davil,* then *Anna Christie.*

8. John D. Williams, New York producer.

9. O'Neill and Nathan finally met in May 1919.

Provincetown, Mass.[1]
Nov. 4, 1919.

My dear Mr. Nathan:

Your letter and the script arrived by the same mail. That you found genuine merit in *The Straw*[2] is the most encouraging boost to my spirits I have received since the play was written. Your stamp of approval gives me renewed confidence in my own valuation.

The Theatre Guild[3] have seen the play and rejected it. They said it was most excellent but not the kind of play for their public. Since *John Ferguson*[4] inoculated them with the virus of popular success—quite contrary to their expectations—I'm afraid they've become woefully worried about the supposed tastes of "their public." I speak not only from my own experience. Before *Ferguson* set them on horseback they had decided to do Susan Glaspell's[5] *Bernice* this season. But now they have discovered "their public" would never—And the latest I hear is that James K. Hackett is to star for them in *Silas Lapham.*[6] My God! The trouble seems to be that you can't eliminate the weakness of the old Washington Square Players[7] by merely changing the name. In my opinion the Guild is doomed to fail through the same timid endeavor to please "their public."

No, even Al Woods[8] is preferable to a success-ridden Guild. He, at least, has few inhibitions. And, although I know *The Straw* stands but small chance with them, I'll have to put my trust in Tyler,[9] Hopkins[10] and

George Jean Nathan and H. L. Mencken, enfants terribles who became partners in promoting a rebellion in American literature through *Smart Set* and the *American Mercury. (Courtesy of Cornell University Library.)*

Williams. Williams has stated that he is willing to reopen negotiations for the play in case I should not sell it elsewhere. As I told you, he was much taken by it, wanted it, but was very vague as to when he could produce.

In the light of the Guild's rejection for popular reasons, I'm sure you'll be interested to know that the Selwyns[11] almost took the play. In a moment of aberration the agent submitted a script to them, and they actually hovered on the brink of acceptance for days. They were quite impressed by its possibilities, it seems. They and Williams are the only commercial managers to pass on it so far.

I'm in daily expectation of a Tyler decision. I wish Hopkins would give it a hearing, but my experience with *Chris* makes me think it's next to impossible to get him to read a play.[12] However, I'm going to have a try at him.

Boni and Liveright are to publish both *Chris*[13] and *Beyond The Horizon*[14] this winter. Perhaps they might do *The Straw* later.

I don't expect to be in New York before the middle of next month but will surely drop in when I do come.

My sincerest gratitude for your words of encouragement. They certainly mean a lot to me!

Cordially,
Eugene O'Neill.

---

1. Remodeled former Coast Guard station on Peaked Hill Bar, Provincetown.
2. Presented 10 November 1921, Greenwich Village Theatre; produced by George C. Tyler. Copyrighted 19 November 1919; published April 1921, by Boni and Liveright, New York, in a volume also containing *The Emperor Jones* and *Diff'rent* (This was the first of a series naming two or more plays on the title page. These volumes often appeared before the plays were produced and were sometimes given newspaper reviews.)
3. A burgeoning new organization, headed by Lawrence Langner (1890–1962), Philip Moeller (1880–1958), actress Helen Westley (1879–1942), and others from the old Washington Square Players.
4. Play by English writer St. John Ervine, presented just as New York's actors, organized by Actors' Equity, went on strike. *John Ferguson*'s non-Equity cast played to full houses for a much longer run than would otherwise have been the case.
5. American playwright and novelist (1882–1948) who, with her husband George ("Jig") Cram Cook, founded and headed the Provincetown Players starting in the summer of 1915, in order to support the serious American drama that the commercial stage was overlooking. The Provincetown Players gave O'Neill his start.
6. O'Neill may have felt justified when the Theatre Guild's production of *Silas Lapham* was "a failure in every way," as he told his wife Agnes Boulton on 29 January 1920 (Sheaffer, *O'Neill: Son and Playwright*, 476).
7. Parent organization of the Theatre Guild. The Players group was founded in the winter of 1914, dissolved in 1918, and returned in 1919 as the Theatre Guild.
8. Albert Herman Woods, New York producer (1870–1951).
9. George C. Tyler (1867–1946), New York producer, was the manager and close friend of the elder James O'Neill. At first Tyler overlooked Eugene O'Neill's talent, believing that his friend showed him his son's plays merely out of parental pride. In 1921, he staged *The Straw*.
10. Arthur Hopkins, New York producer (1878–1950).
11. Archibald ("Arch") (1877?–1959) and Edgar (1875–1944) Selwyn, New York producers who ran the Selwyn Theatre, where *The Emperor Jones* (1920) and *Diff'rent* (1921) played. The Selwyns co-produced *Welded* with O'Neill, Kenneth Macgowan, and Robert Edmond Jones at the Thirty-ninth Street Theatre, New York (1924).
12. Arthur Hopkins, New York producer. He never did give *Chris* a reading.
13. Never appeared in print; was tried on the stage unsuccessfully in Atlantic City and Philadelphia, withdrawn, rewritten, and appeared first as *The Ole Davil*, then as *Anna Christie*, which won a Pulitzer Prize in May 1922.
14. *Beyond the Horizon* was published by Boni and Liveright, New York, March 1920; copyrighted 7 June and 5 August 1917.

Provincetown, Mass.
March 12, 1920.

My dear Mr. Nathan:

This is a late day for me to be writing to thank you for your note of congratulation, but I really have a valid excuse. I have been up to my ears in

Provincetown, Mass.
March 12, 1920

My dear Mr. Nathan:

This is a late day for me to be writing to thank you for your note of congratulations, but I really have a valid excuse. I have been up to my ears in troubles ever since the opening date of "Beyond". First my mother acquired the flu with a touch of pneumonia; then I caught it from her and was laid up in the hotel for four weeks; then my father had a stroke and has been dangerously ill ever since; then, just as I was tottering up to my first "Chris" rehearsals, I received a wire from here calling me to return to a very sick wife! Can you beat it! If this be the payment demanded of me for the big splash made by "Beyond", then I am tempted to remark with Jurgen that "it does not seem quite fair."

Thank you again for your note. I am sure glad "Beyond The Horizon" pleased its godfather.

Sincerely,
Eugene O'Neill.

P.S.

I want to write you much more than this but I'm still too upset mentally, so I'll postpone it.

O'Neill's letter dated 12 March 1920. (The numeral three at the top of the page—designating this as the third letter in the Cornell collection—was added later.) (Courtesy of Cornell University Library.)

troubles ever since the opening date of *Beyond*.[1] First my mother acquired the flu with a touch of pneumonia; then I caught it from her and was laid up in the hotel for four weeks; then my father had a stroke and has been dangerously ill ever since; then, just as I was tottering up to my first *Chris* rehearsals, I received a wire from here calling me to return to a very sick wife! Can you beat it! If this be the payment demanded of me for the big splash made by *Beyond*, then I am tempted to remark with Jurgen[2] that "it does not seem quite fair."

Thank you again for your note. I am sure glad *Beyond the Horizon* pleased its godfather.

Sincerely,
Eugene O'Neill.

P.S.

I want to write you much more than this but I'm still too upset mentally, so I'll postpone it.

---

1. *Beyond the Horizon* was first presented 2 February 1920, by John D. Williams in a special matinee at Broadway's Morosco Theatre; it won O'Neill his first Pulitzer Prize in June 1920.

The production of *Beyond* required about two years, a delay O'Neill found extremely frustrating. He was grateful that his father, with whom he had only recently become reconciled, lived long enough to see the play and perceive his success. (James O'Neill died on 10 August 1920.)

*Beyond* reaped a considerable share of praise from the critics, including Alexander Woollcott, who pronounced O'Neill a "gifted writer" and the play "so full of meat" that it made the rest of the season's offerings "look like the merest meringue" (*New York Times*, 4 February 1920); and, of course, Nathan. He called it "a manuscript of uncommon native quality . . . O'Neill can grasp atmosphere as no other writer for our theater can . . . he is by all odds the most important newcomer the American stage has greeted in many years" ("The Hooligan at the Gate," *Smart Set* 61 (April 1921): 135).

2. A reference to the character Jurgen in James Branch Cabell's *Jurgen: A Comedy of Justice* (New York: Robert M. McBride & Co., 1919).

Provincetown, Mass.
June 19, 1920.

Dear Mr. Nathan:[1]

Many thanks for your note. It is darned encouraging to learn that you think *Gold*[2] is a progressive step beyond *Beyond*. Your verdict is the more welcome because I was beginning to have doubts about it myself. I gave Williams[3] all my scripts of the play right after finishing it, have not had a chance to look at it since, and so, lacking all proof to the contrary, was commencing to wonder what it was all about, and whether I had at all accomplished what I set out to do.

I suppose I shall be credited on all sides with having made *Where The Cross Is Made*[4] into a long play—yet the reverse is the real truth. The idea of *Gold* was a long play one from its inception. I merely took the last act situation and jammed it into the one-act form because I wanted to be represented on the Provincetown Players' opening bill two seasons ago and had nothing else in mind for them at the time. I mention this only because I know how impossible it is to expand a natural short play into a long one and would hardly make such a futile mistake. *Gold* was always full length to me.

I wrote John Williams to be properly persuasive on my behalf in urging you to join him in a visit up here. I hope he has been so, and that you will find time to come. Putting aside the very restorative pleasure I shall feel in having you here, there is for me a very special inducement also. I have wanted for a long time to talk over with you something which has been growing in the back of my head for the past year. It is an idea for future work—a scheme quite on a grand scale, and, as far as my knowledge goes, an original plan in play writing.[5] I do not mean by this that there is any heavy blank verse, soggy symbolism or bizarre innovations connected with it; but it is an idea which is so large in outline that, even having the temerity to grant one's ability for it, it will take some years of intensive and difficult labor to fill in. The question in my mind still is, is this thing as big as I think, is it worth the labor involved, and, from a purely practicable standpoint, can it be done? So, standing on this threshold, I would sure like to have your opinion. At least, whether you find it worth the while or not, I am sure you will be interested.

So regard this letter as an S.O.S.—and do come!

Sincerely,
Eugene O'Neill.

---

1. This salutation is less formal than the earlier "My dear Mr. Nathan."
2. Copyrighted 27 July 1920; published by Boni and Liveright, New York, September 1921. Presented 1 June 1920, Frazee Theatre, New York; produced by John D. Williams. The play was not a success, closing after only thirteen performances. The subsequently written *Where the Cross Is Made*, a shorter play based on the fourth act of *Gold*, was more popular.
3. John D. Williams.
4. Presented 22 November 1918, first bill, Playwrights' Theatre; directed by Ida Rauh. Published in *Moon of the Caribbees and Six Other Plays of the Sea* (New York: Boni and Liveright, June 1919).
5. It is impossible to determine exactly what O'Neill had in mind, but this passage gives a glimpse of his grand ambition to create drama with the scope and depth of the novel.

PREFATORY REMARKS: This, the longest personal letter to this date from O'Neill to Nathan, reveals the strengthening of their bond. O'Neill's continuation of the more familiar salutation underscores his growing willingness to divulge his deeper thoughts and hopes. O'Neill indicates that he values Nathan's letters sufficiently to keep them for at least a couple of years. The pair's rapport is such that the playwright ventures to suggest where Nathan had been mistaken in his *Smart Set* essay (although Nathan never did correct himself publicly).

O'Neill exhibits both humility (in his willingness to make a confessional appraisal of his abilities) and a relentless pride; he is at once, in the words of Nathan, "extremely shy" and possessed of "a vast confidence in himself" (Goldberg, *The Theatre of George Jean Nathan*, 76).

Provincetown, Mass.
June 20, 1920.

Dear Mr. Nathan:

I mailed a letter to you on a trip to the village yesterday—after which I bought the July *Smart Set* and read your article on American playwrights.[1] *After,* s'help me! I underline that word because my letter of yesterday might well appear to you in its too-aptness to have been inspired by what you wrote; and I do not want you to suspect, even for a second, that I would mask my rebuttal that cunningly.

Your criticism of me and mine in the magazine is sure *invigorating*— grateful as keen salt breeze after much hot air puffing from all sides. If my sublime head were bumping the stars askew, your acid test would sure put a blister of truth on my heinie that would disturb any squatting at ease even on the softest complacency. However, I honestly don't need blistering—on that account. My head retains its proper proximity to sea level, I think. But your weighing in the balance is a tremendous lift to me in other ways. For one thing, it gives me the added urge of attempting to make you out a false prophet—in ten years or so. For I refuse to accept your serious doubt, but rather snatch at your "But it may be—that I am wrong" and will try to prove it to you, given the time.

In this connection, I would like to make you my confession of faith where my work is concerned. Honest confession. I am familiar enough with the best modern drama of all countries to realize that, viewed from a true standard, my work is as yet a mere groping. I rate myself as a beginner— with prospects. I acknowledge that when you write, "He sees life to often as drama. The great dramatist is the dramatist who sees drama as life" you are smiting the nail on the head. But I venture to promise that this will be less true with each succeeding play—that I will not "stay put" in any comfortable niche and play the leave-well-enough-alone game. God stiffen it, I *am* young yet and I mean to grow! And in this faith I live: That if I have the "guts" to ignore the megaphone men and what goes with them, to follow the dream and live for that alone, then my real significant bit of truth and the ability to express it, will be conquered in time—not tomorrow nor the next day nor any near, easily-attained period but after the struggle has been long enough and hard enough to merit victory.

*In The Zone*—your "vaudeville grand guignolism"[2] is my own verdict—but I am out of that zone now, never to return. As for *The Rope,* I do believe that is sound enough, although it's a year or more since I looked at it and perhaps I'd agree with you now. But where did you get the idea that I really valued *Where The Cross Is Made?* It was great fun to write, theatrically very thrilling, an amusing experiment in treating the audience as insane—that is all it means or ever meant to me. You will see by my last letter how I came to write it, that it was a distorted version of a long play idea and never intended for a one-act play in my mind. And, by the way, it was not *Where The Cross Is Made* that you advised me to tear up for reputation's sake. You must have confused it with another I submitted to you—*Honor Among The Bradleys*[3]—a very false and feeble piece of work which you "bawled me out" for writing—now in limbo.

To make sure of my accuracy in this matter of *Where The Cross Is Made* I have been looking up your old letters and I find this in one written in October 1918:[4] "I have read *Where The Cross Is Made* and like it very much indeed. It would please me to print it in the *Smart Set.* But I fear that the performance of the play by the Provincetown Players around the first of December would interfere with such a publication. It would be impossible for us to use the play before our January issue"—etc. So you see you have confused *The Cross* with that other play. I am at pains to state all this merely to show you that it was not *The Cross* you advised me to destroy.

Your scheme of measurement to the contrary, I would like to stand or fall by *Bound East for Cardiff*—(with due consideration that it was written in 1914)—*The Long Voyage Home, The Moon Of The Caribbees, Beyond The Horizon, The Straw, Gold*—because these plays are my *sincerest* at different stages. They were written purely for their own sakes. The others had their contributing causes. There are so many intermediate reasons that enter into the writing of a play between the two serious extremes of art and money. Such intermediate dramas are but an instructive form of recreation when one cannot remain inactive—and it takes time to get over the itch to put everything on paper, regardless.

In the light of what you say in your article that you hope I may top my writings from year to year, your later opinion that *Gold* is a better piece of work than *Beyond The Horizon* is more than ever welcome to me.

Let me again urge you to try and make the trip up here with John Williams.[5] I'd sure love to have you.

And again let me thank you for your estimate in the *Smart Set*. Those are the things that count. A prod in the rear and a pointing to a distant goal, not without hope—that is what it means to me.

Sincerely,
Eugene O'Neill.

---

1. Refers to Nathan, "The American Playwright," *Smart Set* 62 (July 1920): 132–33. The thirty-two-year-old O'Neill was stunned and delighted to read the strongest evaluation that Nathan had yet made of him: "Of all the many playwrights that America has produced in the last half dozen years, there is only one whose shoulders begin to lift clearly above the local crowd. That one is Eugene O'Neill: the one writer for the native stage who gives promise of achieving a sound position for himself" (132). This was certainly a turning point in the career of the young playwright.

2. Nathan had used this phrase in his July 1920 *Smart Set* essay. "Grand Guignol" is a genre of short, sensational plays, with a major scene of horror or violence and a surprise ending. It was popular in Paris at the turn of the century and spread to England and America in the early 1920s.

3. A one-acter which was never copyrighted; Nathan criticized its style and O'Neill destroyed it soon after. Agnes Boulton has described the unsavory local characters on whom the play is based: a mother, father, and three beautiful, mysteriously pregnant daughters who eventually vanished.

4. Sometime in 1917, O'Neill and Nathan had started exchanging letters. The earliest preserved letter from O'Neill to Nathan is dated 1 May 1919.

5. John D. Williams, New York producer who had four months earlier staged O'Neill's first play on Broadway, *Beyond the Horizon*.

Provincetown, Mass.[1]
Dec. 11, 1920.

My dear Mr. Nathan:

I am very glad to hear you like *Diff'rent*[2] and especially pleased to learn that you believe I am "edging up to windward" and making progress along the right course.

The Provincetown Players have been dickering with Hopkins to take the *Emperor Jones*[3] uptown. He was quite willing, it seems, but demanded an all-O'Neill bill and insisted on *Diff'rent* being the other play—wouldn't hear of *The Moon Of The Caribbees* or any of my others. This strikes me as strange because Hopkins has never even read *Diff'rent* and can know nothing of its worth. At any rate, his insistence on that play, and that play only, made his proposition impossible for us. We would have to close *Jones*, put on *Diff'rent* (taking the chance that Hopkins wouldn't want it after he had seen it) and postpone an uptown opening for a month and a half, in order to accept his offer. Klauber,[4] for the Selwyns, has offered us the Selwyn theatre for *Jones,* and we can move it up at once if we like.[5] So I think *Jones* is due for the Selwyn at an early date. I would have much preferred the Hopkins' association, of course, but his proposition was too uncertain; and we really couldn't afford to take the chance.

I sincerely trust the neuralgia[6] has let up on you by this.

Sincerely,
Eugene O'Neill.

---

1. O'Neill and Agnes Boulton lived at the old Coast Guard station at Peaked Hill Bar until weather forced them to return to a rented Provincetown house.

2. Presented 27 December 1920 at Playwrights' Theatre by Provincetown Players; published April 1921 by Boni and Liveright, New York, in a volume also containing *The Emperor Jones* and *The Straw.*

3. *The Emperor Jones* had opened 1 November 1920, at the Playwrights' Theatre, to much acclaim; it brought the Provincetown Players their first recognition from Broadway audiences and managers. Charles Gilpin's portrayal of Brutus Jones was the first major role for a black in the American theater.

4. Adolph Klauber (1879–1933), drama critic of the *New York Times* from 1906 to 1918 before he became a theater producer.

5. Klauber, using the original cast (which depleted their Village ranks), produced *The Emperor Jones* at the Selwyn Theatre starting 27 December 1920; it moved to the Princess Theatre on 29 January 1921.

6. Since the age of fifteen, Nathan had suffered chronically from neuralgia in the left side of his face (George Jean Nathan, "oh, doctor!" *Vanity Fair,* January 1930: 36; letter from Julie Haydon Nathan to Nancy L. Roberts and Patricia Angelin, 14 September 1985).

PREFATORY REMARKS: This letter illuminates O'Neill's creative process in writing *Anna Christie* (based on *Chris Christopherson*—also called *Chris*—which failed in road tryouts in Atlantic City and Philadelphia in March 1920; and on *The Ole Davil,* a revised version of *Chris*). O'Neill at the end makes a rare, direct appeal for specific counsel from his critic.

O'Neill was apprehensive when Nathan judged the script's ending unwarrantably optimistic, and he rose to *Anna Christie*'s defense in this reply. The playwright's uneasiness was justified when the play was presented on 2 November 1921 at the Vanderbilt. While critics were generally favorable, quite a few attacked the ending and several in effect accused the playwright of selling out to Broadway. For instance, Burns Mantle in the *New York Mail* called the play "the finest piece of writing Eugene O'Neill has done," but he also charged that "the morbid young genius compromised with the happy ending all true artists of the higher drama so generously despise" (*New York Mail,* 3 November 1921). Mantle was not alone in his criticism.

O'Neill publicly defended *Anna Christie* in a letter to the *New York*

*Times:* "Since the last act seems to have been generally misunderstood, I must have failed in this attempt. . . . A kiss in the last act, a word about marriage, and the audience grows blind and deaf to what follows. . . . It would have been so obvious and easy—in the case of this play, conventional even—to have made my last act a tragic one. . . . But looking into the hearts of my people, I saw it couldn't be done. It would not have been true. They were not that kind. They would act in just the silly, immature, compromising way that I have made them act" ("The Mail Bag," *New York Times,* 18 December 1921, sec. 6).

Ultimately O'Neill was to transfer his resentment of how the play was interpreted to the play itself and consistently to underrate it.

Provincetown, Mass.
Feb. 1, 1921.

My dear Mr. Nathan:

Your criticism certainly probes the vital spot. The devil of it is, I don't see my way out. From the middle of that third act I feel the play ought to be dominated by the woman's psychology. And I have a conviction that with dumb people of her sort, unable to voice strong, strange feelings, the emotions can find outlet only through the language and gestures of the heroics in the novels and movies they are familiar with—that is, that in moments of great stress life copies melodrama. Anna forced herself on me, middle of third act, at her most theatric. In real life I felt she would unconsciously be compelled, through sheer inarticulateness, to the usual "big scene," and wait hopefully for her happy ending. And as she is the only one of the three who knows exactly what she wants, she would get it.

And the sea outside—life—waits. The happy ending is merely the comma at the end of a gaudy introductory clause, with the body of the sentence still unwritten. (In fact, I once thought of calling the play *Comma.*)

Of course, this sincerity of life pent up in the trappings of theatre, is impossible to project clearly, I guess. The two things cancel and negate each other, resulting, as you have said, in a seeming H. A. Jones[1] compromise. Yet it is queerly fascinating to me because I believe it's a new, true angle.

One thing that I realize, on a rereading of the last act, is that I haven't done enough to make my "comma" clear. My ending seems to have a false definiteness about it that is misleading—a happy-ever-after which I did not intend. I relied on the father's last speech of superstitious uncertainty to let my theme flow through—and on. It does not do this rightly. I now have it in my mind to have the stoker not entirely convinced by the oath of a non-Catholic although he is forced by his great want to accept her in spite of this.

In short, that all of them at the end have a vague foreboding that although they have had their moment, the decision still rests with the sea which has achieved the conquest of Anna.

Do you think this would help—in the way of holding up the theme at the end? I sure pine to talk over this play with you, but just how soon I will be able to get to town again is uncertain.

My sincerest thanks for your letter!

Eugene O'Neill.

---

1. Henry Arthur Jones, British playwright (1851–1929).

PREFATORY REMARKS: Nathan must have been flattered by O'Neill's forthright appeal for advice in his letter of 1 February, since he apparently sent off a letter almost immediately in which he approved of O'Neill's suggested revisions.

In reply, the dramatist acknowledged his gratitude to Nathan, then described his difficulties in getting three of his plays, currently under contract, to production. It had become clear that George C. Tyler would produce neither *The Straw* nor the new *Chris* (eventually renamed *Anna Christie*) for the 1920–21 New York season. Burned by the failure of the old *Chris* in Atlantic City and Philadelphia stagings, Tyler wanted to try out *The Straw* as a special Boston matinee before bringing it to New York. A third play, *Gold,* was under contract to John D. Williams, with whom O'Neill tried to confer in mid-February when he visited New York for ten days. Williams was characteristically tightlipped.

Provincetown, Mass.<br>Feb. 5, 1921.

My dear Mr. Nathan:

I am darn glad to know you think I may have found my way out in *The Ole Davil,* and I will get to work on it at once.

The play is at present held by Tyler[1] under the old *Chris* contract but, unless he elects to pay for a large number of performances contracted for but not given during the past year, the rights will be forfeited back to me the first week in March. I hardly think Tyler will go to this expense. He is having enough trouble trying to get on *The Straw* before he forfeits that too.

If you will mention the play to Mr. Hopkins, it will be a great favor. I would certainly like him to read it and have instructed my agent to send him the script. But I suppose he is too busy with *Macbeth*[2] just at present to think of anything else. That goes on the 17th, doesn't it? Perhaps after that he will have free time, and by then I will certainly have completed my revision of the end.

I hear the critics on the dailies have "crawled my frame"[3] for *Diff'rent* uptown, thereby fulfilling your prophecy that they would soon about face.[4] Well, this is rather reassuring. I had begun to think that I was too popular to be honest; but this sort of spanking convinces me that, right or wrong, I am right.

All best wishes.
Sincerely,
Eugene O'Neill.

---

1. George C. Tyler.
2. The controversial 1921 Arthur Hopkins production, starring Lionel Barrymore and Julia Arthur, opened 17 February 1921 at New York's Apollo Theatre.
3. In other letters to Nathan, he occasionally uses the variation "climbed my frame." Both are American slang expressions for "scolded" or "reprimanded."
4. Refers to Nathan's *Smart Set* article the previous month, in which he had prophesied: "Hysterical praise will some day (for such is the way of critics) turn a violently sour tail upon him in an effort to regain its personal equilibrium and to support its own esoteric wiggle-waggle" (*Smart Set* 64 [January 1921]: 137).

PREFATORY REMARKS: This letter illustrates O'Neill's increasing frustration with the dealings of producer John D. Williams; *Gold* was the last O'Neill play he ever presented.

Provincetown, Mass.
March 31, 1921.

Dear Mr. Nathan:

No, there is nothing new about *Gold*.[1] My agent, Richard Madden,[2] has tried vainly to get in touch with him a number of times during the past months. Williams is strictly incommunicado, it seems, and cannot be reached in any way.

I have not attempted to get any word from him myself because I am highly peeved at the way he has acted—especially in one instance where he tried to sell his rights to the Theatre Guild for a large cash sum without letting me know a thing about it. This was not only a violation of the letter of our contract but, what I felt more keenly, a breach of all the ethics of friendly association. He has also hawked *Gold* around to every film company in the country in his efforts to get backing for it. This I know right from the movie people themselves. They were shy of his proposition because his arrangement with the Famous Players[3] had been anything but successful from their standpoint. Naturally, I hardly relish this peddling about of *Gold* to film folk as if it were a dime novel—any more than I like the fact that, as a result of Williams' Famous Player connection last year, that company now owns all rights to *Beyond The Horizon* and will continue to control it for a year to come. So, all in all, I feel that John Williams has given me a pretty rough deal.

Yes, I believe that Gillmore[4] can give a good performance in *The Straw.* The play is now guaranteed a New York showing in October.

All best regards.

Sincerely,<br>Eugene O'Neill.

---

1. Presented 1 June 1921 at New York's Frazee Theatre; copyrighted 27 July 1920; published September 1921 by Boni and Liveright, New York.
2. Richard Madden (1880–1951). Literary agent for the American Play Company (formed by Elizabeth Marbury in 1914), who in 1919 became O'Neill's agent until Madden's death.
3. Famous Players Film Company, headed by Adolph Zukor and Daniel Frohman, had produced a film version of *The Count of Monte Cristo* featuring both James O'Neill, Sr., and his actor son, James, Jr.
4. Margalo Gillmore, a relative newcomer who, after achieving some Broadway recognition during the 1920–21 season, was given the role of "Eileen" in *The Straw,* over O'Neill's initial objections.

EUGENE O'NEILL<br>PROVINCETOWN, MASS.[1]

Jan. 2, 1922

Dear Mr. Nathan:

I have been up here for the past six weeks or so working on my latest, *The Hairy Ape.*[2] The first draft is now completed, with typing and revising still to be done. It is one of those themes where, if the right rhythm is in your system, the whole play just spills forth without interruption save for writer's cramp.[3]

I believe you are going to be very much interested in this play whatever your verdict may be on the complete result. It is a large experimental departure from the form of all my previous work. Perhaps it follows the method of *Jones* closer than any other. But it does not fit into any of the "isms" although there is a bit of all of them in it. I feel confident I have succeeded in what I set out to do but in doing so I have not hesitated to use everything I could find in the theatre or life which could heighten and drive home the underlying idea.

This play is promised to the Provincetown Players but I hope that Hopkins, after he has seen it, will take it uptown after three weeks down there. The production, however, will be pretty well out of the hands of the P. P.[4] Kennedy,[5] a Hopkins man, will direct; Wolheim,[6] a Hopkins actor, will play the lead, I hope. He is the only actor I know who can look it, who has by nature the right manner. Whether he can act it or not, I doubt; but I also doubt if any actor can act it. It is a tremendous part. Finally, Bobby Jones[7] will do the eight sets which must be in the Expressionistic method. So you see it will not be an amateur affair but can be relied on to achieve results. I doubt if any commercial manager, especially this bad year, and including even Hopkins, would be daring enough to give it a thought.

No, I haven't had any word of *The Fountain*[8] being done in the near future. There is no one to play it. Ben-Ami[9] is scratched for the present on account of his Yiddish accent but he is furiously going after English and voice culture and wants to play the part. Jack Barrymore[10] is supposed to have read it but Hopkins is vague on that outcome. J. B.'s frau, I understand, is dead against his acting again—except in the films! It is too bad. He is the real man for it, of course. Well, he isn't definitely out of the running yet, so I will nourish hopes.

Genuine Pilsner! Business of a playwright smacking his lips. It makes me want to grab the first train—but duty demands that I stick here until my *Ape* is typed and revised, a matter of three weeks or so. Will be sure to see you then. In the meantime, if you ever feel so inclined, drop me a line on your opinion of the two plays. I would like to hear what you felt was wrong with the mistitled *Oldest Man*[11] and if you detected many false spots in *The Fountain*. So many folk have objected to the blank verse rhythm in this latter, on the grounds, seemingly, that it is not beautiful verse. Whereas, of course, I used it to gain a naturalistic effect of the quality of the people and speech of those times, to place them, with little care for original poetic beauty save in the few instances where that is called for. I wanted to make ordinary speech of ordinary thoughts stilted, bigoted, narrow, sentimental and romantic, pretentiously ornate.

> All best to you.
> Eugene O'Neill.

1. O'Neill's first use of a printed letterhead in his correspondence to Nathan.

2. Presented 9 March 1922 at the Playwrights' Theatre; produced by the Provincetown Players. It was published along with *Anna Christie* and *The First Man* by Boni and Liveright, New York, July 1922.

3. The next letter (7 May 1923) and many of those that follow were no longer typed, but in O'Neill's tiny, cramped handwriting (until his tremor made longhand all but impossible). O'Neill never did learn to compose on a typewriter, and all his plays were handwritten—some on a single piece of paper in miniscule letters that required a magnifying glass in order to be read. "Writer's cramp" is probably his wry reference to the fact that he wrote the play in longhand in only two and a half weeks.

4. Provincetown Players.

5. Charles O'Brien Kennedy, an aide of Broadway producer Arthur Hopkins, was an Irishman whom O'Neill found congenial.

6. Louis Wolheim, a rugged-looking associate of Hopkins, who played the lead in *The Hairy Ape* in its 1922 debut.

7. Robert Edmond Jones (1887–1954), who codesigned sets for *The Hairy Ape* with Cleon Throckmorton, collapsed from overwork shortly before the play had its première.

8. Presented 10 December 1925 at the Greenwich Village Theatre; produced by Kenneth Macgowan, Robert Edmond Jones, and Eugene O'Neill. Copyrighted 13 October 1921; published in March 1926 by Boni and Liveright, New York, in a volume also containing *The Great God Brown, The Moon of the Caribbees,* and other plays.

9. Jacob Ben-Ami, Yiddish actor who had been acclaimed on Broadway, played "Michael Cape" in the Thirty-ninth Street Theatre's 1924 production of *Welded.*

10. John Barrymore.

11. Refers to *The First Man*, presented 4 March 1922 at the Neighborhood Playhouse, New York; produced by Augustin Duncan. It was copyrighted under the title *The Oldest Man* on 13 October 1921; then published by Boni and Liveright, New York, July 1922, as *The First Man*, in a volume also containing *The Hairy Ape* and *Anna Christie.*

PREFATORY REMARKS: Here there is a gap in the letters preserved. Since his last letter, O'Neill's mother, Ella Quinlan O'Neill, had died (28 February 1922); he had won a Pulitzer Prize for *Anna Christie* (May 1922); he had bought a new home in Connecticut; two of his plays, *The First Man* and *The Hairy Ape,* had opened in New York; and the original Provincetown Players had broken up (after which O'Neill had formed a new Provincetown Players with Kenneth Macgowan and Robert Edmond Jones).

Both Nathan and Mencken judged *Welded* to represent a decline in O'Neill's customary quality, but here the playwright stubbornly argued that it was his "best yet." Ten years later he would label it, along with *The Fountain, The First Man,* and *Gold,* "too painfully bungled" to merit reviving (O'Neill, "Second Thoughts," *American Spectator* 1 [December 1932]: 2).

BROOK FARM[1]
RIDGEFIELD, CONNECTICUT

May 7, 1923.

Dear Nathan:[2]

Nevertheless, I am convinced *Welded*[3] is the best yet. I'm glad to get Mencken's letter but I must confess the greater part of his comment seems irrelevant as criticisms of my play. To point out its weakness as realism (in the usual sense of that word) is to confuse what is obviously part of my deliberate intention.

Damn that word, "realism"! When I first spoke to you of the play as a "last word in realism," I meant something "really real," in the sense of being spiritually true, not meticulously life-like,—an interpretation of actuality by a distillation, an elimination of most realistic trappings, an intensification of human lives into clear symbols of truth.

Here's an example: Mencken says: "The man haranguing the street-walker is surely not a man who ever actually lived." Well, he surely is to me, and what is more to my point, he is also much more than that. He is Man dimly aware of recurring experience, groping for the truth behind the realistic appearances of himself, and of love and life. For the moment his agony gives him vision of the true behind the real.

I can't agree that the speeches in this scene are "banal" or the ideas "rubber stamp." In fact, I'm positive it's the deepest and truest, as well as the best written scene I've ever done. Perhaps it isn't "plausible"—but the play is about love as a life-force, not as an intellectual conception, and the plausibilities of reason don't apply. Reason has no business in the theatre anyway, any more than it has in a church. They are both either below—or above it.

But I won't rave on. I'll grant this much for your criticisms—that parts of the dialogue are still, I find, "speechy" and artificial but that will all be gone over and fixed. It's the slopping-over of too much eagerness to say it all.

Thank Mencken for me for reading it. I'm sorry it didn't "knock him dead" to repay him for his trouble.

Well, just wait until you see it played! (if it's done right) I'm hoping that may make you recant.

My best to you both.

Sincerely,
Eugene O'Neill.

1. Purchased in autumn 1922 as a winter home; Peaked Hill Bar was still used in the summer.

2. O'Neill was now using this more familiar salutation.

3. Presented 17 March 1924 at the Thirty-ninth Street Theatre, New York; produced by O'Neill, Kenneth Macgowan, and Robert Edmond Jones in association with the Selwyns. It was copyrighted 2 May 1923; published by Boni and Liveright, New York, April 1924, in a volume also containing *All God's Chillun Got Wings*.

PREFATORY REMARKS: In this letter, O'Neill is characteristically enthusiastic about the play he has just completed, *All God's Chillun Got Wings*. It was presented 15 May 1924 at the Provincetown Playhouse, directed by James Light. It was first published in the *American Mercury* 1 (February 1924): 129–48—almost three months before its production. (Boni and Liveright brought out an edition of *All God's Chillun Got Wings* and *Welded* in April 1924.)

The Provincetowners had expected the play's racial subject matter to cause some controversy, but no one was prepared for the vituperation that erupted months before the play was staged. The *Morning Telegraph* and Hearst's *American* were especially sharp and often sensational. Shortly before the production, Nathan wrote his reactions to *All God's Chillun:* "His play is unquestionably enfeebled by its sketchiness, by its perhaps too great economy of means, but it nonetheless presents its theme sincerely, intelligently, sympathetically and, it seems to me, dramatically." And Nathan deftly denounced the play's detractors, writing:

> The hoopdedoodle that has been raised over that [racial] theme and over the planned theatrical presentation of the play expounding it must make any half-way intelligent Pullman porter shake his head sadly in pity for the mentality of a certain portion of the race that, by the grace of God, sits in the plush chairs. (Nathan, "The Theatre," *American Mercury* 2 [May 1924]: 114.)

As for O'Neill, in mid-March 1924, he issued his own statement defending the play, decrying the "irresponsible gabble of the sensation-mongers and notoriety hounds." They, and not he, were out to arouse "racial ill feeling." O'Neill argued that "A play is written to be expressed through the theatre, and only on its merits in the theatre can a final judgment be passed on it with justice. We demand this hearing" (" 'All God's Chillun' Defended by O'Neill," *New York Times*, 19 March 1924).

PEAKED HILL BAR
PROVINCETOWN, MASS.

Thursday.
[December 1923]

Dear Nathan:

Well, I've got it done—long-hand first draft—and I'm immensely pleased with it, *but*—here's the rub!—it's a good deal longer than I thought, as long as *The Hairy Ape* perhaps—no, not that long but longer than *Jones*. But here's another thing—it is in "Two Parts"—very definitely so—and might be printed that way. I couldn't keep it shorter; the idea crowded right out of a one-act form. I've had a great splurge of writing it—8 to 10 hours a day—and, whate're befall, it's been great sport.

I hope Mencken and you will like it.[1] I think I've done the right thing by an intensely moving theme and that the result has a real beauty which gives it a blessing.

All best to you both. I'll get it typed as soon as I can possibly get hold of someone to do the job—show it to you and make revisions afterwards. I hope to be down soon for *Fountain* rehearsals. No call yet. This in much haste.

Eugene O'Neill.

---

1. Mencken did not, but Nathan did; and he decided to run it in a single installment, not the two suggested by O'Neill.

BROOK FARM
RIDGEFIELD, CONNECTICUT

Sunday. [December 1923]

Dear Nathan:

Here's the proofs.[1] I won't guarantee that I've been much help on them where spelling, etc., are concerned, but I've done my best.

What do you think of our new group?[2] I think we're going to do some really original stuff in the way of production. My ideas are playing an active part here—not like the old P. P.[3] where I simply handed in plays but kept out otherwise. I think we've worked out an amusing scheme for *The Spook*

*Sonata.*[4] Be sure & see it. I'll bet we do it more interestingly than it's ever been done abroad!

I'm desperate for a production! I no longer believe in Hopkins. When it comes right down to bedrock, he's just another member of the P. M. A.,[5] a bit brainier & more courageous than most, perhaps—but also a lot lazier and less efficient. There's no hope for me with him. He hasn't given me a square deal either. So, as there is no one else I'll have to help create a new outlet—or remain gagged.

I'll be in Town very soon. Shall hope to see you there for a few minutes if you're not too darn busy.

Here's to your first number![6]

Eugene O'Neill

1. Proofs of *All God's Chillun Got Wings*, which was published in the *American Mercury* 1 February 1924: 129–48.

2. The new Provincetown Players, a partnership of Kenneth Macgowan (head of production and business management), Robert ("Bobby") Edmond Jones, and O'Neill (associate directors), formed when Susan Glaspell and George ("Jig") Cram Cook went abroad for an indefinite period, autumn 1923; playhouse reopened in January 1924.

3. Provincetown Players.

4. The August Strindberg play that, at O'Neill's suggestion, became the first production of the new Provincetown Players.

5. Probably the Producing Managers' Association, an organization founded in response to increasing unionism in the theater.

6. Refers to the *American Mercury*, a magazine Nathan and Mencken started in December 1923 as a successor to *Smart Set*.

"Campsea"[1]
South Shore, Paget W.,
Bermuda
March 26, '25

Dear Nathan:

I've been meaning to write to you ever since we arrived here in December to explain why you never got the script of *Marco Millions*.[2] At the last moment, before sending it to you, I reread and decided to rewrite and condense the two nights of play into one long night. The new scripts of play into one long night. The new scripts have been typed and I wrote Madden some time ago to send you one. I'll await your judgment with great interest. Belasco[3] has bought the play and promises to spend the small fortune required to do it right. Give him his due. I think he is about the only one of the lot who would.

The *Desire* censorship mess[4] has been amusing, what? It has a background of real melodramatic plot—the revenge of Banton's enraged Southern Nordic sensibilities on the author of *All God's Chillun* (which he tried so hard to stop, and couldn't "make it").

What I think everyone missed in *Desire* is the quality in it I set most store by—the attempt to give an epic tinge to New England's inhibited life-lust, to make its inexpressiveness poetically expressive, to release it. It's just that—the poetical (in the broadest and deepest sense) vision illuminating even the most sordid and mean blind alleys of life—which I'm convinced is, and is to be, *my* concern and justification as a dramatist.

There's a lot of poetical beauty in *Marco Millions*, I think you'll find. But there the poetic is more or less obviously called forth by the theme and background. It's where the poetic is buried deep beneath the dull and crude that one's deep-seeing vision is tested.

However, I didn't start this letter with any view of boring you by an expounding of inner principles. It was rather to recommend Bermuda to you as a place to "take the waters" in case you're planning a spring vacation. The climate is grand. There's absolutely nothing interesting to do, and the German bottled beer and English bottled ale are both excellent. And the swimming is wonderful, if you like such, which I do above everything. It has proved a profitable winter resort for me. I've gotten more work done than in the corresponding season up north in many years. The frost and hard cider of too many successive New England winters are slowly being rendered out of my system. I've just finished a devastating, crucifying new one called *The Great God Brown*,[5] which I think marks my "ceiling" so far, and I feel right cheerful!

All best to Mencken and yourself. Consider Bermuda.

Sincerely,
Eugene O'Neill.

P.S.

*The Fountain* is again postponed, the delay in completing the new Guild theatre being the reason this time. A play with a jinx attached, I'm afraid!

---

1. O'Neill decided to try the warmer climate and year-round swimming of Bermuda in the winter of 1924–25. Indeed he came to feel that the temperate weather spurred his productivity. Here Eugene and Agnes awaited the birth of their daugher Oona (13 May 1925).

2. O'Neill had finished the first draft in October 1924. The play contrasted Western materialistic values with Oriental wisdom. It was copyrighted as *Marco's Millions* on 28 January 1925; produced 9 January 1928 at the Guild Theatre, New York, by the Theatre Guild (staged by Rouben Mamoulian); published by Boni and Liveright, New York, April 1927.

3. Producer David Belasco (1859–1931), whom O'Neill had once scorned for his showy, commercial productions. But the deal with Belasco fell through and *Marco* was not produced until nearly three years later.

4. *Desire Under the Elms* had its première on 11 November 1924 at the Greenwich Village Theatre (produced by the Provincetown Players). Most critics missed its significance, and many denounced it as morbid and immoral. District Attorney Joab H. Banton, who had not succeeded in closing down *All God's Chillun Got Wings* the previous year, tried to muzzle *Desire*, which he called "too thoroughly bad to be purified by a blue pencil" (Sheaffer, *O'Neill: Son and Artist*, 165). Eventually, *Desire* and other objectionable plays were evaluated by a special, Actors' Equity-backed "citizens' play-jury," outside the customary judicial system; Banton dropped the case. *Desire* was acquitted of indecency, and the notoriety served primarily to boost the play's audience size.

5. Copyrighted 2 July 1925; published by Boni and Liveright, New York, March 1926, in a volume also containing *The Fountain, The Moon of the Caribbees,* and other plays. Presented 23 January 1926 at the Greenwich Village Theatre; produced by Kenneth Macgowan, Robert Edmond Jones, and O'Neill.

KENNETH MACGOWAN   ROBERT EDMOND JONES   EUGENE O'NEILL
GREENWICH VILLAGE THEATRE
SEVENTH AVENUE & FOURTH STREET
NEW YORK CITY[1]

5 Mill Street,
Nantucket, Mass.[2]
[July 1925]

Dear Nathan:

No, I didn't know about Goldberg and the Blue Book.[3] He might have let me in on the secret. I recently authorized Barrett Clark to do a book on me[4] for some McBrides' series in which Boyd did one on Mencken.[5] This rather scrambles the eggs. I don't want to become a five-foot shelf[6] at my tender age!

I'll be in Town in about two weeks or less and will bring a copy of *The Great God Brown* with me when I see you.

All best wishes,
Eugene O'Neill.

---

1. This letterhead is crossed out by hand.

2. The O'Neills, feeling that Peaked Hill would be "too primitive" for their infant Oona, decided to summer in Nantucket.

3. Likely a reference to Isaac Goldberg's biography of Nathan, *The Theatre of George Jean Nathan,* which included fourteen of the young playwright's letters to the critic.

4. Barrett Clark, *Eugene O'Neill* (New York: Robert M. McBride, 1926), the first biography of the playwright. Subsequent editions entitled *Eugene O'Neill: The Man and His Plays* (New York: McBride, 1929; London: Jonathan Cape, 1933; New York: McBride, 1936: Dover, 1947).

5. Ernest Boyd, *H. L. Mencken* (New York: McBride, 1925).

6. Refers to Collier and Son's collection of the world's literary classics, supposedly compact enough to require only five feet of shelf space.

5 Mill Street,
Nantucket, Mass.
[July 1925]

Dear Nathan:

I have been on a trip down the Cape, or would have answered your letter sooner.

By all means use the letters—or rather, let Goldberg[1] use them—if you wish. I rely on you to censor them—(I have forgotten just what they were about)—wherever incoherent.[2] Sometimes my letters get rather scrambled, especially when I am in most deadly earnest.

I shall look forward to seeing you in New York in a couple of weeks. I have a lot to tell you regarding *Marco Millions,* and I want very much to have you read *The Great God Brown.* All best!

Sincerely,
Eugene O'Neill.

---

1. Isaac Goldberg, author of the biography *The Theatre of George Jean Nathan.*
2. Nathan's censorship was minimal; he merely omitted a few of the less interesting letters.


BROOK FARM
RIDGEFIELD, CONNECTICUT


October 31, 1925

Mr. George Jean Nathan,
*The American Mercury*
730 Fifth Avenue,
New York City.

Dear Nathan:

I am at present working hard on a new play[1] but expect to be in town a week from Monday to start rehearsals. I will call you up as soon as I get in.

All best.

Eugene O'Neill.

P.S. By the way, you ask where am I going to stop. I don't know yet. My problem is this: I'll be in New York some four or five days a week steadily for two months as *The Great God Brown* immediately follows *The Fountain.* What I want to do is to find a place where I can work with some degree of quiet until noon, and where my acquaintances can't get at me. Can you recommend The Royalton?[2] I know nothing about it or how expensive it is, but I'd be glad to hear a word from you about it.

---

1. Refers to *Lazarus Laughed.* The play presented a novel concept. Lazarus, having been raised from the dead by Christ (John 11: 1–44), had returned with personal knowledge that an afterlife did exist. He, then, was the one mortal no longer subject to humankind's primal fear of death. Hence his laughter. In trying to imagine what no one has ever experienced, O'Neill was attempting the impossible. Predictably, his execution fell short of his concept. Copyrighted 23 June 1926; its first act only was published in *The American Caravan*, edited by Van Wyck Brooks, Lewis Mumford, Alfred Kreymborg, and Paul Rosenfeld (New York: The Macauley Co., September 1927). On 12 November 1927, Boni and Liveright brought out the first version of the entire play *(Lazarus Laughed, a Play for an Imaginative Theatre)*, with major changes from the *Caravan* publication. *Lazarus Laughed* was presented 9 April 1928 by the Pasadena, California, Community Playhouse.
2. Nathan's New York City home for many years.

PREFATORY REMARKS: When this letter was written, O'Neill was obviously anxious about getting *Marco Millions* produced. George M. Cohan, who almost without exception acted only in his own plays, refused the lead role. (In 1933 he would accept the role of the father, Nat Miller, in *Ah, Wilderness!*)

Producer David Belasco had yielded his option on *Marco Millions* in April of 1925; and both Arthur Hopkins and another major producer, Gilbert Miller, had turned it down. Not until January 1928 would the play be presented, by the Theatre Guild.

BROOK FARM
RIDGEFIELD, CONNECTICUT

Dec. 30th
[1925]

Dear Nathan:

I am sorry to hear the Cohan thing looks to be so hopeless. It would have been such a corking arrangement. I was looking forward to having a real good time out of the association with him and Miller on that production. I would like very much indeed to have got to know Cohan. From what others—like Arthur Hopkins—have told me about him in years past I have always had a great admiration for him. However, I hope there is still hope. He would be grand in the part, I am sure.

I have been going over *Marco*—also *Lazarus*[1]—since I came down here and have made them both better plays than they were, I think, by concentrating a bit and clarifying and cutting off loose ends. The script of *Marco* I have sent on to Liveright[2] for publication. I will get you one of the new scripts of *Lazarus* as soon as some are made. Have only the one here. Reinhardt[3] is very keen about *Lazarus*, so Kenneth[4] writes, and wants very much to do it in New York next season after doing it in Germany first. Kommer[5] is to make a translation for him. So that looks good.

I begin again on *Strange Interlude*[6] tomorrow. But perhaps it won't have that title by the time I get through. I am thinking of *The Haunted,*[7] which fits the play better. Do you like that? Has it been used, to your knowledge?

Mrs. O'Neill joins in all best to you.[8] We sure hope you will try to get down and see us later on when we are settled in our new place.

I'm going to write out the story of that film story soon and send it to Miss Gish.[9]

Cordially,
Eugene O'Neill

---

1. *Lazarus Laughed.*

2. Boni and Liveright first published *Marco Millions* in April 1927.

3. Max Reinhardt was supposedly interested in producing *Lazarus* both on Broadway and in Germany, but such plans never materialized.

4. Kenneth Macgowan.

5. Rudolf K. Kommer, Austrian journalist and translator, who represented Max Reinhardt in the United States.

6. Copyrighted 1 July 1927; published by Boni and Liveright in February 1928. Presented 30 January 1928 at the John Golden Theatre; produced by the Theatre Guild; staged by Philip Moeller.

7. Not an unfitting name, since all the protagonists are haunted in one way or another by guilt. O'Neill ultimately abandoned the title, using it later to name part of the *Mourning Becomes Electra* trilogy.

8. O'Neill wrote nothing to Nathan of his deteriorating marriage to Agnes Boulton, nor of his burgeoning romance with the actress Carlotta Monterey, during this period.

9. Lillian Gish, Nathan's close friend for many years. Born in 1899, she left the stage to become one of the first important film stars. She returned to Broadway in 1930 as Helena in *Uncle Vanya.*

# PART II
## *Colleagues*

# INTRODUCTORY ESSAY

The years 1926–1932 were a time of ascendancy for O'Neill. *The Great God Brown, Marco Millions, Lazarus Laughed,* the Pulitzer Prize-winning *Strange Interlude,* and his mammoth trilogy, *Mourning Becomes Electra* each lit up Broadway. Revivals of *Beyond the Horizon, The Emperor Jones, S. S. Glencairn,* and *Before Breakfast* intensified the luster, leaving no doubt that Eugene O'Neill was America's most eminent dramatist. The failure of *Dynamo* in 1929 hardly affected O'Neill's reputation, so great was the impact of all his successes.

From the vantage of sixty years later we see his best works of this period enjoying revivals while those of other playwrights, highly rated then, can only be found on library shelves. In his vision, his uncanny sense of the dramatic, and the living quality of his dialogue, O'Neill demonstrated over and over a genius not seen in America before or since. This was the period when he continued to experiment and innovate, whether by modifying old techniques such as asides and masks, or by improvising new ones such as "a stage play combined with a screen talky background to make alive visually . . . the memories etc. in the minds of the characters." Tennessee Williams was to use this 1929 "notion" effectively in *The Glass Menagerie,* but not until 1945.[1]

Beyond the talent so essential to the achievement of artistic greatness, one must have the drive and the freedom to create. O'Neill had all three.

His was an incessant urge to write. It sprang, in part, from a longing to enjoy the heights of success his father, touring the country for thirty years as the Count of Monte Cristo, had let slip by. Even more fundamental was his own pressing need to come to terms with his part in the failure of his childhood family to achieve happiness. He was compelled to ponder and to try to resolve his relationships with his now-dead parents and brother. Over the years, his plays became ever more autobiographical. Plagued by sad memories, he dramatized characters tormented by their relationships, especially with their families. *Mourning Becomes Electra,* his great trilogy of 1931, is such a work, for Electra moves through adultery, murder, and proposed incest to a tragic resolution.

Realizing his greatest satisfaction there at his desk, O'Neill labored long, soul-rending hours, often emerging exhausted after sharing the suffering of his characters. Through this identification he gained a necessary psychological relief. It is revealing that an early title for *Strange Interlude* and the actual title of the third part of *Electra* are both *The Haunted*.

For such a man, the regular creation of his work was paramount. This single-mindedness meant that writing precluded everything: family, friends, all pleasures. For example, O'Neill began drinking when he was only fifteen. Like his brother Jamie, he sometimes went on binges that lasted for days. But in 1926, when it came to a choice between alcohol and his work, O'Neill was able to give up alcohol.

Talent and motivation are paramount, but an artist must also have freedom to work. O'Neill's father supported him in his early days. Later, the playwright's own monetary success assured his opportunity to write. But he needed more than this. Isolation became increasingly important, especially after he reached middle age. Agnes Boulton, his wife during the early years, had her own career as a short-story writer. Apparently she did not protect his privacy to his liking. And their two children, Shane and Oona, inevitably made demands on his time to which he did not choose to yield. There were other offspring as well for whom he was, to varying degrees, responsible: Barbara Burton, Agnes's daughter from her first marriage, and Eugene Gladstone O'Neill, Jr., the son born of his own first, brief marriage, in 1910. An artist of O'Neill's intensity needed a spouse devoted to shielding him from all such distractions. Such a protector he found in Carlotta Monterey.

When their romance ignited in 1928, he deserted Agnes and the children to steal abroad with her. Eventually the lovers settled in France. They were married on 22 July 1929, shortly after his divorce from Agnes became final. Like Eugene, Carlotta was strong-willed, but she subordinated her life to his. Warding off all who she felt would interfere with his work, she maintained the domestic order that he found so essential. "I have always attended to everything but the writing of his plays," she once told Nathan.[2] After their marriage she even had the servants wear slippers or rubber-soled shoes so they wouldn't disturb the playwright. She became chatelaine, wife, and the protective mother that Ella O'Neill might have been, just as Nathan fulfilled, in a way, the role of older brother.

O'Neill was aware of his debt to her. In 1930, from France, he wrote Nathan that "Carlotta has been a brick. She has collaborated by keeping the old chateau running with uncanny efficiency so that nary an outside worry has touched me or bogged my stride even for a moment. A most marvelous wife and friend!"[3]

The two had been introduced when she appeared in the New York production of *The Hairy Ape* in 1922. In 1926 O'Neill took his family to Maine for the summer where he again met the actress, this time socially. Their romance did not become serious until 1927 when O'Neill was alone in

New York involved in the productions of *Strange Interlude* and *Marco Millions*. His wife and two children were in Bermuda. Faced with domestic difficulties, O'Neill found the solace Carlotta offered him so irresistible that he fled to Europe with her secretly in February 1928.

From Europe they traveled to the Orient, where a tragicomedy of events ensued, including a bout with flu and a drinking binge of several days in Shanghai climaxed by a spat with Carlotta and a hospital stay. The romance had aroused worldwide interest, and to duck the media O'Neill sailed from Shanghai disguised as the "Reverend William O'Brien." The bickering couple were heading west when Carlotta jumped ship in Ceylon (Sri Lanka), only to relent and sail off again now in pursuit. Wireless operators on the two ships were kept busy until the pair were finally reconciled by radio while the major news services listened in. The lovers continued their cables, sometimes hourly, as her ship chased his across the Indian Ocean. At last the two were tearfully reunited at Port Said, their reunion documented by headlines in newspapers everywhere.

Nathan took a long view of the relationship, seeing it as ultimately best for O'Neill as man and artist. In such a mercurial life, O'Neill found his friendship with Nathan a bracer. It stood on a firm footing of mutual respect. This allowed the two men to differ, sometimes strongly. Writing in his *Intimate Notebooks* in 1932, Nathan revealed that "when . . . he sent me the manuscript of *Lazarus Laughed* and I wrote to him that I didn't care for it, he replied in the next mail that my judgment of it couldn't be taken seriously by him because I was lacking in all religious feeling and was therefore prejudiced against any such play, and that it was really a masterpiece whatever I thought of it."[4] These occasional differences in perspective never stopped the dramatist from seeking the critic's counsel. Moreover, because Nathan saw O'Neill as the shining hope for the American theater, he was usually inclined to aid him in whatever professional way he could. When asked, Nathan willingly evaluated advance scripts and, normally approving, stood ready to promote each he deemed worthy.

Eighteen months before it was produced, *Marco Millions* received such treatment in the June 1926 issue of *American Mercury*, the magazine Nathan had begun with his associate H. L. Mencken in 1924. The critic noted that two Broadway producers had "flatly declined to consider Eugene O'Neill's splendid satiric comedy-romance *Marco Millions* on the ground that the story of Marco Polo is free for use to any moving picture company that wishes to grab it." He went on to decry "the old-line managers' determination to confine themselves only to such plays as may fetch them a subsequent screen revenue."[5]

In August of that year, Nathan again promoted *Marco*, at the same time engaging in a favorite practice, sparring with his fellow critics. This time he countered those who had claimed that O'Neill was an artist "without humor," who "sees the world invariably as of a piece with an undertaking parlor." Nathan asserted, "If ever we have had a dramatist who has been keenly appreciative of the derisory humor that lies imbedded in the heart of even the most tragic dramatic translation of life, O'Neill is that man."[6]

A year later it was *Strange Interlude*'s turn. Nathan wrote that it was "the finest, the profoundest drama of his entire career, a drama, I believe, that has not been surpassed by any that Europe has given us in recent years and certainly none that has been produced in America."[7]

A look at Nathan's criticism of two other plays produced during this period underscores the trust they shared even as Nathan maintained an essential critical distance. *The Great God Brown* had evoked an uneven response. Though one critic called it "ineffective and tedious,"[8] and a second, "jerkily written and pretentious,"[9] another saw it as revealing "O'Neill at both his best and worst,"[10] and still another said it "towers in classic dignity,"[11] Nathan called it O'Neill's "most beautifully imaginative work," but added that, in truth, his imagination had failed him in *Brown* at times.[12]

*Dynamo* was a play over which they sharply disagreed. As it opened in February 1929, O'Neill envisioned it as the first play in his *Myth Plays of the God-Forsaken* trilogy (earlier called *God Is Dead! Long Live—What?*).[13] Nathan, like many of his contemporaries, blasted *Dynamo*. O'Neill had perhaps expected what followed, for he said in one letter, "Not having heard from you about *Dynamo*, I opine it didn't hit you right in the reading" (14 February 1929). This was an understatement. Nathan wrote,

> There is in it, doubly and even triply exaggerated, that note of swollen emotion and indignant vociferation that made *Welded* ineffective and occasionally even absurd and that robbed *Desire Under the Elms* of the slow, smoke-curling force which is drama's most vital attribute. O'Neill betrays himself in so feverish a personal mood that one achieves much the same feeling that comes over one when listening to that boilerworks symphony of Antheil. In place of smooth persuasiveness there is shillaber lapel-tugging and coat-tail pulling; in place of suggestive harmony there is simply an ear-splitting racket.[14]

In August of 1929, however, Nathan put the criticism into perspective. Of all American playwrights, only O'Neill had what Nathan called "size." Even his failures were "distinguished . . . they sink not trivially but with a certain air of majesty, like a great ship, its flags flying, full of holes. He has no cheapness even in his worst plays."[15] And Nathan continued to chart his course with O'Neill.

Perhaps O'Neill's greatest claim to masterpiece during this period is *Mourning Becomes Electra*, his modern psychological trilogy which evokes the Greek sense of tragic fate. O'Neill began thinking about *Electra* in 1926. After marathon writing sessions at Le Plessis, his villa in France, and Las

Palmas in the Canary Islands, from September 1929 to the spring of 1931, he sent the completed manuscript off to Nathan and to the Theatre Guild, who were now producing everything he wrote.

The play opened on Broadway in October 1931 and brought O'Neill almost universal praise. The drama was hailed by Nathan as "one of the most important plays in the history of American drama," and as "not only a monument to O'Neill but to American theatre as well,"[16] and O'Neill's labors would seem to have been justified. Yet in speaking of the play the following year, he commented, "I am very satisfied with it . . . but at the same time, deeply dissatisfied." He complained of the limits of language but felt that, given "the discordant, broken, faithless rhythm of our time," he had done all he could.[17]

O'Neill continually ventured beyond his limits. Sometimes the result was a failure like *Dynamo,* but more often his audience came away moved by the power of his writing and the depth of his vision. He said of *Electra,* "I am always trying to do the big thing. It's only the joy of that attempt that keeps me writing plays."[18] *Electra,* which ran to thirteen acts, was a profound work. Yet O'Neill's finest dramas lay ahead.

## NOTES

1. Letter from Eugene O'Neill to George Jean Nathan, 12 November 1929.

2. Letter from Carlotta Monterey O'Neill to George Jean Nathan, 3 November 1942, Cornell University Library.

3. 19 February 1930.

4. George Jean Nathan, *The Intimate Notebooks of George Jean Nathan* (New York: Alfred A. Knopf, 1932), 24.

5. George Jean Nathan, "The Theatre: Merit and the Managers," *American Mercury* 8 (June 1926): 250.

6. George Jean Nathan, "The Theatre: O'Neill's New Play," *American Mercury* 8 (August 1926): 499.

7. George Jean Nathan, "The Theatre: O'Neill's Finest Play," *American Mercury* 11 (August 1927): 499.

8. Robert Coleman, "God Brown Tedious," *New York Mirror,* 25 January 1926.

9. "Plays and Players," *Town & Country* 81 (15 February 1926): 60.

10. Frank Vreeland, "The Masked Marvel," *New York Telegram,* 25 January 1926.

11. "Great God Brown Ingenious Concept, Towers in Dignity," *Journal of Commerce,* 25 January 1926.

12. George Jean Nathan, "The Theatre: Ut Supra," *American Mercury* 7 (April 1926): 503.

13. *Eugene O'Neill at Work (Newly Released Ideas for Plays),* ed. Virginia Floyd (New York: Frederick Ungar, 1981), 125; Sheaffer, *O'Neill: Son and Artist,* 306.

14. George Jean Nathan, "The Theatre: A Non-Conductor," *American Mercury* 16 (March 1929): 373.

15. George Jean Nathan, "The Theatre: The American Dramatist," *American Mercury* 17 (August 1929): 500.

16. George Jean Nathan, "The Theatre of George Jean Nathan," *Judge* 101 (21 November 1931): 16.

17. Arthur Hobson Quinn, *A History of the American Drama, From the Civil War to the Present Day* (New York: Appleton-Century-Crofts, 1936), 258.

18. Sheaffer, *O'Neill: Son and Artist,* 362, quoting O'Neill's letter to Robert Sisk, 28 August 1930.

# LETTERS: APRIL 1926–APRIL 1931

Cable
"ENEILL"
Bermuda

"BELLEVUE"
PAGET EAST, BERMUDA[1]

April 5th, 1926.

Dear Nathan:

Well, Belasco has passed up *Marco*.[2] The cost frightened him.[3] Who would you suggest now? I have asked Madden,[4] my agent, to phone you in case you might have a hunch. I am submitting it to Hopkins.[5]

My new play about Lazarus[6] seems to be coming along in great shape.

I meant to phone you before I left, but so many things cropped up in the last two weeks that I was out of town most of the time. Will you be coming down here again this year? We certainly hope so. We will be here until the middle of June at least.

Mrs. O'Neill joins me in all best wishes.

Sincerely,
Eugene O'Neill.

---

1. A large estate in Paget Parish with a private beach.
2. David Belasco (whom O'Neill had once disdained for his lavish, commercial productions) had dropped his option on *Marco Millions*.
3. In a note to Belasco on 22 November 1924, O'Neill had indeed acknowledged that the epic-length *Marco* was "costly to put on, involving a forestage, music, many scenes, large crowds, etc." (Sheaffer, *O'Neill: Son and Artist*, 160).
4. Richard Madden, O'Neill's agent from 1919 until Madden's death in 1951.
5. Arthur Hopkins, New York producer.
6. *Lazarus Laughed*.

Cable
"ENEILL"


"BELLEVUE"
PAGET EAST, BERMUDA


April 17, '26

Dear Nathan:

I anticipated the Miller verdict[1]—but not the rejection of Hopkins, the news of which reached me in a note from Madden[2] by the same mail as your last. My hope was that Arthur[3] might take it on, especially as Bobby Jones[4] is so keen to do the sets. His reasons for a negative I haven't heard yet—he is extra uncommunicative with agents!—but Madden says he is writing me, and that he admitted *Marco* was fine writing. At all events, that is that. Harris, I believe, was impressed but unwilling to tackle such a new proposition on his own.

As for Selwyn,[5] I really know so little about what he does and how he does it that my opinion is worthless. An interview he gave out in London in which he condescendingly pooh-poohed my plays and said not one of them had ever made any money—a rather startling statement in view of the fact that no less than six (*Brown*[6] will be the seventh) have had runs in New York of over one hundred performances within six seasons (and comparatively few of these performances were given in the P. P.,[7] too!)—rather prejudiced me against him. Besides being what he must have known was a lie, such spoofing in a foreign land by a brother playwright is not cricket. Perhaps I am unduly irritable about the "regular" theatre cant on how nothing that pretends to art can make a dollar. There is too much inferiority and envy peering through the bursted seams of that old dogma of Managers and Lambs. One reason for my disgust is that I honestly believe the propagation of that theory has done a lot to discourage writers of real sensibility—but who must live—from ever tackling the theatre. And in my case, the notion is completely refuted. I must confess to having made a darn good thing out of my plays financially—a much better thing for the six years, I am confident, than nine out of ten of the professional crafty playwrights of gamblers' guesses at trade goods! Why, even one of my sailor one-acts (*In The Zone*) with a large cast, all men, no love interest, no star, ran successfully as a headliner for from 30 to 40 weeks on the Keith & Orpheum time[8] and paid me good royalties—on which I got married!—way back in 1918! Knowing vaudeville, what greater triumph for the serious playwright can the ages offer? It is true rumors occasionally reached me at the time that the direction had my Cockney stop the show at a crucial point to do a specialty hornpipe and sing "The Old Kent Road," that my Irishman had a few of Jimmy Thornton's[9] stories arranged in his part, etc., but—well, you cannot prove it by me for I never saw it.

I seem to have gone off on a tangent. Aside from the above, Selwyn is O.K. to me but my inner hunch is he wouldn't look at it with any considering eye. How about Dillingham?[10] Or Ames?[11] They have the money, I know, but have they anything else? Do you know of other possibilities? I might try Gest.[12] Or perhaps Walter Hampden[13]—although I have him in mind to submit my Lazarus play to, when completed.

We are sorry about your not coming to Bermuda this year. Still, if your London plans are still unfixed, we'll keep on hoping.

Much gratitude for your efforts on behalf of *Marco*!

Eugene O'Neill.

P.S.

My felicitations to Comrade Mencken![14] It's a case of hands across the continent—while they are at him in Boston (where they have refused to allow *Desire* to play, by the way) they are climbing my frame in great shape out in Los Angeles—for having my Abbie appear in a flannel nightgown, no less! There ought to be a grand quote for "Americana"[15] in that trial out there as reported in the L.A. papers.

---

1. Both Gilbert Miller (1884–1969) and Arthur Hopkins, prominent producers, turned down *Marco Millions*.
2. Richard Madden, O'Neill's agent.
3. Arthur Hopkins.
4. Robert Edmond Jones.
5. Edgar Selwyn, New York playwright and producer, who ran the Selwyn Theatre.
6. *The Great God Brown* was copyrighted 2 July 1925; published by Boni and Liveright, New York, March 1926, in a volume also containing *The Fountain, The Moon of the Caribbees*, and other plays; presented 23 January 1926 by the Greenwich Village Theatre (produced by O'Neill, Kenneth Macgowan. and Robert Edmond Jones).
7. Provincetown Players.
8. Refers to two vaudeville theater chains founded in the late nineteenth century and later merged: the B. F. Keith and the Orpheum chains.
9. James Thornton (1861–1938), actor and songwriter. Famous as a monologist who would make dour comments about imaginary newspaper headlines.
10. Charles Dillingham (1868–1934), New York producer.
11. Winthrop Ames (1870–1937), New York producer. Like Dillingham, he was more interested in serious drama, revolting against Belasco's showy spectacles.
12. Morris Gest (1881–1942), New York producer.
13. Walter Hampden (1879–1955), actor and producer.
14. H. L. Mencken, whose *American Mercury* was fighting a censorship battle in Boston.
15. In his column "Americana" in the *American Mercury,* Mencken presented what he called crack-brained deeds and words.

O'Neill at Bermuda, 1926. *(Courtesy of Thomas Yoseloff.)*

Cable
"ENEILL"


"BELLEVUE"
PAGET EAST, BERMUDA


May 1st 1926

Dear Nathan:

Well, Ames,[1] in addition to the money, has a sort of background in himself from which to give the play the sort of distinction and taste a lot of it needs. Or such is my notion of Ames as garnered from reports of him—a lazy man and a cautious & conventional citizen but an educated American gentleman—but I never met him. I would like to have him read the script, if for nothing more than to hear his reaction. So anything you can do in that direction will be appreciated. I am writing Madden to send him a script if he has not already done so. Also to McClintic.[2] The latter I thought of but dismissed for financial reasons as I know he has no money to undertake so large a thing. But perhaps, as you say, he could get it.

No, I won't let Madden do anything that I won't consider at great leisure.[3] I have even written him not to do any promiscuous submitting on his own. Gest[4] has a script now, I believe, and Walter Hampden[5] asked to read it and has it.

Again thanks!


Eugene O'Neill.

P.S.
Missed mail so am giving this to passenger to mail in N.Y.

---

1. Winthrop Ames, New York producer.
2. Guthrie McClintic (1893–1961), New York director and producer and husband of actress Katharine Cornell (1893–1974).
3. Apparently Nathan had counseled O'Neill to consider carefully the recommendations of his agent Richard Madden.
4. Morris Gest, New York producer.
5. Walter Hampden, actor and producer.

PREFATORY REMARKS: In this letter, O'Neill is still trying to interest a producer in accepting *Marco Millions*. He wants Nathan to use his influence to get Winthrop Ames to read the play.

Bellevue
Paget E., Bermuda
May 28 [1926]

Dear Nathan:

What you can do now which would be a great favor is to persuade Ames to give it a real reading. He has had script for some time without any report, so I conclude he hasn't read it.

You haven't heard from Madden because he is waiting on something definite from Liveright who is crazy about script and is now trying to raise money to back it. This combination might have advantages. At least, any suggestions I made would carry about director, scenic artist, etc.

We sail from here the 15*th*. I hope you will still be in N.Y. then. Want very much to have you read *Lazarus Laughed*, finished now but not typed yet, and want a talk with you.

As ever!
Eugene O'Neill.

PREFATORY REMARKS: There is a discernible tone shift in this letter; the playwright, nervously awaiting Gilbert Miller's decision on *Marco*, seems to think of Nathan not so much as a mentor—but as an equal, a partner.

LOON LODGE
Belgrade Lakes, Maine[1]

Saturday.
[August, 1926]

My dear Nathan:

I wired the *American Mercury* today to find out if you had returned. Something seems afoot with *Marco* and Miller.[2] According to Madden,[3] he says he will do *Marco* if he can get Glenn Hunter and if *Young Woodley*[4] quits soon enough on the road. This is a bit indefinite. Particularly—this is confidential—as the Guild[5] seem to want it if I will give them enough time in which to produce. This latter offer has its bad points, the Guild having a habit of getting cold feet if you give them time to cogitate, especially where money is concerned.

Would Miller's taking it mean the Famous[6] would also buy it as a film, do you think? He seems to have had a talk with Kenneth[7] in which he spoke of my being willing to approve a production with painted drops—wonderfully painted, of course. Now I am all for this method of doing it! I suggested it to Belasco[8] when he first had it and my own ground plans which I use in writing were drawn with this notion in view.

My point in writing to you is that if you see Miller you might tell him this. Also that, other things being equal, I would like to sell it to him. But I really need a quick decision of some sort. I shall have to give the Guild their answer soon. You might let Miller know that there really is another high class producer after it. If my agent or Kenneth told him, he would think it a bluff; but it really looks as if the Guild were serious.

I wouldn't bother you except that I know how interested you are in the play. By the way, your article in the *Mercury* was grand work for me![9] It seems to have stirred them up.

Did you get a chance to read *Lazarus Laughed* before you left? I guess not, from what Goldberg[10] wrote. Madden was a fool to tell you he had to have the script back. I wanted you to read it on the steamer when you had plenty of leisure. It is not a play a person could be hurried at without bad results. Let me know about this, and I will see that a script gets to you at once.

Do you remember that you said you would let me know, if you heard, about what time Miss Gish[11] would be in town this fall? Although there is nothing very definite in my mind I would certainly like to meet her and have a chat so that I could get started thinking definitely about some of the vague film ideas in my mind.

Did you have a good time of it on your trip?

Mrs. O'Neill joins me in all best wishes. The new play[12] is coming forth more slowly than usual—it is damn difficult—but very surely, I feel.

Sincerely,
Eugene O'Neill.

---

1. O'Neill spent the summer of 1926 here.
2. Gilbert Miller, New York producer.
3. Richard Madden, O'Neill's agent.
4. *Young Woodley,* a play by the Englishman John Van Druten (1925). It tells the story of a young man overwhelmed by guilt over his attraction to the wife of his schoolmaster.

5. Theatre Guild.
6. Famous Players Film Company.
7. Kenneth Macgowan.
8. David Belasco.
9. Nathan wrote with enthusiasm about *Marco Millions* in the August 1926 issue of the *American Mercury*, probably hoping to stir up interest and get the production started (George Jean Nathan, "O'Neill's New Play," *American Mercury* 8 [August 1926]: 499–505).
10. Isaac Goldberg, Nathan's biographer.
11. Lillian Gish, a close friend of Nathan's.
12. *Strange Interlude*.

Belgrade Lakes,
Maine.
Sept. 3rd
[1926]

Dear Nathan:

My plan is to get back to town around October the 1st. I would make a special trip down to have a talk with Miller[1] except that I'm going great guns on the new one[2] now, after a month's struggle over one scene that wouldn't come right, and I want to take full advantage of this favorable spell and get as much done on it as possible before cold drives me from these lakes.

I have heard again from the Guild.[3] Their committee has definitely decided they want the play[4]—but they could not do it for over a year. Whether I can make them offer enough advance to make it worth my while waiting so long is a question. At any rate, I will hold them off until I have talked with Miller—and particularly with you for I'd like your advice just as soon as I know that Miller has got an actor and is in a position to "get down to cases." The Guild sale has its advantages, one must admit, although I also know, none better, the disadvantages of tying up with them.[5]

The Actors' Theatre crowd[6] are still in the throes of trying to raise the money to do *Lazarus Laughed* from among the ranks of their million-talking, jitney-giving Scrooges. It will cost around forty thousand. I am getting a bit sick of these groups that never have the dough to do right by me, and always keep me worrying. At the old P. P.[7] naturally one expected it. Yet that group managed to be a good deal more self-sustaining than those that have followed. I am afraid I shall soon have to go on a search for one insane—therefore truly generous—millionaire and start my own theatre.

Seriously, I honestly am getting awfully fed up with the eternal show-shop from which nothing ever seems to emerge except more show-shop. It's a most humiliating game for an artist. Novelists have all the best of it. But I'm beginning to sound like Benny Leonard "panning" prizefighting!

I suppose I'll hear indirectly from Miller what Hunter[8] decides. Do you think he could do it? I haven't seen him since *Clarence*.[9]

All best!
Eugene O'Neill.

---

1. Gilbert Miller.
2. *Strange Interlude*.
3. Theatre Guild.
4. *Marco Millions*, which was still under consideration.
5. O'Neill worried that the Theatre Guild would put box-office considerations above artistic ones, and so he naturally was reluctant to entrust as "experimental" a play as *Marco* to them. But ultimately O'Neill's sole producer *was* the Guild.
6. This was a union of the old Greenwich Village Theatre and the Actors' Theatre, heavily endowed by Otto Kahn (1867–1934), the banker-philanthropist, and supported by the Actors' Equity Association.
7. Provincetown Players.
8. Apparently Miller was still waiting to see if he could get Glenn Hunter to play Marco.
9. *Clarence*, the Booth Tarkington comedy, in which Hunter had starred in 1919.

BELGRADE LAKES, MAINE

Sept. 27th
[1926]

Dear Nathan:

It looks now as if I might not be able to get down until the middle of the month—at the earliest not before the 10*th*. There is something I feel I've simply got to get done before I leave—the first part of *Strange Interlude*—that I'm on.

The Theatre Guild, after doing a lot of Tall Talking, have quit on *Marco* as it was my suspicion they might. And Kenneth Macgowan writes me Miller told him there was no chance of his doing it this year. Did you know this? Perhaps it's wrong. I hope so. I will need a production—financially speaking—badly before the winter is out, and the Actors' Theatre plans for *Lazarus Laughed* continue to drag. *L* is terrifically hard to cast and direct.

All best to you!
Eugene O'Neill.

PREFATORY REMARKS: O'Neill was getting desperate to have *Marco* produced; Miller still hadn't provided a contract.


Belgrade Lakes,
Maine.
Oct. 9 - [1926]

Dear Nathan:

I expect to leave here Wednesday—arrive in New York Thursday morning. Would it be possible to see Miller late Thursday or sometime on Friday? I've got to get a contract out of him at once or else start peddling the play about elsewhere. Baker[1] wants to do it at Yale for the grand opening of his Harkness Theatre there in December. This might be good advance publicity. What do you think? He's going to have a fine theatre there—can get sixty feet depth to his stage—and a wonderful lighting system—and he has two very good men for sets & lights. As for his acting, I don't know—probably bad, but no one would expect good acting there. It might give a good line on the production, this scheme—like an out-of-town opening.

I'll call you up Thursday morning. All best.

Eugene O'Neill.

---

1. George Pierce Baker (1866–1935), who had taught the 1914 playwriting class at Harvard that O'Neill took.


Hamilton, Bermuda.[1]
April 7, 1927.

Dear Nathan:

I have just recently finished *Strange Interlude*—first draft, that is—it will probably need a lot of cutting in a few months when I've gotten far enough away from it to see it critically as a whole. My feeling now is one of particular satisfaction with this play. It does all I had hoped it would do, I think, and seems to me a successful adventure along a new technique that offers limitless future possibilities. It is a "work" in point of size—nine acts, five in the first part and four in the second and will, as I told you, take two full evenings to play. I'm very anxious to have you read it and will see that you get a copy as soon as some extra scripts are made. I've had to send two out at once, one to the Guild[2] whose repertory company and present scheme of production make them first choice as possible producers of such a play, the other to Katharine Cornell[3] who would be ideal for the lead. This haste in order to try and nail down a production for next year. I'm rather desperate in this regard. Nothing definite is scheduled. The Guild are again dickering over *Marco* but have made no decision. Reinhardt[4] is alleged to be mad to do *Lazarus Laughed* in New York next season—but the fact remains that his plans seem still to be nebulous. And, although not costly, *Strange Interlude* presents seeming difficulties at which the run of managers would crawl into holes. And there you are. The old outlet for my stuff, via the P. P.[5] and the Greenwich Village, was certainly not ideal but it had a lot on the present blind alleys. It's hard for me even to think of more than two or three managements that I would care to submit my present work to. The time has come when I ought to have my own theatre, what? Seriously, I've thought of this—or more properly, vaguely dreamed of it.

Lawrence Langner[6] of the Guild was in Bermuda not long ago and I let him read what was typed of *Interlude*—six acts—and he became extraordinarily enthusiastic about it. Perhaps they will do it—I hope so—but he is only one of a committee of six.

(My pen has run out of ink, hence the typing.)

Macgowan promised me two months ago that he would send you one of the revised scripts of *Lazarus Laughed* that he was having typed for me. Did you ever get it? If not, I'll send you mine. I want you to read it over again under more favorable circumstances than when you saw it last.

Is there any chance of your coming to Bermuda this spring? We hope so. It would be fine to see you again. We probably will not come back until late in August. Work on our place is proceeding with provoking Bermudian deliberation, and we have to be around to watch or nothing would ever get done.

A James Cromwell, who married one of the Dodge auto heiresses (Delphine, the motor boat speedster) is visiting our next door neighbors who have become good friends of ours. Cromwell says he knows you quite well. He seems a nice chap. His wife has been next door for some weeks. She also is a good scout.

*Marco* should be out in book form any day now.[7] I am curious to see what reception it will receive. Let's hope it will bring in some money, at least. This season has not been a very productive one for me. I am at present engaged on a story for the movies[8] called *Ollie Oleson's Saga;* but, although this is a comedy of sorts, my past experiences with the film folk do not lead me to expect that they will ever find it suitable. The one I had in mind for Miss Gish is still in my mind, but it doesn't seem to develop into any sort of connected whole.

How is everything with you? Drop me a line when you have the time. Mrs. O'Neill joins me in all best to you.

As ever,
Eugene O'Neill.

---

1. By late November 1926, O'Neill had returned to Bermuda with his wife Agnes and children, Oona and Shane. Except for short visits to New York in May and September 1927, O'Neill stayed in Bermuda until late November 1927.
2. Theatre Guild.
3. Katharine Cornell, a popular young actress who ultimately rejected the central role of Nina Leeds.
4. Max Reinhardt (1873–1943), the Austro-German producer.
5. Provincetown Players.
6. With Philip Moeller, Lee Simonson (1888–1967), and others, Langner revived the Washington Square Players as the Theatre Guild in 1919.
7. Boni and Liveright, New York, published *Marco Millions* in April 1927, and another, limited edition in May 1927.
8. O'Neill occasionally considered movie productions of his plays. A total of seven of his long plays (including the *S. S. Glencairn* plays as a unit) was sold to Hollywood during his lifetime. None was particularly successful, except the Greta Garbo version of *Anna Christie* in 1931.

Hamilton, Bermuda,
April 24, 1927.

Dear Nathan:

You had better wait first and see what you think of *Strange Interlude*.[1] I am arranging it so you will receive a copy in the very near future. Two have been sent up to New York, one to Katharine Cornell[2] and McClintic[3] and the other to the Theatre Guild. I am now waiting for some report on these.

I had read the notice in the papers that Cornell was going to do *The Letter*;[4] but my agents, who are also Maugham's, assure me that she has not yet definitely signed for it but is only under contract to Woods[5] who has the play.

It looks as if the Reinhardt[6] *Lazarus Laughed* thing were off temporarily at least. There seems to be some sort of mix-up between him and Gest,[7] and his plans seem to be very uncertain.

I shall probably be down here until August, so perhaps you may be able to get down before we leave.

Mrs. O'Neill went up to New York a week ago. Her father has been very ill and is not expected to live.[8] I told her to phone you about *Strange Interlude* and to get the script Cornell has to you.

All best wishes, as ever,
Sincerely yours,
Eugene O'Neill.

---

1. When Nathan finally obtained a copy of the play and read it, he was most approving. His article in the *American Mercury* of August 1927 praised it as "the finest, the profoundest drama" of O'Neill's career. It "has not been surpassed by any that Europe has given us in recent years and certainly none that has been produced in America" (Nathan, "The Theatre: O'Neill's Finest Play," *American Mercury* 11 [August 1927]: 499).

In his article, Nathan correctly surmised that critics would question O'Neill's use of asides in *Strange Interlude*. The critic argued that *Interlude*, combining the methods of drama and novel, employed asides in an innovative way that went far beyond the soliloquy or other familiar, somewhat similar techniques.

2. Katharine Cornell.

3. Guthrie McClintic.

4. Cornell did appear that fall in Somerset Maugham's *The Letter*.

5. Albert Herman Woods, New York producer.

6. Max Reinhardt.

7. Morris Gest, New York producer.

8. Agnes visited her dying father at the Laurel Heights Sanatorium (originally the Fairfield County State Tuberculosis Sanatorium) in Shelton, Connecticut—on the same site where O'Neill had been a tuberculosis patient in 1912.

Hamilton, Bermuda
May 2nd [1927]

Dear Nathan:

The reason Mrs. O'Neill didn't get the script of *Strange Interlude* to you was that Katharine Cornell took it upon herself to walk off to England with it—a futile bit of business[1] that annoys me a lot. The only other script except for the one I have here is the one the Guild has. It looks possible now that they may do both it and *Marco*—but with the Guild I make no statements of fact until the contracts are signed and sealed.

There is no question of a three years' contract with them—only of my giving them a first reading option on my next three plays. If they meet me halfway on the other terms of the contract, I really think it would be to my advantage to do this, don't you?

You must have misunderstood me in my last. What I meant was a jape to the effect that after you had read the play you might not want to do an article on it, hence had better wait till you read it before volunteering.

I expect to come up to argue matters out with the Guild within the next two weeks. I'll get in touch with you as soon as I get in.

All best.
Eugene O'Neill.

---

1. Futile because Cornell had already agreed to star in Somerset Maugham's *The Letter* that fall.

Hamilton, Bermuda.
June 16*th*. '27

Dear Nathan:

Many thanks for your note. I will look forward to reading the article on *Strange Interlude*.[1] It is hard for me to say how deeply gratified I have been ever since you read the play to know your high opinion of it. I am not, except for rare monomaniacal moments, one of those to-be-envied ones who seem so happily certain that everything they write is "a darb." My days of doubt can do with a lot of reassurance and your appreciation is, as always, capable beyond all others' of reviving my groggy self-esteem.

Have you sent the script to Madden? I ask merely because, in that case, I must write him what to do with it.

Do you think Hopkins would be a good producer for *Interlude?* As I told you, the Guild is not definitely committed, and I am entitled to submit it elsewhere, provided I let the submittee know the circumstances of the option which expires Oct. 15th. There is a twofold advantage to be gained here: I might find a producer ready to take it up immediately: [if] the Guild let go—and if the Guild knew someone else wanted it, it would help them to decide to do it! But, at that, I think they will do it anyway.

All best to you,
Eugene O'Neill.

---

1. George Jean Nathan, "The Theatre: O'Neill's Finest Play," *American Mercury* 11 (August 1927): 499–506.

SPITHEAD
BERMUDA

July 15*th* '27

Dear Nathan:

I am immensely pleased with your article on *Strange Interlude!* Much gratitude! It should certainly be of great assistance in helping the cautious Guild bunch to come to a favorable decision—or, for that matter, Hopkins or any other to whom it might be submitted.

Poor Otto![1] I already hear his protest that he *did* contribute to the Provincetown Player and Greenwich Village funds to start their seasons— but they had always lost all that before they came to my plays. I suspect that you or I or both of us will hear from the Great Kahn or his press agent.

I'm going to send *Strange Interlude* to Hopkins just as soon as the cutting and minor revising are finished. I spoke to him about the play when we had lunch together during my last trip up, and he is expecting the script. Of course, anything you say, when you see him, to get him more interested would be greatly appreciated.

All best wishes—and again thanks!

Eugene O'Neill.

---

1. Here, O'Neill is reacting to Nathan's attack on Otto Kahn, the New York philanthropist, in the *American Mercury.* Nathan had criticized Kahn for having "regularly been deaf to every appeal made to him to support anything that O'Neill has done" (Nathan, "The Theatre: O'Neill's Finest Play," *American Mercury* 11 [August 1927]: 499).

SPITHEAD
BERMUDA

August 11*th* '27

Dear Nathan:

Many thanks for the *Times* editorial.[1] Your article[2] has certainly stirred them up! Did you see something by Allison Smith in the *World?*

And speaking of your article, I have read it over again a good many times since I last wrote you. It is certainly corking stuff! I only hope the play, when produced, will live up to what you have written of it. I have been doing a lot of work on it lately, thinking carefully over every line in it and cutting and rewriting a bit in a few spots—a job that has taken a great deal of time but has resulted in a much better play. I've also gone all over *Lazarus Laughed* and done quite a bit of changing to simplify it. It is going to be published in October.[3] I'm thinking of writing a brief introduction explaining what I'm driving at in it, my use of masks in P. P.[4] productions since *The Hairy Ape*, my notions of what an Imaginative theatre should be, etc.— What do you think of this idea?

I suppose the *Times* editorial was written by Corbin.[5] Only Corbin would hold up Montrose Moses[6]—God save the mark!—as an alive authority on drama. And calling me a "dark giant"! Makes me feel like a member of a colored baseball team!

I'm coming up about Sept. 1st. Will you be in town around then? There are many things I'd like to talk over.

It has been, physically speaking, a bad luck summer for me[7]—I've had a case of Bermuda summer flu that hung on for five weeks and only yielded finally to a lot of vaccine injections—but it has been very fertile for my work. In addition to the long intensive jobs on *Interlude* & *Laz.* I've got my next, *Dynamo*,[8] ready to start the dialogue and I've had four ideas for new plays that I think are real stuff!

Mrs. O'Neill joins in all best.

As ever,
Eugene O'Neill.

1. Charles Morgan's "An Analysis of Current Plays," *New York Times*, 24 July 1927, sec. 7, which criticized *The Great God Brown*'s use of masks.

2. A reference to Nathan's preproduction praise of *Strange Interlude* in "The Theatre: O'Neill's Finest Play," *American Mercury* 11 (August 1927): 499–506.

3. By Boni and Liveright, New York, November 1927.

4. Provincetown Players.

5. John Corbin (1870–1959), *New York Times* drama critic.

6. Montrose J. Moses (1878–1934), American drama critic and scholar.

7. O'Neill left Bermuda at the end of August for New York, where he courted Carlotta Monterey (while his family remained in Bermuda). He probably did not tell Nathan about this. O'Neill returned to Bermuda for October and part of November—the last time he ever lived there.

8. *Dynamo* was copyrighted 4 October 1928; published by Horace Liveright, New York, October and December 1929; presented 11 February 1929 at the Martin Beck Theatre (produced by the Theatre Guild).

PREFATORY REMARKS: In February, O'Neill left Agnes Boulton and sailed to Europe with Carlotta Monterey. He did not mention his tumultuous personal life to Nathan here—although he had in great detail to Kenneth Macgowan in a letter just two days earlier.

O'Neill was to remain three years abroad. Meanwhile, Nathan evaluated the state of American drama; he claimed that "with O'Neill . . . the native drama has begun to take on at least a measure of the significance that it previously lacked . . . O'Neill has shown the aspiring American playwright that there is a place here for a whole-hearted integrity in dramatic writing" (Nathan, "The Theatre: The American Prospect," *American Mercury* 15 [October 1928]: 248).

THE BERKELEY
London, W. 1.
GERRARD 4321
"SYBARITE" LONDON

Feb 24*th* '28

Dear Nathan:

Well, after a week in London I am strong for it. It seems to me that if it were possible for me to live contented in any city this would be the one. There is something so self-assuredly nerveless about it. Of course, the weather has been unexpectedly fine—warm and sunny every day—and that helps. Also I've kept strictly incognito, and it is a grand relief to live as an unknown private citizen for a change with the security that my intimate affairs[1] are not being kept tabs on by the gossips and the *Graphic*,[2] *Mirror*[3] & Co.

In short, I've been happier since I left New York than ever in my life before. One can't say more. It is like a rebirth, really, after a long period in which I existed with resignation because, after all, there was always my work to escape into—but from now on I expect to live as well as work—without any disadvantage to the latter. Rather I know my work will gain an added vitality.[4]

Madeira is out. The more I found out about it the less I liked the prospect. So it will probably be the south of France or Italy—motor around until the right spot is found on the coast. I'm leaving for Paris on Monday.

My address until I get definitely put will be c/o Guaranty Trust, Pall Mall. Write me a line when you get the chance.

All best always!

Eugene O'Neill.

1. O'Neill is referring to the scandal over his desertion of Agnes Boulton.
2. The *New York Graphic*, a sensational tabloid published by Bernarr Macfadden.
3. The *New York Daily Mirror*, a sensational tabloid published by William Randolph Hearst.
4. He was correct; his best work did indeed lie ahead.

[postcard postmarked "Espana"]
[1928]

Dear George:

Hope that taxi bump didn't bother you much! Tough luck!
This is the best shore place[1] I have struck in Europe really good stuff!
All best [to] you both from us.

Gene

1. The reverse side of the postcard shows Málaga, a city on Spain's south Mediterranean coast.

PREFATORY REMARKS: This is one of the longest letters O'Neill ever wrote to Nathan.

Paris, August *26th*
[1928]

Dear Nathan:

I've started to write you about a half-dozen times in the past few months, but something always came up to switch me off of it. In a *Paris Herald* that I happened to pick up I saw where you had been over here and were sailing for home. Were you in France at all? I wish I had known you were coming. We might have been able to hook up some place. There is nothing I would have liked better than to have had a long talk with you. So much water has flowed under so many bridges since I last saw you. Well, better luck next year!

I have spent most of my time (this is confidential, of course) in Guéthary near Biarritz down in the Basque country. Of course, there has been a lot of touring about but my headquarters, where I have written *Dynamo*, has been in Guéthary. I have a fine old villa there right on the sea.[1] The Basque country and the Basques hit me right where I belong. According to present plans and inclinations it is there that I shall settle down to make a home for the rest of my days—and I feel that this time it's going to prove what none of my other attempts were—a real home!

Europe has meant a tremendous lot to me, more than I ever hoped it could. I've felt a deep sense of peace here, a real enjoyment in just living from day to day, that I've never known before. For more than the obvious financial reasons, I've come to the conclusion that anyone doing creative work is a frightful sap to waste the amount of energy required to beat life in the U.S.A. when over here one can have just that [much] more strength to put into one's job.

*Dynamo* is finished and is now in process of being typed. I want you to see a script of it as soon as possible. It is real stuff, I am sure—a good symbolical and factual biography of what is happening in a large section of American (and not only American) soul[s] right now. It is really the first play of a trilogy[2] that will dig at the roots of the sickness of Today as I feel it—the death of the old God and the failure of Science and Materialism to give any satisfying new one for the surviving primitive religious instinct to find a meaning for life in, and to comfort its fears of death with. It seems to me anyone trying to do big work nowadays must have this big subject behind all the little subjects of his plays or novels, or he is simply scribbling around on the surface of things and has no more real status than a parlor entertainer. But more of this when we talk. The two other plays will be *Without Endings Of Days* and *It Cannot Be Mad.* These two plays will be greater in writing scope than *Dynamo*—which has a direct primitive drive to it and whose people are psychologically simple, as compared to *Interlude*'s—and will give me a greater chance to shoot my piece as a writer—but *Dynamo*, believe me, has taken all I have to give as a dynamist of the drama, and it should make its power felt terrifically when once it is skillfully produced. I'm quite proud of it and anxious to get your reaction. It is going to bring all the pious sectarians down on my neck in hell-roaring droves, I prophesy—and should be as much argued about, I think, in its different way as *Interlude*. It will require some expert directing to get its full values across, but I hope this will be safe in the hands of Phil Moeller.[3] Unfortunately I won't be there to help and will have to take my chance on being present only in a detailed list of written instructions. The snarl in my domestic situation, with my wife still playing financial hold-out and making all sorts of impossible demands, has rather forced the decision on me of fighting shy of the U.S.A. for another year and continuing my travels. I am sailing for the Far East early in October—expect to be in India a bit, then settle down in Hong Kong for a spell of work, then to Java and way stations and so on down to South Africa for another settling down and more work, back to France in June. This ambitious scheme may vary in detail but the general plan of it will be carried out. I think this trip is going to give me a lot I need and I'm certainly looking forward to it.

The aspect of life has certainly changed for me in the past six months. For the first time in God knows how long I feel as if life had something to give me as a living being quite outside of the life in my work. The last time I wrote you I said I was happy. A rash statement, but I can make it again with tenfold emphasis! And, believe me, it has stood tests that would have wrecked it if it weren't the genuine article, for everything has been done from the outside that malice and revenge could dope out to ruin it! But it has come through finer and deeper and is the wealthier for all the knocks. As I approach my fortieth birthday, I feel younger and more pepped up with the old zest for living and working than I've ever felt since I started writing. I may seem to slop over a bit about this, but no one really knows into what a bag of tedium and life-sickness I was sinking. I was living on my work, as one does on one's nerves sometimes, and sooner or later my work would certainly have been sapped of its life because you can't keep on that way forever, even if one puts up the strongest of bluffs to oneself and the world in general. Now I feel as if I'd tapped a new life and could rush up all the reserves of energy in the world to back up my work. Honestly, to me it is a sort of miracle, so resigned had I become to being resigned to the worst, and you'll have to be indulgent to my wishing a bit of my pop-eyed wonder at it on you!

In addition to the plans for near future plays I've also done a lot of thinking on my idea for the Big Grand Opus.[4] It's too long for me to try to go into here, but much of it when I see you. I want to give about three years to it—either one long stretch or, more probably, that amount of working time over a longer period with intervals of doing a play in between times. This G.O. is to be neither play nor novel although there will be many plays in it, and it will have greater scope than any novel I know of. Its form will be altogether its own and my own—a lineal descendant of *Interlude*, in a way, but beside it *Interlude* will seem like a mere shallow episode! Does this sound ambitious? Well, my idea of it as it is growing in me certainly is aiming at stars, and I only hope to God I have the stuff in me to do it right— for then it will be One of the Ones and no damn doubt about it!

So you see I'm feeling fairly fit when I'm dreaming of championship belts! I hear a lot of the boys in N.Y. are feeling very sad about the future of my work, fearing that it will be ruined by the fact that I had the guts to make a grab for happiness.[5] I feel sorry for these melancholy ones whose wish is so obviously the father of their apprehension! They are going to be terribly disappointed! I wonder why the hell it is that even the people whom you would think were free from the banal dogmas of Main Street always believe that every artist's wife collaborated in his work and he couldn't have done it without her companionship (when more often he is driven to work to escape from her)? I'll be damned if I don't think it's the fool authors themselves who are responsible for this myth, what with their propitiatory dedications to their fraus stuck in the front of nearly every book one comes across.

I've also heard reliable gossip of much more serious rumors about what I have done and haven't. Of course, I expect this, knowing the original source of all such hooey. Some wives turn out that way and are only spiteful when they have promised to be sporting and come clean. But it's all rather nauseating. In all my life among all kinds—and a good part among the so-called worst kinds—of people, I've never been double-crossed before. Not because I couldn't be. I was always easy and wide open, but I always found that men and women knew they could trust me so they never gypped my trust in them. This is a new experience. Frankly, I don't care for it. Somehow it reflects on a humanity that is already too reflected on for much faith. At first, I was a bit hurt by it, but now I'm only peevish.

But enough of that! It's not worrying me much really, and I don't know why I'm bothering you with it except that you may have heard said dirt and wondered what my reaction to it was.

I'm sending this letter by Louis Kalonyme.[6] I'm also giving him a letter of introduction to you. He has been an intense and loyal admirer of yours for a long time and wants very much to meet you. He's an old friend of mine. You've probably seen a lot of his art criticism (and for one season, theatre) in *Arts & Decorations*. He's got real stuff in him but has had a rotten hard break from fate in that serious trouble with his eyes has kept him barging back and forth from one specialist to another in U.S., Germany & England. I've known Louis for six or seven years. He's a good guy. Well, that's about all about me, I guess.

I know this is a hell of a late date to be expressing my grateful appreciation of your article on the *Interlude* critics. I meant to write you at the time, but I was dodging around so much then.

I'm in Paris for a few days—then back to Guéthary for two weeks. You'd better address any letter care of Guaranty Trust Co., 50, Pall Mall, London.

All good wishes always,

As ever,
Eugene O'Neill.

---

1. O'Neill had taken a six month's lease on the Villa Marguerite with its own private beach on the Bay of Biscay. Close by were the Pyrenees.

2. The other two were to be titled *Without Ending of Days* (later renamed *Days Without End*) and *It Cannot Be Mad*. The overall title was first *God Is Dead! Long Live—What?*, then changed to *Myth Plays of the God-Forsaken*.

3. Philip Moeller directed most Theatre Guild productions, and later directed the original

productions of *Strange Interlude* (1928), *Dynamo* (1929), *Mourning Becomes Electra* (1931), *Ah, Wilderness!* (1933), and *Days Without End* (1934).

    4. First reference to his ambitious cycle of plays, which he never finished.

    5. O'Neill is referring to the New York critics, who suddenly seemed to wax disapproving.

    6. Louis K. Kalonyme (1900–1961), contributing art critic to the *New York Times;* art and drama critic for *Arts & Decoration.*

PREFATORY REMARKS: This letter contains one of the most personal written statements O'Neill made to Nathan about his turbulent private affairs.

> Villa "Les Mimosas"
> Boulevard de la Mer,
> Cap d'Ail, A.M., France.[1]
> February 14*th* 1929.

Dear Nathan:

I've been meaning to write you as soon as we got settled and at last we are. It's a good villa finely situated right on the Mediterranean and will be just the spot once the weather decides to behave normally. It's been snowing nearly every day and colder than the devil so far. Sacha Guitry[2] lives about a stone's throw away on the waterfront.[3] I hope if you come over later on you'll be able to pay us a visit.

The trip to the Far East was all I expected of it and more. I got an enormous lot out of it in spite of being really pretty ill for three weeks—a touch of sun in swimming at Singapore followed by flu in Saigon and finishing in a Shanghai hospital.[4] Also the publicity mix-up in Shanghai & Manila[5] was particularly exasperating and threatening at the time although the humorous side of it strikes me now. It was really the most ridiculous farce I've ever run into! I'll have a lot of amusing dope on it to tell you when I see you. It's too much for a letter.

Not having heard from you about *Dynamo,*[6] I opine it didn't hit you right in the reading. Perhaps when you saw it on the stage, you got a new light on it. I hope so. In rereading it lately it seemed so essentially a thing that must be seen and heard in a theatre in order to appreciate its true value.[7] It also seemed badly in need of cutting. I hope Moeller made a good job of this.

The East and the tropics are no place to work—at least not for me. I felt the itch to get back on the job and vetoed our original plan of going to South Africa on the way back—was afraid I might not work there either. As it is I'm on a new play[8] now but the idea is still doing unexpected somersaults in my planning it out—the last part of it, at least, for it will be in two parts like *Interlude*—and I haven't begun actual dialogue yet.

All is well with us, and my latest news is that Mrs. O'N. will shortly be going honestly to Reno, so when that is gone through we'll both be able to have a little peace.[9] We've sure earned it. "God only knows the trouble we've seen"—quite enough!—through A's willful waiting. Her motives are not mercenary either. That end of it was settled long ago. The delay has been caused by her refusal to accept a clause specifying that she should write no articles about me or our married life or thinly-disguised autobiographical fiction exploiting me. Can you beat it? The necessity for such a clause, from my standpoint, is that even before we separated I knew she was dickering with an agent about an article of that nature.

An ugly business, the whole affair! I shall be so damned relieved when it's all over. This living on the brink of a scandal, with families and children on both sides to be protected, is a wearing business which lets one in for a lot of humiliating experiences. If C and I didn't have such considerations to watch, it would be so easy to come out in the open and tell everyone to learn to like it or go to hell!

Well, it's been as hard a test of our relationship as one could imagine and has done a lot for us we ought to be—and are—grateful for in that respect. So it's an ill wind that—

Carlotta joins me in all good wishes. Write when you get a chance. I hope all is well with you and that the weather, which I hear is as rotten in N.Y. as elsewhere, hasn't laid you out.

Good luck!<br>
Eugene O'Neill.

---

1. Just outside Monte Carlo; the O'Neills stayed about five months, leaving in late May.

2. Sacha Guitry (1885–1957), French actor, film director, and dramatist.

3. Ultimately, O'Neill found the villa not secluded enough, and he and Carlotta moved to Le Plessis.

4. O'Neill glosses over some events: he went on a drinking binge (his first major relapse) and quarreled with Carlotta.

5. Alfred Batson, an old acquaintance of O'Neill's now working as a reporter for the *North China Daily News*, recognized the playwright in Shanghai. Shortly after Batson's modest article appeared, American news media (including the *New York Times* via the Associated Press) invaded the city. Journalists scoured Shanghai for a glimpse of the famous playwright, reporting any gleanings of information, sometimes with humorous results. Disguised as a priest, O'Neill fled to Manila on the German liner *Coblenz*.

6. O'Neill was correct. Nathan had hinted as much in his *American Mercury* columns (*American Mercury* 15 [December 1928]: 505; *American Mercury* 16 [January 1929]: 119–20). The critic didn't reveal the full extent of his displeasure with *Dynamo* until after it opened in February 1929.

7. O'Neill would eventually take the opposite view, shunning production as a diversion of his energies from the only aspect of the theater that truly interested him—writing.

8. Probably *Mourning Becomes Electra*, which was copyrighted 12 May 1931; published

November 1931 by Horace Liveright, New York; presented 26 October 1931 by the Theatre Guild, Guild Theatre.

9. Agnes Boulton obtained a Reno divorce on grounds of desertion on 3 July 1929. On 22 July, O'Neill and Carlotta Monterey were married in Paris.

PREFATORY REMARKS: Critics pounced upon *Dynamo*. A reviewer for the *New York Telegram* wrote that O'Neill "shook his fist at God and blew kisses in the general direction of Electricity" (Robert Garland, "Eugene O'Neill's Dynamo Displayed in 45th Street," *New York Telegram*, 12 February 1929). Only a few critics—notably Brooks Atkinson in the *New York Times*—thought the play had merit.

Nathan judged the play "an extremely poor one" which was "miles below his better work." It was crude, childish, trivial, and a "dud" (Nathan, "Judging the Shows," *Judge* 96 [9 March 1929]: 18, 29). But Nathan also attacked the critics who were deriding O'Neill; he accused them of castigating the man as much as the artist.

In his second post-opening review of *Dynamo* (in the *American Mercury*), Nathan was waggish as usual, but also much sharper. *Dynamo*, he wrote, "is almost completely without shading"; its "final effect is of a calliope going down for the third time and tooting at the top of its remaining strength for help." To make his point, the critic printed all of the heavyhanded stage directions from Act One. He added that subsequent acts "are every bit as rich in 'fuming impatiences, snorts of contempt, fuming longings, flyings into a rage, defiant sneers, taunting laughs, dire booms of foreboding,' and 'terrible looks'" (Nathan, "The Theatre: A Non-Conductor," *American Mercury* 16 [March 1929]: 373–78).

Villa Les Mimosas,
Cap d'Ail, A.M., France.
March 19, 1929

Dear Nathan:

Your letter arrived yesterday and I was damned glad to hear from you. Yes, I've read your second article[1]—didn't see the first[2]—and I thoroughly disagree with you about the play. Not that you're not right about the excessiveness of the stage directions, but then I thought you knew that my scripts get drastically weeded out in that respect when I read proof, and that I always let them slide as they first occur to me until then. A slovenly method, perhaps, but the way I've always worked.

Then again, I don't think it's fair to take the speeches of a lot of admittedly inarticulate characters in a particular play as expressions of the general underlying theme of a trilogy—which I obviously never intended them to be. But here again I was wrong in laying such stress in my letters on what is, and was, a very general and indefinite meaning I took those three plays to have as examples of American blundering in search for some satisfying and sustaining faith. The stories of the plays came to me quite independently of one another, as separate entities with no reason for being written except their own particular dramas of people's lives. The notion that the three had a general underlying spiritual theme which related them only occurred to me long afterwards, and I had no business to lay stress on it to the damage of what was my proper and inspiring job,—each play on its own as a drama of human interrelationships. For what is *Dynamo* primarily but the story of a minister's son and the psychological mess into which hatred and fear of his bullying Fundamentalist father and an over-emphasis on love for the mother who betrays his trust, lead him when his life suddenly becomes complicated by love for an atheist's daughter. When this is further complicated by his devouring popular science manuals—in final rebellion against his father and his father's god—and weaving a new besotted dogma out of them, never really getting away from his mother (witness the postcards) and then finding she has died wanting him, longing for him—why then in his unbalanced state of mind he makes his mother into an atheistic deity out of the popular science books,—a dynamo, since dynamos fascinate him—and, when he is unfaithful to her with the girl she hated, kills the girl as an expiating sacrifice and then runs back into his mother—death in her, one with her, possessing her again—as his final effort in flight from life to security.

Now to me this story of the play, *Dynamo*, is almost too obvious in my script—but no one writing of the production, seems to have seen it. And that, I take it, is my own fault for throwing sand in their eyes with my ill-advised—and, in any event, premature—announcement of my personal interpretation of three ideas for plays.

There's a lot more to say by way of explanation—but, oh hell, it can wait until I see you, in case what I've said above isn't clear. I'm to blame, too, for letting the play out of my hands too soon, and while I was in such an upset and uncritical state of mind. There is much to be done on it clearing it up and this I am now doing on the proofs. And I'm to blame for letting it go on without my being there. I mean no reflection on the Guild production, but I always sense a lot of good and bad values I was blind to before when I *hear* my plays in rehearsal. And, especially with a difficult play like *Dynamo*, no one can really substitute for the author in such matters.

But *Dynamo is not* far, far below me. I'm sure of that! Wait and see! It will come into its own some day when it isn't judged as a symbolical trilogy with a message to good Americans about what's wrong with them and what to do about it. Most of "the boys" seem to have mistaken it for just that! And I think you're wrong, too, this time—as wrong as about *Desire* & *Lazarus Laughed* (*Lazarus* is *far* the best I've ever written!).

As for the wave of denunciation, I expected that. It was as sure to come as it was with *All God's Chillun*. But I'm getting awfully callous to their braying, for or against. Ervine,[3] as I once told you, I've thought ever since he started as critic was the biggest fool writing English. But, psychologically, he's easy to see through—a disappointed playwright gangrened with his failure. Broun[4] ought to write a final sequel to his first novel and call it *The Boy Doesn't Grow Older.* He runs true to dishonest form in criticizing stuff of mine he's neither seen nor read—a practice he began with his wife's criticism of *Diff'rent,* if you'll remember.

But what the devil, they're really boosting me with their wholesale condemnations for the reaction against such nonsense will come soon enough. And these teapot turmoils at least keep me shaken up and convinced I'm on my way to something. I know enough history to realize that no one worth a damn ever escaped them—so it gives me hope. When I'm generally approved of I begin to look in the mirror very skeptically and contemplate taking up some other career I might succeed at. So it's all tonic!

But what I really started to write this letter about—(dismissing *Dynamo* with a joking word or two!)—was this. Will you surely plan now to come and see us when you come over? Carlotta joins her urgings to mine. We will, by that time, be settled somewhere along the Loire between Nantes and Tours (the loveliest part of France, to my mind)—a fine motor trip, not too long, from Paris. We will come to Paris and motor you down in our car—and it is a fine car, for I am a "bug" and a snob where cars and boats are concerned, and I try to have the best or nothing. We have a fine cook—and although it is a tee-total household, we are not bigoted; and you shall not go thirsty. And we hope to have a decent house. So there you are! What could be fairer? And I further urge it on you as a personal favor to me because I'd sure like a long talk with you on many matters.

So in your next letter, make your reservations with us—at least to the extent of promising you will come, and never mind the "God willing"!

All best from us both.
Eugene O'Neill.

P.S.

You might be just in time to be a "best man" at a ceremony in some French village!

---

1. *American Mercury* 16 (March 1929): 373–78.
2. *Judge* 96 (9 March 1929): 18, 29.

3. St. John Ervine, playwright and *New York World* critic, who had written of *Dynamo:* "The Greenwich Village atheist prepares to meet his God" (*New York World,* 13 February 1929).

4. To Heywood Broun, the play was further proof "that O'Neill has no message" except "that of a saturnine sophomore" (Heywood Broun, "It Seems to Me," *New York Telegram,* 14 February 1929).

Villa Les Mimosas,
Cap d'Ail, A.M., France
March 29*th* '29

Dear Nathan:

Just a line to retract about thirty percent of my defense of *Dynamo* in my last! After laboring for ten days on the proofs I have to admit that the play as it reached you in script sure had its slovenly muzzy defects! The last act was particularly messed up and incoherent. I say "was." I hope I've cleared the whole play up by the drastic treatment I've given it and that it is now thirty percent better.

I let it out of my hands too soon, before I had any perspective on it. And I did too much writing in the medium of sets throughout. This last cannot be remedied at this late date. It's inherent in my idea of the play. But it's boring and confusing for a reader. As far as sets are concerned I'm going in for absolute simplicity in future—a dome[1] and a few suggestive details—plenty of lighting—complete freedom of movement. At least that's how I've felt about it for the past four months—perhaps a reaction I got from the Chinese theatre.

But more of this when I see you.

I still claim *Dynamo,* as will be in the book,[2] is a sound piece of work, in spite of some questionable technique, and really represents me on a good level.

This is all confidential, of course. I don't want to appear to be defending this play, or to admit, as a lamentable post-mortem that the Guild[3] might justly resent, that I sent it to them too soon—or to give out any detail of my future plans at present. Mum and then again mum is the proper course for me now.

Carlotta joins in all best to you. We are counting on your visit.

As ever,
Eugene O'Neill

---

1. A plaster cyclorama.
2. Perhaps the Liveright (New York) edition of *Dynamo,* October 1929.
3. Theatre Guild.

Villa Mimosas
Cap d'Ail, A.M., France
April 5th 1929

Dear Nathan:

Well, after much struggling with *Dynamo* as is in the proofs, I've decided the last half of the play absolutely can't be made to do, and I'm rewriting extensively throughout the whole play to let my main idea emerge from the mess I got it into. I'm also introducing two scenes that I had mapped out before but never wrote in because I felt they would throw the play between two stools—too long for a single play and too short for a double one. Also because I felt them unnecessary! Now I feel they're absolutely essential! I feel very strongly that in its new form *Dynamo* will certainly justify itself both in publication and when it is produced over here. I wouldn't waste this hard labor on it unless I felt sure of this.[1]

And that's that.

The snide boys, I gather from clippings, have certainly seized on your stage direction compilation with howls of low glee.

All best from us both. See you in June or so, we hope.

As ever,
Eugene O'Neill

---

1. But *Dynamo* stands as one of O'Neill's least praised plays. Nathan cited it as an exception to O'Neill's genius ("The Theatre: O'Neill: A Critical Summation," *American Mercury* 63 [December 1946]: 717; "The Theatre: The American Dramatist," *American Mercury* 17 [August 1929]: 500).

Villa Les Mimosas
Cap d'Ail, A.M., France
April 29th [1929]

(On second thought a
better address in future c/o Guaranty
Trust Co., 50, Pall Mall, London
—we're moving in a couple of
months and I don't know the P.O. of
it yet.)

Dear Nathan:

I have been touring about home-hunting in Touraine and did not receive Miss Gish's[1] first cable until I landed in Paris (mailed to me—about four days

Villa Thimeras,
Cap d'Ail, A.M., France.
April 5th 1929.

Dear Nathan:

Well, after much struggling with "Dynamo" as it is in the proofs I've decided the last half of the play absolutely can't be made to do and I'm rewriting extensively throughout the whole play to let my main idea emerge from the mess I got it into. I'm also introducing two scenes that I had mapped out before but never wrote in because I felt they would throw the play between two stools — too long for a single play and too short for a double one. Also because I felt them unnecessary! Now I feel they're absolutely essential! I feel very strongly that in its new form Dynamo will certainly justify itself both in publication and when it is produced over here. I wouldn't waste this hard labor on it unless I felt sure of this.

And that's that.

The snide boys, I gather from clippings, have certainly seized on your stage direction compilation with hands of low glee.

All best from us both. See you in June or so, we hope.

As ever,

Eugene O'Neill

O'Neill's letter dated 5 April 1929. The effects of the playwright's tremor on his handwriting can be seen here. *(Courtesy of Cornell University Library.)*

late). Then I went back to Touraine and didn't get her second cable until I got home here—again a few days late. It would be a favor if you would explain the delay in my answer, when next you communicate with her. And I couldn't make any definite answer as the Theatre Guild own half the rights. Madden had already set her a price, I guess, before she heard from me. Then there was some misunderstanding—on my part, at least—as to whether I was expected to make the version or not. If so, naturally I didn't want to split what my labor was worth with the Guild. Madden's price seemed right to me. *Strange Interlude* should be worth a hundred thousand, if other film prices are any standard of comparison. I am greatly interested in the idea of Miss Gish doing it and hope something will come of all this cabling back and forth.

No, I didn't see the article you wrote on the obvious venom displayed.[2] Would like to. Have you a copy of it? The clipping bureau[3] always lets me down on the ones I want while swamping me with the bunk.

Will look forward to seeing you. Carlotta sends her greetings.

As ever,
Eugene O'Neill

---

1. Lillian Gish, who was considering making a film of *Strange Interlude*.
2. Indicates, perhaps, the exiled O'Neill's dependence on Nathan to provide information and gossip about the New York theater. Probably O'Neill is referring to Nathan's first post-opening review of *Dynamo* (*Judge* 96 [9 March 1929]: 18, 29).
3. While living abroad, O'Neill subscribed to the International News Clipping Service to keep track of his productions.

## LE PLESSIS
## SAINT-ANTOINE DU ROCHER
## INDRE-ET-LOIRE

June 23*rd* [1929]

Dear Nathan:
I was damn glad to get your cable that you are surely coming to France. We are looking forward to seeing you here for a visit.[1] I remember saying in my letter I would drive up to Paris and get you but that part of it looks impossible now as I've just had a disagreement with the chauffeur and given him the gate and how soon I'll have a new one, don't know. Moreover I'm none too sure you wouldn't prefer the train to a long motor trip, in any

Nathan in a typical pose. *(Courtesy of Cornell University Library.)*

event—in fact, imagine you would. Let me hear from you by telegram as soon as you decide when you can come. Tours is, of course, the station, and there are fine trains. Will meet you at the Tours station. It's only a few hours' ride from Paris.

You'll like it here, I know. Hope you can surely make it. See you soon!

As ever,
Eugene O'Neill.

P.S.

If you should happen to run into Kalonyme[2] in Paris, he doesn't know this address, and for the present I don't want him to.

---

1. Nathan came, bringing Lillian Gish. According to Arthur and Barbara Gelb, during this visit O'Neill began finally to address the critic as George (instead of Nathan), although O'Neill's letters to him did not reflect this change until a year later (Gelb and Gelb, *O'Neill*, 705).
2. Louis K. Kalonyme.

LE PLESSIS
SAINT-ANTOINE DU ROCHER
INDRE-ET-LOIRE

August 31*st* '29

Dear Nathan:

I was damn glad to get your letter. We both were—for Carlotta was delighted with it. I have been intending to write to you or Lillian about the *Interlude* suit,[1] but there isn't any news except the discouraging fact that the case is on the calendar and may not come up for trial until a year and a half! This business of the law irritates me to the exploding point! Here is a case manifestly absurd and cooked-up on the face of it and yet our legal lights of the Guild, Liveright[2] & O'Neill can't seem to do anything to get it dismissed. We have to go through with it at endless trouble and much expense.

I told Harry Weinberger[3] to get in touch with you and send you the lady's book and her claims of similarity to look over. You'll get a big laugh out of the book which I advise you to read. It handed me a laugh, and I didn't approach it in a comedy vein. It's the damnedest piece of writing I've ever run across—a mixture of Laura J. Libbey, Elinor Glynn, and the Young Visitors! Harry W. sent it to me for my comment—which is that the lady-author is undoubtedly a bit loose in the head.

No need to say how grateful I will be for your help in this affair. What is needed most are examples of the use of the hereditary insanity and the eugenic baby motive in modern literature.[4] Of course, these themes are old as the hills but what Weinberger wants are specific works in which they figured.

I'm still stewing around on the preliminary mulling over of the work[5] I outlined to you—and there is still a lot to get thought out clearly before I start actual dialogue. It is going to be difficult, this! It would be so easy to do *well*. The story would see to that—and that's the danger I want to avoid. It has got to have an exceptional quality to lift it above its easy possibilities and make it worthy in some sense of its classic antecedents—or it will be a rank flop in my eyes no matter what others may think of it. So I'm going to do a lot more of tentative feeling out and testing before I start.

Also I'm waiting until I see many uninterrupted months straightaway before me. There have been visitors, necessary trips to Paris, etc. breaking in. And the latter part of Sept. I've got to go through a long painful session with the dentist (extractions & new bridges). So I won't be on my way until October. But I grow more and more enthused by this idea for the next work. It keeps growing richer and I don't grudge the delay because I know it's moving.

My nineteen-year [-old] son, six foot-two, 180 lbs., Eugene Jr.[6] has been visiting us after a tour of Germany I staked him to. He seems to have got a lot of valid stuff for himself out of Europe. He isn't the usual college youth from Yale; and yet he has enough of that about him to be no intellectual young prig. A fine youth, truly! I am proud of him—and I think he is of me—and our relationship is naturally brotherish with none of the forced "pal-father-son" bunk to it. When I survey his merits and think of the rotten mess of a life I was at his age, I have no fatherly superiority assumptions, believe me! He fits in very well with us. Carlotta likes him and he likes her, and I'm sure he feels more at home with us than he ever did when with me in the past. So all's well.

You don't say anything about the English plan?[7] Are you going to take them up?

It was grand to have you here, and it was grand to get to know Lillian.[8] She is simple and charming, and I sure admire her! Carlotta aussi! Put it down in the old date book that you're coming to us next year—and really stay for a while!

And think upon this: There are lots of chateaux for sale in this neighborhood. You had better look them over when you visit us.

All our affectionate best to you both!

As ever,
Eugene O'Neill.

1. Refers to the plagiarism lawsuit against O'Neill filed on 27 May 1929 by Georges Lewys, who claimed *Strange Interlude* had borrowed wholesale from her novel, *The Temple of Pallas-Athene*, which had been published in 1924. After a much-publicized trial in March 1930, the suit was dismissed.

2. Horace Liveright (1886–1933), founder of the publishing house Boni and Liveright; also theater producer.

3. O'Neill's personal lawyer and the Provincetown Playhouse's counsel.

4. O'Neill wants Nathan to identify other literary treatments of these themes, which Lewys claimed *Strange Interlude* had stolen from her novel.

5. *Mourning Becomes Electra.*

6. O'Neill's elder son, born 5 May 1910 during his marriage to Kathleen Jenkins.

7. Perhaps a reference to the *London Daily Express*'s invitation to Nathan to become an editorial contributor and guest critic, which he did the following year.

8. Nathan and Lillian Gish had been among the first visitors to Le Plessis in the summer of 1929. He was linked romantically with her for many years, until both finally told the *New York Times* that they were not engaged but were "good friends" ("Nathan Denies Betrothal," 23 June 1927).

## LE PLESSIS
## SAINT-ANTOINE DU ROCHER
## INDRE ET LOIRE

Oct. 12, 1929

Dear Nathan:

No, the copy of *Monks Are Monks*[1] has not arrived up to date. I saw a review of it in a Sunday *Times* but that's all. How has it hit them? Has Hergesheimer[2] made any comment on the tibia motif?

The Boston-*Interlude* mess[3] is sure ridiculous but the Guild seems to have got around them and made asses of them in fine shape, from what I hear. I think the whole affair will have a good effect, quite outside of the advertising in that it will make the censor boobies in the other cities a bit leery of stepping on it. The Quincy notion[4] strikes me as a good stroke, judging from results.

I'm breaking off work to go to the dentist in Paris for the prolonged session I've been ducking so long. The prospect doesn't fill me full of cheer, but I've had hellish toothaches lately, and that has forced the issue.

I've made two false starts on the big job.[5] It is going to give me an awful battle, I'm afraid, before I hit the right note. There are so many ways it might be done but none of them yet impresses me as *the* one way for it.

How is the New York season promising so far? *The Hairy Ape* is still on in Paris at the Pittoëffs' theatre.[6] I haven't seen it. Its reception was mixed. Most of the usual press critics were thumbs down, either resenting its alleged

Communistic message or resenting the American invasion of their theatre. The more radical papers were, of course, for it. But outside of these two prejudiced groups, it got some very fine appreciations from men like Antoine,[7] etc. which pleased me a lot. And it seems to have created a lot of talk and argument, mostly stupid stuff about its philosophical message, it is true, but useful in the long run. I hear the N.Y. papers said it was universally panned. This is not true at all, not even where the morning-after dailies were concerned. It really came out much better than I had expected. *The Hairy Ape* can't ever really be translated, in the first place. It is bound to lose in translation just the quality of it that is most worthwhile—its rhythm of colorful dialogue, its dynamic drive of language. And its emotional significance and meaning is nothing the French rational mind could ever get in a million years. The French theatre is dead from the neck down—and that means all dead where a theatre is concerned, no?

Carlotta joins in all cheeriest to you. Give the same to Lillian[8] when you see or write to her. We are fine. The chateau can easily be kept warm, we find. The heating system really works. So we're looking forward to winter without apprehension. The country is beautiful these days—the leaves just beginning to turn.

> Again, all best!
> As ever,
> Eugene O'Neill.

---

1. *Monks Are Monks*, published by Alfred A. Knopf (New York) in 1929, is a comic novel which features the characters of O'Neill, Nathan, and Mencken, thinly disguised.

2. Joseph Hergesheimer (1880–1954), American novelist and short-story writer. In his early career, he wrote historical novels, including a three-part saga of a Pennsylvania iron-founding family.

3. Arousing much protest from theater people and civil libertarians, Boston had banned *Strange Interlude*.

4. *Strange Interlude* had moved to the nearby city of Quincy, drawing much national attention.

5. *Mourning Becomes Electra*.

6. Georges Pitoëff (1887–1939), Russian-born French actor and director who founded a theater in Paris after World War I.

7. André Antoine (1858–1943), French actor, director, and theater manager; prominent in theatrical reforms in the late nineteenth century.

8. Lillian Gish.

LE PLESSIS
SAINT-ANTOINE DU ROCHER
INDRE-ET-LOIRE

Nov. 12*th* 1929

Dear Nathan:

Your letter arrived a few days ago and we were both damn glad to hear from you. We had just returned from Paris where we spent three weeks—I with a daily visit to the dentist all that time! Now my teeth are fixed for the present and I can concentrate on work. Which I have been doing since our return, and I now feel I am at least off on the right foot. It should come with a rush from now on. All elaborate schemes have been cast aside and the aim now is to do this big job[1] with the utmost simplicity and naturalness. I had gotten myself terribly messed up searching for new ways and means and styles—but the idea just wouldn't fit in with any of them. They only got in its way. So I'm going ahead and let it write itself. The result will probably be a modified, simplified, *Interlude* technique. My plan is to work like hell, hold myself to doing an act a week at all costs, and get the first draft of the twelve acts in the three plays done by Feb. 1*st*. Then I'll set it aside for six months—take a trip somewheres and then write the first draft of another idea that has grown ripe.[2]

One thing that has made the preliminary work on this new trilogy extremely arduous has been the tremendous difficulty of seeing every character through all the situations in different plays. With *Interlude* that was simple. They followed fairly straight lines of development in that work. But this is another story.

In Paris I saw Lenormand's[3] *Mixture*[4] and liked it quite well—a strong play that sort of fizzles into anti-climax in the last two scenes. I like Lenormand himself immensely—a fine sensitive artist. His wife, the Dutch actress,[5] is also very much of a person. They are coming down to visit us soon. I also met the Pitoëffs[6] in Paris and liked them. She (Ludmilla) wants to play *Desire Under the Elms* and I've given the translation rights to Madeleine Boyd[7] (who visited us here) and Strowski,[8] the Parisian critic, as collaborators.

And in Paris I saw my first "Talkie"—*The Broadway Melody*—and, think what you will of me, I was most enthusiastic! Not especially at the exhibit itself, naturally, but at a vision I had of what the "Talky" could be in time when it is perfected. Looked at from the personal angle, I saw how its technique could set me free in so many ways [that] I feel still bound down— free to realize a real Elizabethan treatment and get the whole meat out of a theme. Not that the "Talky" folk are ever liable to let me realize any of these dreams but I think the day may come when there will develop a sort of Theatre Guild "talky" organization that will be able to rely only on the big cities for its audiences. As for the objection to the "talkies" that they do away with the charm of the living, breathing actor, that leaves me completely cold. "The play's the thing," and I think in time plays will get across for what their authors intended much better in this medium than in the old. Also I believe a play written for the "Talkies" can have just as much literary value in printed form as any done for the regular stage. And again I am certain plays can be written that could be played as written on either the regular stage or as a "talky"—with a little help in the way of elasticity in the contrivings of our stage scenic designers. At any rate, my inspirations on this subject have had one practical result that I see the next play after the trilogy (an idea I set aside because I couldn't see how to do it) as a stage play combined with a screen talky background to make alive visually and vocally the memories, etc. in the minds of the characters. Keep this notion of mine a secret, of course.

I am most eager to talk to Lillian[9] about all this—after she has made *The Swan*[10]—hear all about the inside of this new technique. Perhaps we can eventually get together on something worth doing for both of us. Be sure to bring her here next summer!

Does my "talky" enthusiasm strike you as idiotic? Be frank and write me at some length when you've got the mood and the leisure, and let me know what you think, not of the "talky" as is being done but as a medium for real artists if they got a chance at it.

*Interlude* got a bad spanking from the critical boys in Berlin. They say I have no roots (being a Yank!) except in Ibsen and Strindberg, forgetting that that, if true, is equally true of their own playwrights. One even objects to the play bitterly because I stole the aside from Shakespeare! It is all too damn dumb! Judging from the stupidity of their comments, I think Percy Hammond[11] would be a Georg Brandes[12] in Berlin! But the thing that makes me especially sick about the discussions of this production and that of *The Hairy Ape* in Paris is the evident fierce animosity to Americans as artists. They are forced to see our industrialism swamping them and forcing them to bad imitations on every hand, and it poisons them. They are bound they'll die at the post rather than acknowledge an American has anything to show them in any line of culture. It's amusing—and disgusting!—this clinging of theirs to their last superiority out of the past!

I see by the Paris *Herald* that Sinclair Lewis, Dreiser and I (in the order named) have been mentioned in the current Nobel Prize consideration—which mention is at least a step forward for us Yanks! (By the way, speaking of Sweden, when *Interlude* was done so successfully there, no one mentioned my imitation of Ibsen & Strindberg, it remained for the non-Square-head Berliners to discover that). They say Thomas Mann[13] is sure to get the award. I hope so. He deserves it. I think his work, with a few exceptions, is great stuff, don't you?

Carlotta joins in all good wishes to Lillian & you. We are looking forward to your coming here next year. Don't let anything stop you!

As ever,<br>
Eugene O'Neill

P.S.

Where is your book?[14] We've never received one. Do you mean to say I'm going to have to buy it? If I don't get it soon, I will! That ought to shame you!

---

1. *Mourning Becomes Electra.*

2. Possibly *Days Without End*, which was copyrighted 20 July 1933; published by Random House, New York, January and February 1934; first performed at the Plymouth Theatre, Boston, 27 December 1933; presented by The Theatre Guild at the Henry Miller Theatre, New York, 8 January 1934.

3. Henri-René Lenormand (1882–1951), French playwright, critic, poet and novelist; sometimes called the "Eugene O'Neill of the French stage" because his tragedies explored, often in a dreamlike way, the torturous effects of the unconscious and other mysterious forces.

4. Written in 1927; focuses on a woman of questionable virtue who is remarkably perceptive about the problems of existence.

5. Marie Kalff.

6. Georges and Ludmilla (1896–1951) Pitoëff.

7. A literary agent (and wife of critic Ernest Boyd).

8. Fortunat Strowski de Robkowa (1866–1952), French educator and literary critic.

9. Lillian Gish.

10. The 1930 United Artists comedy that Gish contracted to star in (a deal that ultimately fell through; when director Max Reinhardt withdrew, so did Gish).

11. (1873–1936), outspoken American drama critic for the *Chicago Evening Post, Chicago Tribune,* and *New York Tribune* (later *Herald Tribune*).

12. Georg Morris Cohen Brandes (1842–1927), Danish drama critic and scholar famous for his six-volume *Main Currents of Nineteenth Century Literature* (1872–1890).

13. Mann did receive the Nobel Prize that year.

14. *Monks Are Monks*, published by Alfred A. Knopf in 1929.

LE PLESSIS<br>
SAINT-ANTOINE DU ROCHER<br>
INDRE-ET-LOIRE

Jan. 7th, 1930

Dear Nathan:

I have been working like the very devil or I would have answered your letter and acknowledged the receipt of your book[1] long before this. Aren't you very well pleased with the book? Seems to me you certainly ought to be.

Your scheme worked out wonderfully. It is so damned amusing and it draws all the criticism together and takes the curse of straight criticism off it in such a novel way.[2] It has handed me endless guffaws—and also much serious appreciation. I was afraid the tibia[3] might be deleted before publication and was delighted to find it in! Thank you very much indeed for sending the book!

It's good news about your finally getting free of the *Mercury*[4]—since I know how fed up you had got. And the idea of an international critical review[5] is certainly a grand one! I'm anxious to hear in detail what your plans are about it. Will hope to see you both[6] here as soon as it's convenient for you after you get over. We're going on a motor trip—either through Spain or Italy—as a vacation after my first draft[7] is off my hands. By the first of March I figure that will be—with good luck. We'll be gone maybe a month but will be "at home" again by the time you get over.

I'm on my seventh act now—the third act of the second play—which means the job is a little over half completed. I am working longer hours than I ever have before as a day after day stint. Sometimes I think it's grand and other times that it's rotten—as usual. The dialogue hasn't taken any turn outside of my method in *Brown, Desire,* etc. Everything I tried by way of experiment along the lines I spoke of last summer simply wouldn't work. And an *Interlude* technique would only be in my way—these are plays of direct passion and intensity and involved inhibited cerebrations don't belong in them. I monkeyed around with schemes for dialogue and ideas for production until my head ached—but the story I had to tell made all such stuff seem futile, and I finally settled down to the direct and least noticeable way. And I find I can get everything said about these characters' souls, hearts, and loins that can be said. But more of all this when I see you.

Carlotta joins in all affectionate best to Lillian and you. Good luck! We're enjoying the winter here. Plenty of gray days and much rain but very mild temperature. It seems to agree with us.

As ever,
Eugene O'Neill.

P.S.

I'm telling Weinberger[8] to be sure and see you about the plagiarism stuff[9] before you leave.

---

1. *Monks Are Monks.*

2. The plot revolves around the beautiful Lorinda's unsuccessful attempts to seduce a series of hardly disguised literary figures, among them O'Neill, Mencken, and Nathan. Finally, after the literati's only response to her charms is to intellectualize in comic form, Lorinda gives up and enters a nunnery.

3. O'Neill is referring to the book's bawdy "fibula" motif. (For example, Gilbert Hemingham [a.k.a. Hemingway] is greatly concerned with "the length of his fibula.")

4. The *American Mercury*, which Nathan had cofounded with H. L. Mencken in 1924 as a successor to *Smart Set*. From the beginning, the two had been at odds over the editorial direction of the *Mercury*. Mencken wanted it to include more serious content in politics, sociology, economics, and history, while Nathan, as usual, was mainly concerned with the arts. In July 1926 Nathan resigned as coeditor, remaining a contributing editor and dramatic critic. In 1930, he left to join the staff of *Vanity Fair*.

5. The *American Spectator*, launched in late October 1932 by Nathan, with O'Neill, Theodore Dreiser, Sherwood Anderson, James Branch Cabell, and Ernest Boyd as joint, unpaid editors. Other contributors included Joseph Wood Krutch, Havelock Ellis, Lincoln Steffens, and Clarence Darrow. Inspired by the eighteenth-century English *Spectator* of Addison and Steele, it was a folio-sized monthly focusing on the arts. It sold for ten cents a copy and included no advertising. The *American Spectator* ceased publication in 1935, a casualty of the Depression.

6. Nathan and Lillian Gish were still close friends at this time.

7. Of his trilogy, *Mourning Becomes Electra*.

8. Harry Weinberger, O'Neill's personal attorney.

9. Georges Lewys's plagiarism lawsuit against O'Neill, which went to trial the following spring.

LE PLESSIS
SAINT-ANTOINE DU ROCHER
INDRE-ET-LOIRE

Feb. 12*th* 1930

Dear George:

As Carlotta wrote you, I postponed reading *Testament of A Critic*[1] until I got off the night-and-day shift on the trilogy and had a little sane mind to give to it. I read it last night and like it immensely. In fact, it seems to me the best of all your books. At any rate, whatever your own opinion is, I know I enjoyed it more. It had the effect on me of striking a deeper vein. My congratulations on a fine piece of work! I see, via the clipping bureau,[2] it has infuriated Arnold Bennett.[3] Well, that's good!

*Interlude* seems also to have roused the ire of a number of the "Limey" critics, while others praise it fulsomely. The sedate ones are outraged by the frank sex and offended by the length. None of them on either side of the fence seem[s] to know what it's all about. I think English criticism is a pretty dumb brother. They seem to be lost in the past somewhere—the classic Pinero[4] past.

Our respective healths are better but still far from fit. Since the return from Spain we have had a poor time of it. The weather continues incredibly depressing. Rain and filthy lowering sky, muggy air, day after day. I never experienced anything like it. It has got on our nerves and spirits. We sail from Lisbon for Las Palmas in the Canary Islands on the 25th. There let us hope there is sunshine and warmth and maybe a canary bird still singing.

Re the trilogy: I put in six weeks' hard work making a change in the first two plays that I thought would improve them—and as soon as it was finished and typed saw it was no benefit at all but a mistake and threw it away. Since returning from Paris I have been busy restoring the status quo. What a damn fool one can be at times! Well, for better or worse, when this rechange is typed, I will have *a* version which I will let rest until two or three weeks of Canary sun have restored me. Then I'll read it and try to discover what all the writing is about. If what I discover merits your consideration, I will send you a script then—also submit to the Guild. If not, I will give it to the Canary Islanders for toilet paper, call this grand opus stillborn triplets, and try and think of something less wearing on the inner gent than fashioning tragedies in the Soviet and machine age. For your private ear, I reiterate that I feel up a stump about *Mourning Becomes Electra*. I can only catch glimpses of an act here or an act there, at most a day's slant at one play, but the whole work entirely eludes my eye except as a vast blur. As a result, I am a bit confused and harassed in spirit, wondering what I have or haven't done with it. I have simplified it greatly—to its advantage, I know—and probably on a last reading may decide to simplify it still more. It still needs a lot of cutting. I know that, but am too weary now to do it.

All best to Lillian and you from us both. And again let me tell you how very much I liked the *Testament*.

As ever,
Gene.[5]

---

1. Published by Alfred A. Knopf, New York, 1931.
2. International News Clipping Service.
3. (Enoch) Arnold Bennett (1867–1931), English novelist, dramatist, journalist, and critic.
4. Sir Arthur Wing Pinero (really Pinheiro) (1855–1934), English actor who became a dramatist recognized chiefly for several excellent farces, including *The Schoolmistress* (1886), *Dandy Dick* (1887), and *The Cabinet Minister* (1890). However, his *The Second Mrs. Tanqueray* (1893) helped pave the way for more serious drama.
5. The first time O'Neill uses this more informal form.

## LE PLESSIS
## SAINT-ANTOINE DU ROCHER
## INDRE-ET-LOIRE

Feb. 19*th* 1930

Dear Nathan:

Have been waiting until my first draft[1] was done before answering your letter. Well, it is finished now, thank God, and I am very well pleased with it.

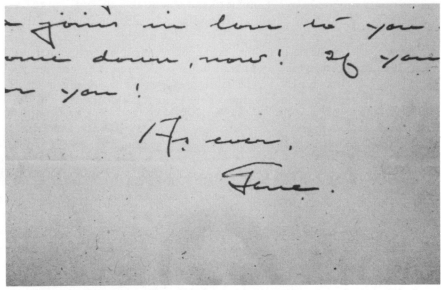

O'Neill's familiar closing. *(Courtesy of Cornell University Library.)*

Of course, there is a devil of a lot to be done on it yet. I rate it as about two-fifths finished in terms of the labor the final script will have taken. My plan now is to let it rest a bit while Carlotta and I take a few weeks' motor trip in Italy, then write the whole damned thing over in longhand, copying and revising, then let it rest for a longer spell while I do a first draft of my next one, and then copy and revise in longhand a third time for the final product. When you consider that there are twelve full-sized acts—four to a play—in this opus, you can see I am a glutton for punishment! But I think the results will justify the pains taken. By this method, which I think I will adopt hereafter with all my stuff, I think I should get all out of my material it's possible for me to get.

As a tentative title for the whole trilogy I have *Mourning Becomes Electra*, which you will see the full ironic force of when you have read the work. The first play is "Homecoming," the second "The Hunted," the third, "The Haunted." I think this is a good lay-out. This is confidential, of course. You are the only one who knows anything about what I'm doing.

Needless to state, I'm a bit fagged. I've been writing half a day, getting up at eight every single day for nearly four months—and thinking about the work most of the rest of the time. This doesn't count all the preliminary work I did on it for months. I've never had anything ride me so hard. Each play is pretty intense from beginning to end and it takes the guts out of one. Carlotta has been a brick. She has collaborated by keeping the old chateau running with uncanny efficiency so that nary an outside worry has touched me or bogged my stride even for a moment. A most marvelous wife and friend! I am steeped to the ears in gratitude—and more than gratitude! And though it has been lonely for us collectively and individually at times, nevertheless, we've been happy and made quite a pleasant life of it alone together here. The vacation we're about to embark on to Italy will be welcome, however. We're going to Paris first for a short stay. Carlotta's eyes are glittering with that new clothes look—while I'm due, as usual, for a few happy hours with the dentist.

But we'll be back surely by the time you hit the continent. So plan accordingly and come to us, both of you,[2] whenever you like.

I see Mencken[3] is on his way home and I can imagine with what whoops of welcome you'll greet his taking the office off your hands.[4]

From what I read in the *Times* and *Variety*—yes, I subscribe to *Variety* for road news—the lay-out of dramas on Broadway this season must be extraordinarily lousy and your critical work more than usually boring. Judging by your article in the *Mercury*,[5] you don't seem to have found much of interest.

Carlotta joins in all best to Lillian and you. We'll be seeing you—before long, we hope.

As ever,<br>
Eugene O'Neill

P.S.

Have you and Lillian seen the Garbo talky of *Anna Christie*?[6] What is the bad or good news on it? I am interested because the silent film really was excellent.

---

1. Of *Mourning Becomes Electra*.
2. Nathan and Lillian Gish.
3. H. L. Mencken.
4. Nathan was eager to relinquish his post at the *American Mercury;* he had been minding the shop while H. L. Mencken visited Europe on an extended vacation (*Publishers Weekly,* 116 [28 December 1929]: 2925).
5. *American Mercury.*
6. This, the second film version of *Anna Christie,* was the talking debut of Greta Garbo. It was the only film of an O'Neill play that was a big financial success.

LE PLESSIS
SAINT-ANTOINE DU ROCHER
INDRE-ET-LOIRE

April 10*th* '30

Dear Nathan:

I note we'll hear from you before May 1*st* as to when you'll arrive in France. Plan to come here whenever it suits you best. Outside of a few days in Paris around May 1*st* to get out my income tax, etc., we'll be here all the time from now on. We got back from our vacation tour ten days ago. Never got beyond France but saw a lot of it we hadn't seen and had an enjoyable time.

What you say of Jed Harris[1] sounds fine! The Guild may get cold feet about this one when they're faced with the finished product. And what you tell me about the *Freeman*[2] sure is fine news! I used to subscribe to the old one and have always considered it the most interesting periodical we've ever had.

I saw in the *Times* that Lillian[3] was to be in *Uncle Vanya*.[4] Give her our affectionate cheers for a grand success! She ought to be fine in the part, as I remember it.

Yes, I hear the director did a lot of improvising for the *Anna C.* talky—but somehow I can't seem to care much of a damn about it.

Carlotta says for you and Lillian to plan to stay here longer than you did last year—if it doesn't conflict with your schedule.

All our best to you both! See you soon!

As ever,
Eugene O'Neill.

---

1. (1900–1979), New York producer and director.
2. In 1930, Nathan was dramatic critic for the newly revived *New Freeman*.
3. Lillian Gish.
4. Gish had returned to Broadway in 1930 as Helena in Anton Chekhov's *Uncle Vanya*, to critical acclaim. Nathan had advised her not to accept the role, fearing she might be overwhelmed in it.

PREFATORY REMARKS: Nathan and Lillian Gish had visited the O'Neills at Le Plessis during the summer of 1930, and plans were made for a Mediterranean cruise the next summer by chartered yacht, with just the

O'Neill at Le Plessis, the chateau near Tours, France, where he lived from May 1929 to May 1931. There he worked on *Mourning Becomes Electra*. O'Neill dated the photograph July 1930 and inscribed it thus: "To George, with all friendship, Gene." *(Courtesy of Thomas Yoseloff.)*

O'Neills, Nathan, and Gish. The playwright devotes a major portion of this letter to stating his reservations about the addition of a couple, friends of Nathan's to the cruise. The letter suggests O'Neill's seclusiveness, his reluctance to admit others to his tight circle. Eventually, plans for the trip were dropped; Gish could not go the following summer, and O'Neill believed Nathan would not go without her. Also, the O'Neills were tiring of France and beginning to think about returning to the United States.

LE PLESSIS
SAINT-ANTOINE DU ROCHER
INDRE-ET-LOIRE

Sept. 4*th* 1930

Dear George:

Yes, I have heard the news about Horace,[1] but I am also assured by Manuel Komroff[2] and others on the inside that those who have finally taken over the firm are all square-shooters and will carry on in good shape. So for the present I will mark time and await future developments. I don't believe the company is any longer for sale—not the last I heard. If anything comes up that prompts me to make a change, I will let you know at once—and much gratitude to you for offering your help in this matter!

What you say of the Oelrichs preparing to join our cruise gives me pause—Carlotta also. I am going to be quite frank. I am afraid of it. You see we don't know them at all, and who can tell whether the four new interrelationships involved would click or not? Just one miss would spoil the whole affair for all concerned. A yacht is a damn small place, and you have got to be pretty sure of real friendship and compatibility before you risk a month on a small boat together. We four are fine. We are sure of that. And, since none of us is likely to do this stunt again, and we do so much want it to be a happy and memorable occasion, I think we ought to keep it a closed corporation and not run any risk of it becoming just another one of those yacht cruise things. Then there is the fact to consider that both you and I may find we want to get in some work on this voyage. But I won't go into this any further. You understand all I'm driving at as well as I do. It's in no sense any personal feeling about Oelrichs. I would feel the same about anyone I didn't know—and about nearly all the people I do know! Carlotta feels the same way. It just seems to us as if this were a case where absolutely no chances of any sort should be taken.

I appreciate that this probably places you in an embarrassing situation in regard to the Oelrichs, especially when he is doing the fixing and is so kind about it. Would it help if you dropped the matter of arranging the cruise through him? I know George Draper[3] well and he knows or is good friends with most of the N.Y.Y.C. important yachtsmen. Through him through them I am sure I could readily get all the necessary dope on where, how and what for a Mediterranean charter. This would let you out gracefully—in case you think the Oelrichs would be offended if, after he went to so much trouble, we didn't ask them in.

Oh hell! It's too bad, all this! But it seems to me a time where each of us four has got to be stubbornly selfish—for the benefit of this four!

I've finished going over the second draft of the first two plays[4] and am now starting on the last. I've made quite a few improvements during this process and am well satisfied. Once the going over of the third play is done, I will give them all a rest for a while before starting to type the third—I hope, final—version of the whole opus.

Carlotta has written you all there is of news, I guess. The weather has finally changed, thank God, and we have been having sun and heat and the swimming pool comes into its own.

We join in all affectionate best to you and Lillian!

As ever,
Gene.

---

1. Horace Liveright, who had just stepped down from his publishing firm. Partially to recoup Wall Street losses, Liveright had sold what amounted to a majority of his shares in his business to the head bookkeeper, Arthur H. Pell, who then assumed control of the firm.

2. O'Neill's veteran editor at Liveright, whose letter gave him the detailed inside story of the takeover.

3. O'Neill's physician.

4. Of the trilogy *Mourning Becomes Electra*.

LE PLESSIS
SAINT-ANTOINE DU ROCHER
INDRE-ET-LOIRE

Oct. 3rd 1930

Dear George:

I have been waiting until the going over of the trilogy[1] was finished before writing you. There has been so much revising done on this going over the second draft that it really amounts to a third draft. It is in pretty good shape now, I think; and when I get back from Spain,[2] I will type the fourth and (I hope) final edition. The scheme I discussed with you for doing the soliloquies did not pan out well and I finally dropped it, and cut out most of them. They were all right in themselves but they got in the way of the play instead of helping it. This is not to say by any means that they are all out, but I found I could do without a number of them, especially in the first play where they appeared particularly uncalled for.

It is good to know that *Testament of a Critic* is coming along so well and that you are pleased with it. I will surely look forward to reading it. What you say of all the different work you are doing[3] certainly sounds like sweating blood! Aren't you letting yourself in for too much?

Of the two yachts you mention I should say the all-British one seemed like the choice. Don't you think so?

We are leaving for Spain for a three or four weeks' tour on the *8th*. It should prove darned interesting and I am looking forward to a change—and some sun! Touraine has been almost continuously gray and wet since we saw you. It gets on one's nerves—after nearly a year of the same stuff! Moreover, having come to a period spot in work, I am suffering from reaction and my tail is dragging on the ground. Have also been taking my yearly anti-cold vaccine treatment and that makes me feel low as hell while it's going on, although it does the trick and make me immune to the colds and sore throats that used to bother all my winters.

Carlotta joins in all affectionate best to you and Lillian. We will let you hear our reactions to travel in Spain.

Wall Street seems to keep right on crashing! Is the theatre showing the effect of this more than previously?

All best!<br>
As ever,<br>
Gene.

---

1. *Mourning Becomes Electra.*

2. After a summer of continual rain, the O'Neills were eager for sunshine, which they found in Spain and Spanish Morocco.

3. Nathan was writing or about to write for a number of publications at this time, as he was ending his association with the *American Mercury.* In 1930, he was dramatic editor of the *New Freeman,* a contributing editor of *Arts & Decoration,* an editorial contributor and guest critic for the *London Daily Express,* and drama critic of *Vanity Fair.*

LE PLESSIS
SAINT-ANTOINE DU ROCHER
INDRE-ET-LOIRE

Dec. 1*st* 1930

Dear George:

I note your delight that your book[1] is on the presses—and I hugely envy you! Would to God this damned trilogy of mine were off of my neck! I'm beginning to hate it and curse the day I ever conceived such an idea. The notion haunts me that I've bitten off a good deal more than I can chew! On my return from Spain the first two acts of the first play struck me as not right, so I've started to rewrite them. And so it goes on! It looks as if the rest of my life was doomed to be spent in rewriting the damned thing! I honestly feel very low about it and anxious to get done with it and free my mind from the obsession of it and get on to something else! When these two acts are done, for better or worse I'm going to call quits. I don't think I can go through the ordeal of typing it myself now. I'm too fed up. Think it wiser to get it typed. It would bore me so that before the end I would probably burn it.

Yes, I wrote Bob Sisk[2] a brief general outline of the scheme but that's all. No details about the plays. I much appreciate your offer about the essay. You know that. But first you better have a good look! I don't know whether it will be worth an essay or anything else.

This isn't an author's immodest hokum! I really feel most low about it.

The Guild seems to be starting their season on the right foot—to judge, if one can, by the *Times*. At any rate, financially!

Have you read Maugham's[3] latest, *Cakes and Ale?*[4] The last thing I have read in a long time. He evidently took some pains on this one. I am glad. I like him, the little I've seen of him.

I sent Lewis[5] a cable of congrat. when I heard the news in Madrid—several days late. Hope he got it. I don't envy him. On careful consideration—and no sour grapes about it because I had no hopes!—I think the Nobel Prize, until you become very old and childlike, costs more than it's worth. Lewis will find, I think, that it's an anchor around his neck he'll never be able to shake off.

But I'm so pleased the award infuriated Henry Van Dyke![6]

How did friend Dreiser[7] take the blow? Too bad! He deserved it more than any American.

Let me say again, you must see Spain! It is really extraordinary! And I liked Tangiers a lot!

Love to you and Lillian from us both!

As ever,
Gene.

---

1. *Testament of a Critic*, published in 1931.

2. Robert Sisk, publicity agent for the Theatre Guild; eventually a film executive. He was one of the very few who remained on close terms with Eugene and Carlotta O'Neill.

3. W. Somerset Maugham (1874–1965), English novelist, short-story writer, and dramatist.

4. Novel (London: Heinemann, 1930; Garden City, N.J.: Doubleday, Doran, 1930).

5. Sinclair Lewis, who was awarded the Nobel Prize that year.

6. A Presbyterian minister who had become professor of English literature at Princeton in 1900. As a Princeton freshman, O'Neill had balked at required attendance at Van Dyke's sermons, which he found dull.

7. Theodore Dreiser. In November of the previous year, just before Thomas Mann had won the Nobel Prize, the *Paris Herald* had listed Lewis, Dreiser and O'Neill, in that order, as possible Nobel laureates.

Hotel du Rhin,
Paris, France.
January 27th 1931.

Dear George:

This is a hell of a late date to be answering your letter, but as Lillian has learned from Carlotta, we have been having more than our share of troubles. Carlotta is now in the American hospital here—and has been for a week—and won't be out for another week at least. We both had a bad attack of grippe around Christmas time and were laid up in bed for a week. Carlotta got up too soon, and when we came to Paris to convalesce, she broke down with the after-effects. It is nothing serious. It is simply that she is worn out. I am also still feeling pretty punk. I am getting my play[1] typed here and at the same time rewriting part of the second play which does not yet please me. It is tough to have to do this when I do not feel up to snuff, but I do want to get the whole thing typed and off my mind for a time. I ought to have it ready to submit to the Guild within a month or two now. And I will be sending you a script at the same time. I won't give you any opinion of it. It is so on top of me that I do not know anything about it.

Your book[2] has not arrived yet. I am eagerly looking forward to reading it. Perhaps it may be down at Le Plessis waiting but I do not think so as they have been forwarding everything here to the hotel.

Yes, I read Sinclair Lewis' address to the Swedish Academy.[3] Quite outside of the fact that I was very grateful for the fine stuff he said about me, I was tickled to death with the whole address, especially the part which referred to Henry Van Dyke. His knock at Lewis made me fume inwardly. I hold Van Dyke in grudging memory because when I was at Princeton, at Sunday chapel, his sermons were so irritatingly stupid that they prevented me from sleeping.

What do you mean, "hornswoggle me into the local Academy?" I do not belong to any Academy. You are thinking of the Institute. If you will look up the members of that, you will find there are a good many real people in it!

Will you kindly tell the *Freeman*[4] for me that I do not care to do any article on drama for them now.[5] I might if I can ever regain my interest in drama which is now at very low ebb. I simply do not see anything to write about.

*Strange Interlude* is to open up in London on February 2nd. Needless to say, I will not be there to see it, although if it runs long enough I will go over later on. I would like to see Mary Ellis[6] as Nina. I have a hunch she will be better in the part than anyone who has played it. However, I do not imagine it will last very long in London. The dear old "Limies" will never stand for being yanked from their afternoon tea to the theatre—especially by an Irish-Yankee.

I go out to the hospital every day to see Carlotta. She is steadily picking up and gaining strength. A good rest was what she needed. She says to send her best love to you and Lillian. She is writing Lillian, I think.

We are planning to go away some place where there is sun soon after she gets out—either the Canary Islands or Sicily. I can give the play the last going over there. Le Plessis has been a failure this winter owing to the incredible weather. It has rained nearly every day and the whole atmosphere has been highly depressing.

All best to you, as ever,

Gene

Mr. George Jean Nathan,
The Royalton,
44 West 44th Street,
New York City.

P.S.

Excuse the typing. I'm still a bit shaky in knees and hands.[7] That's the reason.

---

1. *Mourning Becomes Electra.*
2. *Testament of a Critic.*
3. In his acceptance speech in Stockholm on 12 December 1930, Lewis praised O'Neill, saying he "has done nothing much in the American drama save to transform it in ten or twelve years from a false world of neat and competent trickery into a world of splendor, fear and greatness."
4. The *New Freeman*, for which Nathan was dramatic critic that year.
5. O'Neill was not inclined to explain his play ideas in formal writing of this nature.
6. British actress.
7. This may be O'Neill's first reference to Nathan of the tremor that later made writing all but impossible for him.

PREFATORY REMARKS: About this time, Carlotta began to add postscripts to her husband's letters.

## LE PLESSIS
### SAINT-ANTOINE DU ROCHER
### INDRE-ET-LOIRE

Feb. 21*st* 1931

Dear George:

Well, we are off for Lisbon tomorrow and sail from there on the 25*th* for the Canary Islands. Las Palmas is the particular spot we are heading for. Let's hope we will escape the eternal damp and chill and greyness of Touraine and be able to wallow in sun and sea for a bit and buck up. We are both still a bit seedy and need a bracer. But I have recounted all this to you before, I guess. We return about April 1*st*—and begin to pack up. Our plan now is to cut our lease and return to the States in May—perhaps for good, perhaps only for a visit; we are not absolutely certain on that point yet. It all depends on how we like the homeland once we are there. Carlotta wants very much to see her mother and child, after so long a spell away from them, and so we are going direct from here through the Canal to California. There is a good Swedish line of ships that runs from Antwerp to Los Angeles and, as we want to look over Cal. first with a view to making a home there eventually, it will be simpler to go direct instead of via New York with a long train trip and much

O'Neill acquired Silverdene Emblem (nicknamed Blemie), a Dalmatian, while he lived in France. The inscription is Carlotta O'Neill's: "To Uncle George, with love, Blemie." *(Courtesy of Cornell University Library.)*

bother with luggage, Blemy,[1] the Renault (possibly), etc. to face. New York will come afterwards on our itinerary.

I need not tell you that this is all under your hat. We don't want it known we are coming back until we are in and any reporters' welcoming committee is avoided. Of course, this lets us out of the yachting plan we made—but, from Lillian's letter to Carlotta I judge she is very uncertain if she will be able to do that anyway and I know you wouldn't without her. You haven't mentioned it in any letter of late so I guess the yacht is off from your end too. Well, it is a pity but, to be frank, we are both horribly fed up with life in France and our chateau in the drear wintertime. You would be too if you tried to live over here at long length. The first year and a half was fine—but now it just simply bores us. You get that feeling of not really belonging, of having no affinity with land or people—of being rootless and growthless. In a word, we have got all out of it there is in us to get; and, after the saturation point is reached, the life becomes dull beyond bearing. Perhaps, if the weather had not been so constantly lifeless and depressing, we might have stuck out another six months with a little enjoyment. As it is, we are through and it would be idiotic to linger.

I have put aside the trilogy[2] until the latter part of our stay at the Canaries. Then I will look it over in type and decide if it is right yet or not. I learn, via A.P. inquiries, that the news of it being a trilogy is out. Well, that's all right. But I do want to keep title and idea dark for a long while yet—at least, until it is scheduled for production at a definite date. Any dope on the Greek trilogy connection would be very injurious, I think—and misleading because

O'Neill and Blemie at Le Plessis. *(Courtesy of Cornell University Library.)*

beyond the general plot outline of the first two plays there is nothing of the Greek notion about it now. I have simplified it until all its Greek similarities are out—almost. And it has gained in directness and clarity in the process. But you will note all this when you see it.

Your idea for the new book,[3] as I told Carlotta to tell you in her letter, sounds fine to me! But then I am an interested party!

Carlotta joins in all affectionate best to Lillian and you. We will write and let you know what the Canary Isles are like.

As ever,
Gene.

[Handwritten note by Carlotta
directly below O'Neill's:]

Dearest George Jean,

In looking over some clippings today I found one in which you stated that "Eugene O'Neill was happy in his new marriage!" I thank you.——We're both for matrimony——you'd better try it!!

Carlotta

---

1. Also spelled Blemie, nickname for Silverdene Emblem, a beloved Dalmatian the O'Neills acquired from England while they lived at Le Plessis.

2. *Mourning Becomes Electra.*

3. Perhaps *The Intimate Notebooks of George Jean Nathan,* published in 1932 by Alfred A. Knopf, New York. The book includes essays on O'Neill, Dreiser, Lewis, Mencken, and others.

Hotel du Rhin,
April 7*th* 1931.

Dear George:

This is to be about the trilogy which I am sending you by this same mail. I won't mention that damned suit[1] except to tell you how deeply grateful I am for what you did as a witness! It must have been a disagreeable ordeal for you and I appreciate accordingly! As for the "vain, conceited fellow," that was a damned clever bit. It was fortunate for me circumstances kept my stuff to a deposition. I am the world's worst actor in a courtroom scene as has been proven on the two occasions when I figured as a witness, to the detriment of my side, and was almost fined for contempt. I cannot retain my goat under a snooty lawyer's fire but lose my nerves and temper completely—which is duck soup for the enemy! The deposition let me keep the proper dignified poise. Why the hell they take testimony in these cases is beyond me. It is simply a case of two books and their sources, etc.

Your opinion of the trilogy will be anxiously awaited. It still needs the final trimming and toning down it will get before production or publication. Please allow for this in the reading. As you will see, no departures in technique are involved. *Interlude* soliloquies and asides only got in the way in this play of intense passions and little cerebration. The mask idea has also gone by the board. It simply refused to justify itself. It confused and obscured instead of intensifying. All that is left of it is the masklike quality of the Mannon faces in repose, an effect that can be gained by acting and make-up. The dialogue is colloquial of today. The house, the period costumes, the Civil War surface stuff, these are the masks for what is really a modern psychological drama which has no true connection with that period at all.

It has been one hell of a job! Let's hope the result in some measure justifies the labor I've put in. To get enough of Clytemnestra into Christine, of Electra in Lavinia, of Orestes in Orin, etc. and yet keep them American primarily; to conjure a Greek fate out of the Mannons themselves (without calling in the aid of even a Puritan Old Testament God) that would convince a modern audience without religion or moral ethics; to prevent the surface melodrama of the plot from overwhelming the real drama; to contrive murders that escape cops and courtroom scenes; and finally to keep myself out of it and shun the many opportunities for effusions of personal writing about life and fate—all this has made the going tough and the way long!

And even now it's done I don't know quite what I've got. All I do know is that after reading it all through, in spite of my familiarity with every page it leaves me moved and disturbed spiritually, and I have a feeling of there being real size in it, quite apart from its length; a sense of having had a valid dramatic experience with intense tortured passions beyond the ambition or scope of other modern plays. As for the separate parts, each play, each act, some seem better than I hoped, some not so good. I don't know much about them anymore, they fade out into the whole.

And that's that. Let's hear your judgment.

A word about the chanty "Shenandoah" that runs like a theme song through the plays. You will have to hear it to understand the effect. It's the most haunting of all the old chanties—a yearning melancholy tune with a beautiful sad sea rhythm to it—a longing for escape.

I saw the trilogy announcement that leaked out. But that's all right. What I want to keep dark is the title of the whole thing—those of the separate plays don't matter, they reveal nothing. I want, if possible, to conceal the Greek plot foundation until the plays are given. I don't want people to come with Agamemnon & Co. in their heads expecting this or that to happen in a certain way. It would confuse and put a wrong emphasis on my use of the plot. Let the boys deduct the secret from the first play. That seems to me good showmanship. The accent will then be in the proper place. What are your ideas about this?

But I'm talking as if production were certain. I don't feel it is. What with the censorship howl and the difficulties of production, I have my doubts.

Carlotta has, I know, written Lillian all our news so I won't repeat. Our late experience on a small steamer in a hellish storm has made us veto the long California voyage I told you we'd decided on. We will come via N.Y. and to Cal. by rail. I hope we will hit N.Y. before you leave and get together there. I'll let you know definitely when we're coming as soon as we know. It depends on the time necessary to close up Plessis. We will leave most of our stuff here and will come back in the fall for a while. This, of course, is under the old hat. I don't want my former frau to know I'm in N.Y. until I've come and gone. I think I can frame it to get in without being noticed.

All affectionate best from us to you both!

As ever,
Gene.

P.S. (over)

I am writing Saxe Commins,[2] a very old and close friend of mine who is now working for Liveright, to phone you and call to get the script from you when you are *quite through* with it. I want him to read it and he will know who to show it to at Liveright's who can be trusted to keep mum. I have to work each script overtime because I've only three available for duty and two have to go to the Guild committee to insure quick action there.

And Saxe is a great worshipper of yours, and I want you to meet him. He is a fine simple rare person. Carlotta likes him as much as I do—and that's a lot—and we know you'll like him.

---

1. Georges Lewys's plagiarism suit against *Strange Interlude* came to trial in New York on 11 March 1931. Nathan's testimony helped O'Neill win the case. The critic retained his equanimity in the face of sarcasm and outright belittlement from the plaintiff's chief counsel, Daniel F. Cohalan.

2. Commins became O'Neill's trusted editor at Liveright (as successor to Manuel Komroff).

# PART III
## *The Nobel*

# INTRODUCTORY ESSAY

Eugene and Carlotta returned to the United States in May 1931, landing in New York. After the boredom of long lonely months in France, Carlotta looked forward to what she felt was her rightful recognition as the wife of the playwright. She and Eugene were reasonably active socially as they spent their time in the city and at a rented estate on Long Island. But his work and the isolation necessary to it always came first. After an autumn vacation at Sea Island just off the Georgia coast, the two became enthralled with the idea of a palatial dream house there. To free her husband and protect his privacy, Carlotta took complete charge of both the planning and the building. The groundbreaking took place in early spring, and by June she was supervising the furnishing of their Spanish-style mansion. In early July 1932 they were in residence; but, like so many dream homes, Casa Genotta (a name combining "Gene" and "Carlotta") cost much more than planned. The O'Neills found themselves financially squeezed.

Still the playwright chose to continue his isolation from the theater. A decade earlier, he had yearned for frequent productions; now he was not particularly dismayed when only two new plays reached the stage from 1932 to 1936: *Ah, Wilderness!* (1933) and *Days Without End* (1934). *Ah, Wilderness!*, O'Neill's only comedy, came relatively easy. He had awakened one morning with the play complete in his mind and was able to write it in less than a month. It was as if, after years of stress, his creative self demanded some comic release. O'Neill fondly dedicated the play to Nathan and described it as picturing the childhood he would like to have had. *Ah, Wilderness!* was generally well received by the critics. Referring to O'Neill, a fellow editor of the *American Spectator*, Nathan quipped, "Although the Editors . . . are not supposed to say anything decent about one another in the pages of the paper, *Ah, Wilderness!* is an American comedy of the first rank."[1] O'Neill, Nathan crowed, had proven his comic sense rivaled the very best of his contemporaries'.[2] Now the dramatist's artistry was demonstrated to command a full range.

*Ah, Wilderness!* was a fortuitous interruption of the work O'Neill had been struggling with. Almost as soon as he had arrived at Sea Island, he had begun writing *Days Without End*. His customary method was to create a scenario for his play, then a succession of drafts that filled in the bare outline.

In the process, he usually overwrote the dialogue and stage directions, then whittled the play for performance. But *Days*, intended as the second play of the *Myth Plays of the God-Forsaken* trilogy—the first was the ill-fated *Dynamo* of 1929—presented fundamental problems with its ending. The *God-Forsaken* trilogy presumed that science and materialism had destroyed the old concept of a humanlike deity. The purpose of the trilogy was to explore the twentieth-century dilemma of finding a satisfactory replacement. *Dynamo* had concluded with humankind reaching toward union with the machine. Now O'Neill would explore further solutions in *Days*. After changing his ending several times, he finally decided to adopt an affirmative Christian conclusion, thus denying the death of God and, hence, violating the basic premise of his trilogy. He later repudiated his choice, and working against his natural inclination had probably increased his considerable difficulty in writing the play. Endless revision had not saved it; in fact, Nathan declared, it had ruined it.[3]

Such outspokenness hardly damaged the pair's friendship. Indeed, when Sean O'Casey observed playwright and critic together in 1934, he remarked, "It was plain to me that these two men loved each other."[4] By now, Nathan was long accustomed to addressing O'Neill affectionately by his middle name "Gladstone." And after more than a decade, the reticent dramatist had finally begun to write "Dear George" rather than "Dear Nathan" and to sign his letters "As ever, Gene."

Nathan well knew that his personal friendship with the playwright could compromise his own professionalism. It was becoming widely known that, as a New York columnist would later put it, "Their friendship is one of the longest and strongest in the American theatre . . . they sit and meditate at home on nice things to say about one another in public."[5] To protect the integrity of his criticism, Nathan published in *Vanity Fair* a fanciful conversation with the O'Neills at Sea Island. In it, Nathan had Carlotta complain at some length about the harsh things Nathan had said about O'Neill's weaker plays: "Did you read his unspeakable reviews of *Dynamo*? I hadn't met him then, but I said to myself, 'Anyone who could be that nasty and unfair to Gene . . . would never be allowed within even hailing distance of me!' Then what of the unholy ridicule he poured on *Welded*, and what of his abrupt dismissal of *The First Man*? What, too, of his criticism of *Lazarus Laughed*? Why, the fellow even found fault with one or two things about *Mourning Becomes Electra*, which even the critics most hostile to Gene praised wholeheartedly!"[6]

Having Carlotta do all the complaining increased the critical distance between the two men while allowing the dramatist, silent and relaxed during Carlotta's complaints, to emerge from the description as changed from the old, nervous, worried O'Neill to a more stoical person, "at peace with himself and the world." At the same time it brought out for the record the bad notices the critic had given his friend the playwright whenever Nathan thought O'Neill's works warranted such judgment. Thus Nathan proved his point without pleading his own case. His method deftly allayed at least some of the questioning of his close association with the O'Neills.[7]

The article was one of several Nathan published on O'Neill the man, beginning in 1932. The critic would write more of these profiles in succeeding years, especially as no new O'Neill plays presented themselves for production and review. Seeking to broaden the common perception of the dramatist as serious, brooding, and pessimistic, Nathan described him in conversation as easygoing, with an informality that would surprise and delight an apprehensive interviewer, a man of few words, and those spoken slowly, but a man of humor, who enjoyed his camaraderie with intimate friends, singing around Rosie, his player-piano. He was "fundamentally a cheerful and at times even a waggish fellow, with a taste for low barroom chatter, bordello anecdotes, rough songs and other such forms of healthy coarseness."[8]

So eager was Nathan to show the lighter side of the playwright that he created the legend that O'Neill was expelled from Princeton for an act of vandalism against the university's president. As Nathan had O'Neill recounting the story, "Princeton . . . [kicked] my tail out of [the] place . . . because I was too accurate a shot with an Anheuser-Busch beer-bottle and hit a window in Woodrow Wilson's house."[9]

It was about this time that Carlotta started writing occasional letters to Nathan. One gives some credibility to the critic's lighthearted portrayal of the dramatist. "What you and Frau Edelbrau have done to our household is shocking," Carlotta began, acknowledging Nathan's gift of a keg of beer. "Casa Genotta is completely demoralized." She recounted how O'Neill, in particular, had enjoyed beer at lunch, beer in place of tea, beer for dinner, and beer for a nightcap. "Rosie plays and the Edelbrau flows!"[10]

Nathan also portrayed the playwright as a lover of sports. O'Neill would spiritedly discuss them at length with the most casual of acquaintances, and enjoyed going incognito when he could to watch for hours the six-day bicycle races in New York. He also read all the mystery and detective novels he could lay his hands on. He was a man of modesty and courtesy with a willingness to forgive, but an independent thinker. Nathan warmed his accounts with sketches of O'Neill's home life: Carlotta coming downstairs to dinner in a stunning gown and the playwright's obvious pleasure but boyish reticence to admit it.[11] To Nathan, O'Neill was one of "the happiest, most contented and most genial practitioners of belles lettres that I know. And excepting only [Sinclair] Lewis, he can laugh louder and longer when the occasion warrants."[12]

As his legend grew, the man whose whole life was characterized by introspection and the quest for privacy to pursue it was near collapse. After frustrating, tedious months writing *Days Without End*, he had thrown himself into casting, rehearsals, and the many details of production, all of which further drained his energy. Panned by critics as one of O'Neill's poorest plays, *Days Without End* rang down its last curtain after only fifty-seven performances. It would mark the end of O'Neill's use of experimental dramatic techniques. When he learned of the closing, O'Neill could feel only relief from "hoping against hope" for the success of *Days*.[13] To his friend Kenneth Macgowan, he declared: "I feel as stale as mousetrap cheese on the theatre. I won't start anything new for a long while. I'm fed up."[14]

He headed home and, following his physician's advice, avoided writing. Instead he and Carlotta went north, spending time in New York City and the Aidrondacks. In the wilderness, swimming, fishing, and rowing gradually renewed him, and he returned to his work with some zest. Even while loafing he had probably never quite stopped thinking about it. After a visit to Casa Genotta, Nathan once reported that a "dozen times a day he will stop in the middle of a sentence and, without a word of apology or explanation, depart, head dejected, to his writing room to make note of a line or an idea that has just occurred to him."[15]

O'Neill was never without an abundance of ideas. He had what he called "an embarrassment of riches."[16] These he mused over in odd moments shaping and reshaping, never forcing, but allowing each to gestate until one was so much in his consciousness that he felt driven to give it form. Then he would create a scenario, placing it with those for other plays he was developing. When he found one of these pressing on his mind, he would begin the often arduous task of fleshing out the play itself, working at his desk daily, interminably, for months at a time. The process often required several drafts. When the play was finished, O'Neill almost always found himself drained.

And now there were portents of a time when the task would become still more difficult. Dire world news had begun to trouble him. He cringed at reports of Hitler's treatment of the Jews, although it was not until World War II became inevitable that international events became a paralyzing depressant. It is significant that after *Days Without End*, all the plays he completed were set in the past. Finally, an unevenness in his handwriting, still mild at this time, loomed as a threat to his work, for O'Neill could not compose his plays any other way than by hand.

Yet his writing would go on for some years, although his active participation in the theater was over for a while; and he would not see another new play produced for twelve years. He was not only geographically but mentally removed from the theater. There were several reasons. He was disgusted with what he referred to as "the eternal show-shop," the artificiality of the theater world. Related to this was his increasing distaste for the productions of his plays, for he found them inferior to those he had conceived in his imagination. Actors also usually displeased him. He felt their egos distorted their performances, so that on stage they were untrue to his personal concept of his characters. In later years he remarked, "There have been only three actors in my plays who managed to realize the characters . . . as I originally saw them"—Charles Gilpin in *The Emperor Jones,* Louis Wolheim in *The Hairy Ape,* and Walter Huston in *Desire Under the Elms*—". . . only those three lived up to the conceptions I had as I wrote."[17] By 1945, O'Neill would confess to Nathan, "I have become so apathetic about the theatre that I really don't give a damn whether any play of mine is ever produced again or not. I have to fake an interest."[18]

In mid-1933, O'Neill negotiated an excellent contract with Bennett Cerf, the publisher of Random House, which assured him of financial security. (O'Neill's published plays always sold well, often better than highly successful novels.) Now he had no pressing need for stage productions and could devote more time to writing. There was time to dream of his magnum opus, a great cycle of plays, envisioned as five, then expanded as more plays were added until it numbered eleven in all, the saga of an American family traced from 1828. The idea for the Cycle grew directly out of the ill-fated *Myth Plays of the God-Forsaken* trilogy and would be his supreme comment on the failure of American science and materialism to provide a spiritual answer to humankind's inherent fear of death and to its need to see a meaning in existence. It was to tell the tragedy of America, corrupted by greed, as it reached for but failed to realize its magnificent potential. The theme was not a new one to O'Neill. Both *The Fountain* and *Desire Under the Elms* allude to it, and O'Neill voiced it in interviews.[19]

O'Neill called the Cycle *A Tale of Possessors Self-Dispossessed.* It was to become awesome in its demands, for the interrelationships of the lives of successive descendants, with events in one play affecting the plot of each succeeding one, would become increasingly complex. Thus the need for detailed planning and the prospect of countless revisions of earlier plays if the master plan failed to anticipate events in later ones, especially if the playwright decided later to extend the Cycle.

By early spring of 1936, O'Neill had a first draft of *A Touch of the Poet,* originally the first play of the Cycle, set in 1828. He decided, as he wrote it, to extend the Cycle to eight plays by an earlier beginning in 1806. He had written a first draft of *And Give Me Death,* the new first play in the Cycle, by mid-August.

Although his last production, *Days Without End,* had failed and no new O'Neill play had enjoyed production in 1935 or 1936, his reputation was already sufficient to bring him the Nobel Prize in 1936. He had once said the Prize meant one's great work was over, but O'Neill, at forty-eight, was far from finished.

## NOTES

1. George Jean Nathan, "Nathan Digests the Theatre," *American Spectator* 2 (December 1933): 2.

2. George Jean Nathan, "The Theatre: A Turn to the Right," *Vanity Fair* 41 (November 1933): 66.

3. George Jean Nathan, *The Theatre Book of the Year: 1946–1947* (New York: Alfred A. Knopf, 1947), 104.

4. Gelb and Gelb, *O'Neill*, 786.

5. Louis Sheaffer, "Gossip of the Theatre: Wherein O'Neill and Nathan Are Friends—Helen Hayes Teaches—Fred Allen Mourns and Katharine Cornell Studies," *Brooklyn Times Union*, 28 February 1937.

6. George Jean Nathan, "O'Neill," *Vanity Fair* 41 (October 1933): 31.

7. Nathan, "O'Neill," 31.

8. George Jean Nathan, "The Recluse of Sea Island," *Redbook* 65 (August 1935): 36.

9. George Jean Nathan, *The Intimate Notebooks of George Jean Nathan*, 22.

10. Letter from Carlotta Monterey O'Neill to George Jean Nathan, 19 December 1935, Cornell University Library.

11. Nathan, *The Intimate Notebooks of George Jean Nathan*, 31.

12. George Jean Nathan, "The Cosmopolite of the Month: Eugene O'Neill," *Cosmopolitan* 102 (February 1937): 11.

13. Sheaffer, *O'Neill: Son and Artist*, 433, quoting Eugene O'Neill's letter to Russel Crouse, 12 February 1934.

14. Letter from Eugene O'Neill to Kenneth Macgowan, 14 February 1934, collected in *"The Theatre We Worked For": The Letters of Eugene O'Neill to Kenneth Macgowan*, ed. Jackson Bryer and Travis Bogard (New Haven: Yale University Press, 1982), 208.

15. Nathan, "O'Neill," 54.

16. Letter from Eugene O'Neill to George Jean Nathan, 19 September 1941.

17. Sheaffer, *O'Neill: Son and Artist*, 157.

18. 16 September 1945.

19. Sheaffer, *O'Neill: Son and Artist*, 441, 442.

# LETTERS: JUNE 1932–DECEMBER 1936

PREFATORY REMARKS: During the winter of 1931–32, the O'Neills had lived in a New York City apartment. There they had seen Nathan occasionally. In the summer of 1932, they moved to their newly built home, Casa Genotta (a neologism based on their first names), on Sea Island, Georgia. From here O'Neill again wrote Nathan letters, although almost exclusively for five months, perhaps because his finances were precarious at this time, he used up his old stationery from Le Plessis (carefully marking through the letterhead).

CASA GENOTTA
SEA ISLAND
GEORGIA

June 9th [1932]

Dear George:

The enclosed, as you will note, was written some ten days ago. Like a damned fool I stuck it in my pocket to mail and then forgot it. But all in it re Cerf[1] still holds good—in fact, everything there is now just about set.

It's fine to know we're to see you soon!

As ever,
Gene.

---

1. Bennett Cerf (1898–1971), who had bought his way first into a vice-presidency at Liveright's (O'Neill's publisher). In 1925, in partnership with Donald S. Klopfer, Cerf had bought the Modern Library, Liveright's most lucrative subsidiary, and had become its president. The Modern Library would publish many O'Neill plays, as did Random House, founded by Cerf and Klopfer.

Casa Genotta, Sea Island, Georgia, O'Neill's home from the summer of 1932 to November 1936. Casa Genotta (the house of Gene and Carlotta) boasted Spanish architecture, while the playwright's study recalled a captain's quarters on an old sailing ship. While he lived there, O'Neill completed and saw produced *Days Without End* and *Ah, Wilderness!*. *(Courtesy of Cornell University Library.)*

PREFATORY REMARKS: Nathan had requested that O'Neill contribute an essay for his new venture, *American Spectator* (for which O'Neill was listed as an editor). The playwright labored over this assignment at length, for he never found it easy or enjoyable to write expository prose about his plays. O'Neill's essay on his use of masks was split into three parts and published in the first three issues of the *Spectator* ("Memoranda on Masks," 1 [November 1932]: 3; "Second Thoughts," 1 [December 1932]: 2; "A Dramatist's Notebook," 1 [January 1933]: 2).

Sea Island Beach
Georgia

August 6*th* 1932

Dear George:

Well, I'll have another shot at the darned article, but if nothing evolves more satisfactory than my three previous attempts, you will have to count me out. You wouldn't want poor stuff anymore than I would want it used. It would simply give the "literary newspaper" a black eye on its first number—and do me no good, in the bargain. You see you're really yanking me entirely out of my class. I've never written an article on anything in my life that I can remember, except small town newspaper junk.[1] My old bean simply can't seem to get started functioning on such lines. It's the same as if I asked you to write a play. The three attempts I made hadn't even got started on what I was trying to say at the end of a thousand words. I can't think that way. So you see the predicament. It's the flesh that is weak and not the spirit, believe me, George! And I am too enthusiastic about the scheme of the paper to send in any misbegotten amateur (which is what I am in this) effort, even if you would consent to publish it.

A play, can do. Might even do a short play still, although I have no idea for one. A novel, given the next ten years to learning how to use that form, maybe. But short stories or articles, no. Things appear too complicated and involved to me.

But, as I promised above, I'll have another shot. A plea for the adoption of masks as a needed—and practical—convention for the modern theatre is about the only subject I can get up any interest in. None of the things you suggested hit any response. I don't know enough about O'Casey's[2] plays, for example.

But one thousand words! I honestly don't see how I can do it, George! Supposing it's two thousand? Could you run it in two sections?

I'm working hard. Finished three acts of the new one,[3] first draft, but then hit on what I believe is a better scheme for it so am at that now. What I had seemed fine for what it was, but this new plan will keep all that and give scope for a lot of new values.

Come down and see our Home!

As ever,
Gene.

P.S.
When would this here article have to be sent in?

1. O'Neill had been a cub reporter on the *New London Telegraph* (Connecticut) from August to November 1912 when he was twenty-four, shortly before he decided to be a playwright.

2. Sean O'Casey (1880–1964), the Irish dramatist. When O'Neill and O'Casey finally met in 1934, they did so almost as old friends, for each had heard much about the other from their mutual friend and champion, Nathan.

3. *Days Without End.*

Sea Island Beach,
Georgia

August *27th* 1932

Dear George:

Much gratitude to you for the inscribed book![1] I am damned glad to have it to add to your others. Read it last night until 2 a.m. It strikes me as the most interesting of them all, George—your best! Although I was familiar with a lot of it from your articles, and seeing the biographies[2] in script, I couldn't leave off until I had finished it. The biographical part has gained a lot by the omissions, it struck me. Those others were a bit out of line with the spirit of the ones you have retained. The acid taste is now out.

I've labored for eight days on the stuff for your first issue.[3] You probably will doubt this when you see the mousey result, and I don't blame you—but such is the fact! Carlotta is now retyping the stuff and it will go off to you within the next few days. What I've done is to expand scraps of old notes on the use of masks, but they had better be presented just as notes from a notebook. This will help to explain—or excuse—their incoherencies! Reading them over I feel they are fairly lousy—that they get at so little of all I feel about what masks might do in the theatre as to be ridiculously misleading. But you will judge about this. If you think they're badly done and not interesting in content, for God's sake, have no hesitation in junking them! I won't feel hurt! I'll feel relieved! And if you think anything ought to be cut, just let me know what it is and I'll probably agree with gusto! The stuff now should run to about 2000 words.

Think you will be able to get down here? Sure hope so! I've hit a dead spot in the play[4] and am not feeling like a writer at all. This happened before I began expanding the notes, so that's not to blame. One of those blind alleys, that's all.

All best!

As ever,
Gene.

O'Neill at Sea Island, Georgia. *(Courtesy of Cornell University Library.)*

1. *The Intimate Notebooks of George Jean Nathan.*
2. The first section of Nathan's new book contained autobiographical sketches of literary personalities, including O'Neill.
3. O'Neill was still laboring over his essay for Nathan's *American Spectator.*
4. *Days Without End.*

Sea Island Beach,
Ga.

Sept. 1*st* '32

Dear George:

And this is this![1] I haven't gone over it carefully for foibles in grammar, relying on you or your proof reader to spot those, if any. Same applies to punctuation at which I'm usually a bit hither & yon.

Let me impress on you again that if this strikes you as at all flat, stale, etc., you can junk it without wounding my vanity in the least. But let me know about any cuts you may wish to make—for, whatever its worth or worthlessness, I did try to cover many angles in the related parts as comprehensively as possible under the circumstances.

This, a scribble in haste.

All best!
As ever,
Gene.

1. O'Neill had finally finished his essay on masks for the *American Spectator.*

Sea Island Beach
Georgia

Oct. 16*th* 1932

Dear George:

Well, forty-four today—and I don't feel a bit younger. Ought to be a lucky year—here I knock wood!—if there's anything in Numerology, what?

I've postponed answering your letter of the 10th until I came to the end of the act I was on.[1] Finished that yesterday. I've been working like hell ever since we arrived the first of May—except for the two weeks in July when the kids were visiting with us—but with extra intensity since Sept. 1st—nine a.m. to four or five p.m. continuously every day—lunch sent up to study so there will be no interruption—etc. Have got a lot done—and much that will surprise and interest you—nothing in final shape yet, of course. But tell you all about it when I see you. Will you ever be able to get down here? There's small chance of us coming up for some time to come.

I was so damned sorry to hear about your Mother.[2] I can be understandingly sympathetic there. I went through that—under particularly harrowing circumstances. But here's hoping your fear may turn out to be unjustified.

The beautifully engraved stock certificate[3] arrived this a.m.—by way of a birthday gift, it seemed. Good omen. I'm damned sure it will be worth something. But can't see how it's coming to me, in justice. You know how little of value I'm able to contribute. And a check for my mask notes[4] also arrived. Here I howl! I can't accept that, George, and am enclosing it back to you herewith. Please understand my feeling. I worked hard on those damned notes—even though it would be hard to prove it by their excellence! I hated the job but got a real kick out of the fact that it was being done because *you* wanted it for *your* new periodical—and an added kick when you wrote saying the stuff pleased you and would fit in all right. Well, this check stuff sort of spoils my feeling, even if the amount involved matters nothing one way or another. I just can't accept payment for my contribution, whether it's ten cents or ten grand. For me, it's a personal matter concerning our friendship, and money is out. Perhaps this may seem [a] silly punctilio to you—but there you are—and I know you will understand. Don't spoil my gratification in that first issue! Really selfish, all this argument, you know— Boy Scout—Good Deed stuff!

What do I do about the five bucks?—I mean, to conform to all the legal formality re corporations & stockholders, etc. Send a check to *American Spectator* or to what? I suppose the Corp. has got to have definite record of it, somehow, to comply with law? Let me know.

No news much—except that the Book of Month is getting out a volume of nine of my plays for a gift book for their subscribers.[5] They were hot at first to go after you to select the plays and write an Intro. But I vetoed that. I felt that in your book just out, with its many O'Neilliana, you had more than done your bit by me for 1932! Also, I suspected you were too up to your neck in the *Spectator* and your other work to be bothered. And there were other reasons which I'll disgorge when I see you.[6] So I suggested Krutch[7] for the Intro, and myself to do the picking of plays. Krutch has been settled upon, has agreed, and that's that. Whether I'll be allowed to do the picking [of] plays is undecided yet. I don't want *Anna Christie* in. They do. It's all further involved by the number of pages allowed to the book, etc. It's all a teapot tempest—a premium book to encourage the subscribers to keep on subscribing, as I understand it. But it means a bit of added royalty I can't afford to ignore—especially this year.

*Electra* is going to be done in Berlin, Prague & Stockholm this season—and thank God I won't have to see any of that!

Carlotta joins in much love to Lillian & you, and in the hope that you both may be guests at Casa Genotta before too long!

As ever,
Gene.

---

1. Probably *Days Without End*. (O'Neill was also working on *Ah, Wilderness!* in September and October of 1932, but he told Nathan nothing about this play until the following June.)

2. Nathan's mother, Ella Nirdlinger Nathan, was ill with cancer.

3. Nathan had sent O'Neill, who was one of the editors of his *American Spectator*, stock in the publication.

4. O'Neill's essay on masks, which appeared in three segments in the first three issues of the *American Spectator*.

5. The Liveright firm, in financial difficulties, had made an arrangement whereby a volume of nine O'Neill plays would be distributed to Book-of-the-Month-Club members as a bonus. O'Neill himself selected the plays: *The Emperor Jones, The Hairy Ape, All God's Chillun Got Wings, Desire Under the Elms, Marco Millions, The Great God Brown, Lazarus Laughed, Strange Interlude,* and *Mourning Becomes Electra*. This same book was reissued by Random House in 1936 as a "Nobel Prize Edition."

6. Perhaps the real reason was contained in a letter O'Neill wrote to Saxe Commins around this time, in which the playwright explained that such a volume would "stand in everyone's mind as representing the whole significant trend of my work, and, between us, I don't like leaving such a choice to Nathan" (Sheaffer, *O'Neill: Son and Artist*, 408). Apparently O'Neill felt Nathan had some blind spots about his work. Playwright and critic were frank about such differences, however, and no doubt O'Neill discussed it in person with Nathan, as his letter suggests.

7. Joseph Wood Krutch (1893–1970), American writer and journalist who was dramatic critic for the *Nation* from 1924 to 1959.

Telegram—Brunswick, GA.

Western Union

1932   OCT 22   AM 12   36

Received at
      BRUNSWICK GA
GEORGE JEAN NATHAN =
    44 WEST 44 ST NYK =
CONGRATULATIONS ON SPECTATOR AM ENTHUSIASTIC IT
HITS JUST THE RIGHT NOTE IN EVERY WAY =
      GENE.

PREFATORY REMARKS: In the following letter, O'Neill neglected to mark through the Le Plessis letterhead.

Sea Island Beach
Georgia

Oct. 22, 1932.

Dear George:

Your letter arrived this a.m. I had wired you after going over the first number of the *Spectator*[1] and I hope it gave you a hint of my enthusiasm. Everything about it struck me as exactly the right note. The appearance, particularly! What I mean is that I can't see how the dignified simplicity—and uniqueness!—of that can fail to touch a grateful spot in anyone of intelligence and good taste. That's a stroke of genuis! And it seems to me just the right time for that appearance to appear, if you get me. And it looks so distinctly what it is, it leads you by the eye to expect just what you find in its reading matter. Two of the articles I didn't think much of—one being by O'Neill and the other by that other Mick, O'Flaherty.[2] The first seems to me poorly written and the second—well, I'm fed up with the personal feud note of all O'F.'s bickerings with "the priests." It's a subject, not a personal vendetta. As the latter it bores me. But maybe it's just the Irish parish priest who bores me and I'm incapable of indignation over his preordained imbecilities.

But everything else about the *Spectator* I am delighted with! Again, my congratulations, George! You certainly have started a splendid thing! If it doesn't meet with immense success, then good taste and intelligence are dead, and we better all get together and pray for the Second Flood!

I note what you say about "The Editors Believe" sentences,[3] and if any occur I'll send them on. But there's not much chance while I'm working on a play.[4] As soon as the old pencil stops, my mind goes dead each day— nothing but mechanical, automatic—and idiotic—conversations move in the old bean.

I'm immensely pleased O'Casey[5] sent his regards. Will you give him my best when you write. I'm looking forward to his article.[6]

Carlotta and I are overjoyed at the grand news about Lillian. She must be gorgeous in that, and I know Bobby's work would be just right for it.[7] I think that may be a knock-out in New York, don't you? Here's hoping!

All best from us both!<br>
As ever,<br>
Gene.

---

1. The November 1932 issue.

2. Liam O'Flaherty (1896–1984), Irish novelist and short-story writer. His article objected to the "tyranny of the Irish Church," which had imposed censorship upon his work, since he had decried "the sordid filth around the altars" ("The Irish Censorship," *American Spectator* 1 [November 1932]: 2).

3. Probably O'Neill was responding to Nathan's call for contributions for these occasional editorial quips in the *American Spectator*.

4. *Days Without End.*

5. Sean O'Casey, Irish dramatist, who also contributed to the *American Spectator*.

6. Sean O'Casey, "Laurel Leaves and Silver Trumpets," *American Spectator* 1 (December 1932): 4.

7. Lillian Gish was going to play the role of Marguerite Gautier in Alexander Dumas's *Camille* at the Central City (Colorado) Opera House. Robert ("Bobby") Edmond Jones directed the play and designed the sets and costumes.

Sea Island Beach,<br>
Georgia<br>
Nov. 3rd 1932.

Dear George:

Grand news, that of your card of the 28th! About the 4th printing,[1] I mean. Damned if I would ever have believed such was possible in this depressed era! It trends on the miraculous! But it's grand stuff, eh? You must feel very gratified after all the time and thought you have put in on it.

Hmmm. That stock certificate. You wouldn't care to give me some more in exchange for some St. Louis & San Francisco Pfd., would you? No? Why, that's strange! Well then, make a suggestion: What can one do with Frisco Pfd.? Even the receivers don't seem to want it. I hope you appreciate these remarks are richly humorous—born of a twenty thousand dollar & more experience in R.R. financing by a playwright.

Working hard but bogged down in a bad spot.[2]

C. joins in love to Lillian & you. We have seen no reports of *Camille* but hope it was a grand smash. As ever,

Gene.

---

1. Probably the very popular *The American Credo* (New York: Alfred A. Knopf, 1920), revised edition, 1921; then revised and reissued, as *The New American Credo,* by Alfred A. Knopf, 1927, and by Blue Ribbon Books, Inc. (New York), 1927.
2. O'Neill found the writing of *Days Without End* to be frustratingly arduous.

Sea Island Beach,
Ga.

Nov. 28, 1932

Dear George:

Well, how is the *Spectator*[1] coming along on its second number? If it's out, none have come this way yet. I have tried to think up something to send in but nothing whatever has come to me. This damned play has a strangle hold on the old bean. And, I'm sorry to say, without any satisfying results. I just finished what amounts to a second draft[2] and am already starting to rewrite from top to bottom. Read what I'd done and it seemed to me a horrid mess—not even worth getting typed. At this rate, there won't be any play ready for production next season, either. Which, from what I hear of prevalent conditions in the N.Y. theatre—and due to get worse instead of better—may be just as well. *Electra* on the road is doing miserably. I expect any day to get the bad news that it has been called in.

Carlotta and I were planning to take a trip to N.Y. sometime around New Year's but we've had to call that off. Simply can't afford it, the way things are shaping up. Is there any chance of you and Lillian getting down here? We hope so but are afraid you are too tied up with the *Spectator* to make it. It's too damned bad we are so far off and it's such a jump to get here. But it's worth it, in weather and health, once you're here!

I have no news of any kind. Got a few English clipping[s] about *Spectator* which were very superior and snotty. You will have seen them, of course. All I see now are International clippings[3]—and that only to track down productions over there. I cut out the American clips before I left New York. Expensive, and not one in a hundred that was worth a nickel to look at.

We're both "in the pink" in spite of various worries. Here's hoping you and Lillian are!

What do you hear now about the financial outlook for us [in the] U.S.? Love from us to you both!

As ever,
Gene

---

1. The *American Spectator.*
2. Of *Days Without End.*
3. O'Neill subscribed to the International News Clipping Service.

CASA GENOTTA
SEA ISLAND
GEORGIA

Dec. 29*th* 1932

Dear George:

My deepest sympathy![1] I know what you have been going through and what it must have done to you. I also realize how futile it is for me to say anything that can mean anything—but again, my deep sympathy.

Don't you think that possibly if you got away down here now for a few days, it would be a good relief for you after such a prolonged period of mental and nervous strain? You know, just wire you're coming any time you care to.

As ever,
Gene.

---

1. Nathan's mother, Ella Nirdlinger Nathan, had died on 23 December 1932 in Philadelphia.

Sea Island, Ga.
Jan. *2nd* 1932
[1933]

Dear George:

I didn't write you about the second and third issues[1] because I imagined you must be so upset over your mother's illness that you wouldn't care to be bothered with letters. My opinion of the two numbers was that they kept up the high average established by the first. I liked them immensely and I'm looking forward to the next with the Mooney[2] story. It was a grand stunt, your getting that!

I realize how the four of you must feel about a fellow editor who toils not. But what's to do about it? I've searched the old bean but cannot dig up anything suitable for an article or comment that I believe in enough to consider worth the expressing or fit for print. Moreover, I am at present all up a stump over this damned play[3]—disappointed, disgusted, seeing no way out for it, and thinking seriously of junking the idea entirely—after six months' work. As a result, for the past two weeks I've been enjoying an attack of nervous indigestion—a new one, this, for me!

But quite aside from these complications, it would still remain a fact that as a contributing editor, I am and always will be a washout. As I stated at length to you before the *Spectator*'s first issue, you are expecting something for which I haven't the slighest aptitude. It simply is not in my makeup. And never has been. My ideas absolutely refuse to take that form.[4]

So think or feel along that line. It's the same as if someone asked you to write a play.[5] With the best will in the world, you couldn't get your ideas to fit, you couldn't force your interest in your own expression into it.

You have got to realize this—I mean, accept it as unalterable fact, act of God, and not as a temperamental whim of mine which I can change by the wishing to do so. Otherwise, there will be continued misunderstanding on both sides.

I think the only thing to do in the interest of the *Spectator*—the above being recognized as first—will be for you to eventually ease me out as a contributing editor and put someone else (Brooks, for example) in my place who can really contribute and give you value, and let me then turn over my stock to be redistributed. I mean this seriously. After all, we can both discuss this objectively and frankly from the standpoint of the ultimate goal of the *Spectator*, which, you must believe, is foremost in my mind as it is in yours. You can't afford to carry deadwood beyond a certain point. My name and mask stuff in the opening issues were probably of some help in advance interests and the launching but now the *Spectator* is established and flourishing mightily, my slight usefulness becomes monthly more a thing of the past which you no longer need at all. I don't mean that I should necessarily be abolished entirely—that is, certainly not as long as you feel my by nature restricted participation (and enthusiasm for the *Spectator*) are of any service—but it seems to me I could easily be shifted to some honorary berth like Advisory or Associate Editor or something of that sort, which would keep me belonging to the *Spectator* family but not imply the active contributing for which I am so unfitted, and which my present editorship connotes.

The above is only a suggestion to get you thinking on the situation. You will see the last thing to be done when the time comes. You will understand all I am seeking is what will be fair to you and the other editors. The present status would be grossly unfair to the active workers, if it were allowed to run on too long—and to the best interests of the *Spectator.*

No, unfortunately, there is no likelihood of our coming to N.Y. The trip and stay there would be too expensive. What with *Electra* closing and the income tax wolf again on the mat, plus the enormous overhead of alimony & educating kids, things are down to cases and all but the necessary is out.

You are damned right! The *Spectator* is the only optimistic note—that I hear, at any rate. It's extraordinary how it has flourished—damned fine news and good to hear! Again, all congratulations to you for this achievement!

Carlotta joins in love to you and Lillian!

As ever,
Gene.

---

1. Of the *American Spectator.*

2. Thomas J. Mooney was a minor labor leader who had been arrested and tried in connection with a bomb explosion in San Francisco at a Preparedness Day parade on 22 July 1916. He was given a death sentence, but the evidence was so questionable that in 1918 President Woodrow Wilson asked the Governor of California to delay execution. Labor and other organizations championed Mooney's case, and eventually his sentence was commuted to life imprisonment. In 1939 he was pardoned and released.

3. *Days Without End.*

4. O'Neill is referring to his difficulty in writing expository prose.

5. Actually, Nathan had written plays, including *The Eternal Mystery,* produced in New York in 1913, and *Heliogabalus* (with H. L. Mencken), published in 1920, as well as several scenarios (some of which are included in Goldberg's *The Theatre of George Jean Nathan*).

PREFATORY REMARKS: In the next five letters, O'Neill continued to use up his old stationery, marking through the letterhead which read "1095 Park Avenue."

Sea Island,
Ga.

Jan. 29*th* 1933

Dear George:

I was among the eager listeners-in last evening and, outside of a distant background of jazz from some Southern or Cuban stations that wouldn't be cut out, everything came over well.[1] Your voice came over very distinctly, the others' not so good but good enough to make out all right. My reaction was that it was a damned amusing stunt, and an ad. for the *Spectator*[2] that ought to cause a lot of comment—but how disappointed a number of hearers must have been who were expecting something of the usual solemnly pontifical editorial crap!

Did you by any chance see the opera of *Jones*[3] at the Met.? Madden[4] wrote you had told him you might go. I've heard conflicting reports and would like your judgment. Couldn't get it on the radio—too much static that day.

As Carlotta wrote you, we never got a copy of the Mooney issue.[5] I don't want to miss that. We missed out on another number, if you'll remember, until I wrote about it. Perhaps the mailing dept. have a wrong address or something.

I'm still in the creative doldrums and not getting ahead much on either of the plays.[6]

It's grand down here now—and will be until the June heat arrives. You & Lillian better plan a vacation!

As ever,
Gene.

---

1. Nathan and two other *American Spectator* editors, Theodore Dreiser and Ernest Boyd, had made a broadcast, "American Criticism," which was carried by WABC (New York) and other CBS-affiliate stations.

2. The *American Spectator*.

3. An operatic version of *The Emperor Jones* had opened at New York's Metropolitan Opera House, starring tenor Lawrence Tibbett, who won critical praise. O'Neill, in need of cash, was to receive a royalty of eighty dollars a performance.

4. Richard Madden, O'Neill's agent.

5. He is referring to the February 1933 issue, which contained Tom Mooney's article, "Sixteen Years" (*American Spectator* 1 [February 1933]: 1, 2).

6. *Days Without End* and *The Life of Bessie Bowen*. The latter was actually a new title for *It Cannot Be Mad*, the third play in his *Myth Plays of the God-Forsaken* trilogy (following *Dynamo* and *Days Without End*). Later, *The Life of Bessie Bowen* would be part of his general plan for his Cycle of eleven plays.

Sea Island,
Ga.

Feb. 6*th* 1933

Dear George:

The two *Spectator* numbers duly arrived. As it turned out, Carlotta was wrong about the January number, we had already had that. It was the Feb. that had never reached us. I've just finished reading it. The Mooney article is fine stuff.[1] So is yours on censorship.[2] That was an eye-opener to me. As you know, I never see Talkies. I had absolutely no idea they had dared to become that raw. It's an amazing angle on these U.S. when you come to think of it, what? I also liked Beer's[3] stuff and Dreiser's on Bourne,[4] whom I knew slightly. And this whole number keeps up the high average of the preceding ones, I think. The main impression I get is that the *Spectator*, even where one can't agree with this or that comment, has guts and a virile distinctive life of its own.

Yes, I've been working on a second play—*The Life of Bessie Bowen*— having put aside *Without Endings of Days*[5] as, for the present, a blind alley. But, although I'm keen on the possibilities of this second opus, I haven't got beyond a detailed outline stage yet. The answer is I just don't feel like working at anything—much! My long battle with *Without E. of D.* has left me fed up with myself as dramatist and washed up of creative energy. Fishing seems more important. In fact, the more I read the world crisis news in the papers, the more important fishing appears as against play scribbling!

Yes, do try and get down in late March! It should be beautiful here then. Love from us both to Lillian & you!

As ever,
Gene.

---

1. Mooney's article, a description of his daily prison routine, dramatized the monotony of incarceration.

2. George Jean Nathan, "The Smutty Censors," *American Spectator* 1 (February 1933): 2.

3. Thomas Beer, "Death at 5:45 P.M.," *American Spectator* 1 (February 1933): 1, 4. In this article, Beer poked fun at Hemingway's "baroque hokum."

4. Theodore Dreiser, "Appearance and Reality," *American Spectator* 1 (February 1933): 4, was a poignant personal reminiscence of the critic Randolph Bourne.

5. This was O'Neill's tentative title. After several changes he finally settled upon *Days Without End*.

Sea Island,
Ga.

Feb 16*th* 1933

Dear George:

Just to say I just finished reading the lynching story[1] and your article on Radio City.[2] The former is sure horrible—and a corking fine piece of work!—the best thing of its kind I've read, I think.

I was wondering whether you were going to give the Rockefeller opus a treatment. God, what an imbecile mess that must have been—and be! And to think that when Macgowan, Jones & I were trying to raise backing for our G.V. and P.P. enterprise—with a record of sound achievement behind us—all of the plutocrats disdained us or cried poor and parted reluctantly with petty doles, so that we were finally forced to quit! Your cutting this Radio enterprise into shreds sure found a grateful satisfaction in me.

All best!
As ever,
Gene.

---

1. Vernon C. Sherwin, "Souvenir," *American Spectator* 1 (March 1933): 1, 2, was a harrowing account of an Alabama lynching.

2. George Jean Nathan, "Historiette of an Episode in the Art Life of America," *American Spectator* 1 (March 1933): 1, 2. In this, Nathan took a critical look at the Rockefeller family's creation of the Radio City cultural complex in New York City. After detailing the enormous sums that had been spent to build this citadel of the arts, he snidely described its opening night performing artists: "a couple of radio performers, . . . a clog dancer . . . [a] vaudeville comedian, and a troupe of Japanese acrobats" (2).

Sea Island
Ga.

April 27*th* 1933

Dear George:

Yes, I've been working like hell on the play[1]—fifth draft, this is, and I think I will have something that is worthwhile getting typed, at least, although it's still far from what I want a final draft to be. It's too involved to go into a letter, but the technique I'm now using is a new revealing angle on the material and, as far as I know, new to modern drama. You remember what I said in the *Spectator* Notes[2] about the modern psychological significance of *Faust* being that Faust & Mephistopheles are the same person—or something like that. Well, my scheme derives from that intuition. Title now is *An End Of Days*—but not final. I'll tell you all about it when you at last pay us that visit. Think you will be interested. I'll get what I want in the end, I hope, but it's a difficult job to work out.

As Carlotta wrote you, I thought the number before last of *Spectator* was the most stimulating of all, but the last one I found, by comparison, rather flat.

The Liveright collapse?[3] Well, I wish to hell they would either crash or not crash and get it over with! It still seems there's a chance for them, the last I heard. Frankly, I've been keeping it out of my mind until I have to think about it. Madden[4] & Weinberger[5] are keeping in touch for me. I had a note from Knopf[6] and told him to talk with Madden—same with Harcourt, Brace & Smith & Cape. Naturally, it will all boil down to who has the most to offer in the way of advance & terms—and, most important, who is financially in the best shape to carry on through these bleak days. I would certainly appreciate your advice on this last—I mean, what you hear. The firms above are those which have gotten in touch with me direct, but I imagine there may be others interested that you know of. I am going to hold out for the biggest advance possible. That is about the only protection against future uncertainties.

I hope *9 Pine Street*[7] gives Lillian her chance. It seems to me that's long overdue her now. But I feel sorry that story wasn't tackled by someone who could really handle it in a play. It's grand material but it takes doing. And what you say about the play tells me that a great opportunity has been muffed.

Carlotta is fine. So am I. Good swimming weather again and our grounds, sand a year ago, are burgeoning with lawn and trees and flowers and shrubs. I get a kick out of this place I never got out of a home before. So does Carlotta. We have a creative sense about it—of having made it out of nothing, of helping it grow. You never get the full benefit out of that when you buy a built place.

Think you & Lillian will get a chance to come down later on? We hope so. We know you'll like it.

Love from us to you both!

As ever,<br>Gene.

---

1. *Days Without End.*
2. A reference to his "Memoranda on Masks," *American Spectator* 1 (November 1933): 3.

3. As O'Neill's publisher edged close to the brink of financial collapse, a number of publishers began to woo the playwright.

4. Richard Madden, O'Neill's agent.

5. Harry Weinberger, lawyer for the Provincetown Players and later for the Theatre Guild, who had become O'Neill's personal attorney and old friend.

6. Alfred A. Knopf, Nathan's long-time publisher.

7. Written by John B. Colton and Carleton Miles (1933), the play is based on the famous Lizzie Borden case. Gish played the heroine, Effie Holden.


Sea Island,
Ga.


May 9th 1933


Dear George:

Well, the publishers are now on my neck in droves—or rather Madden's neck—and there have been some pretty good offers by way of preliminary sparring. Of course, I'm doing no deciding yet. There's no hurry, and I want to do a lot of looking into before I leap.

But of all the offers, I've got to tell you that Knopf is by far the lowest—so low as to be ridiculous!—and I'm afraid I'll have to scratch him off my list. He wrote Madden a letter giving his terms and the reasons for them which has got my back up, because I don't like to be treated like a moron and he ought to know that I know damned well his statements are bunk. I happen to have very fine inside information and check ups on those profits on my books with Liveright giving me 17½% and for Knopf to try and tell me a publisher can't afford honestly to pay more than 15% is ridiculous! Why even *Dynamo*, a flat failure in production, made a good profit for L. at 17½ with its sale of 17000—three times what the average novel sells! And there is not a book of plays on my list which has not sold from 12 to 15 thousand since original publication! And *Electra*, published in the leanest of lean days, has already sold 55000. Later still, the Book of Month Club *Nine Plays* after an original edition of 5000, has taken 14000 beyond that and Liveright's edition of the same volume had sold 1000 in addition up to Jan. 1st. Everyone ought to know that my stuff has been a financial mainstay for Liveright and their failure has been due to flagrant mismanagement and not because my books haven't been profitable. And I would be a dunce, knowing what I do, not to demand a raise over what I've been getting from L. on any new contract. I want 20% and I want a big advance to safeguard me— and, by gosh, I'm going to get it. I've already been offered the 20% part of it.

I'll get Madden to get in touch with you when things come down to cases.

Or, better still, if, as your letter makes us hope, you will manage to get away down here soon, we can talk it all over.

It's fine about the *Spectator*'s continued success. Even after making all due allowances for its outstand[ing] worth, still, damn it, it *is* a bit of a miracle in these days for it to go on succeeding after the first flair is over. But, somehow, I don't like the idea of increasing its size.[1] Its form at present seems to me to be so exactly right I'd be superstitiously afraid to tamper with it.

I hope you do the *London Express* thing[2]—and give them hell again! It will lend a nice touch to that International Conference of Brotherly Boodle there in June, what?

Carlotta joins in love to Lillian & you. We'll keep on hoping to see you both soon.

As ever,
Gene.

---

1. *The American Spectator* expanded from four to six pages for the August and September 1933 issues. A year later, in August 1934, it had grown to sixteen tabloid pages.

2. In 1930, Nathan had been an editorial contributor and guest critic for the *London Daily Express*. Perhaps he was considering further writing for that publication.

CASA GENOTTA
SEA ISLAND
GEORGIA

May 31*st*, 1933.

Dear George:

I have practically settled that I will go with Random House as soon as a few things get ironed out. To me their proposition is particularly attractive and presents an exceptional setting. I don't want to go with a big firm with a large mixed list but to place my stuff where it will be concentrated upon. Random House, with its surefire commercial background of the Modern Library, and its other background of the Random House fine books, will have no one but Robinson Jeffers[1] and me as a starter on the new selected trade list they are starting. And Jeffers is the kind of company I am proud to be in.

I needn't add that they are offering me all I was after financially—and then some. And, what is more important to me, they are giving Saxe Commins[2] a fine job on a three-year contract. I have been holding out for this—was determined the Liveright mess was not going to throw Saxe out on a cold, unemployed world. As you know, he is one of my oldest and most loyal friends and I want to do all I can to help him. He has two kids and he and his wife have been putting up such a courageous battle with the breaks constantly coming against them. So I've wanted to seize my opportunity to make sure that they get a good break at last. He will be getting a real chance in the right spot at Random House—where, with most of the other publishers, he would be out of it as far as real opportunity goes, even if I could make them take him on.

Another important point is that according to the report on the financial status of every publisher that has made me an offer (which I had the Guaranty Trust Co. make for me) Random House is in an exceptionally sound position as compared with even the most favorably situated of the others.

So you see, I think you will agree with me that my choice is a good one and based on a pretty sound survey of the field. I've been doing nothing for a month but look over publishers' lists—and God, what strings of junk most of them put out!—and read the financial reports from the Guaranty and Madden and Saxe's dope. I think with Random House I will feel my stuff is at home—and darned if I felt that about any of the others! Also I like Cerf and know we can work together—especially with Saxe there in personal charge of my end as part of his Random House job.

It's damned good news to hear, via your note to Carlotta, that you've about decided to pay us that visit! Fine! There's a lot I want to tell you, too lengthy for a letter, and a lot I want to ask your advice about.

As ever,
Gene.

P.S.

Thanks for your information about the royalty guarantee form of contract! But, thinking it over, I have decided I don't need it when I have the security I am getting in Random H. contract.

---

1. John Robinson Jeffers (1887–1962), American poet. His "The Tower Beyond Tragedy," a long narrative in *Tamar and Other Poems* (1924) was based on the story of Orestes and Electra.
2. O'Neill's Liveright editor and one of his closest friends. In early April, Commins had tipped off O'Neill that his publisher was close to bankruptcy. Commins had then quickly persuaded the firm to pay O'Neill all his outstanding royalties.

CASA GENOTTA
SEA ISLAND
GEORGIA

June 14*th* 1933

Dear George:

Nothing in those reports. No one has seen the play[1] except Saxe Commins who types my stuff, and you can bet he has said nothing about it. I gave Lawrence Langner a verbal outline of my treatment when he was here, but told him I didn't know if the play would be ready for next season or not. And I don't. All depends on how much work there needs to be done on it— to be decided when I read it over. I am sure there will be a lot. Can't imagine how such reports get out. The script was only typed a couple of weeks ago— after Langner left. As for Parker,[2] that sure is a mystery. But then, I got an authoritative rumor a while ago that I was known to be writing an historical play! So it goes. Someone about the theatre evidently possesses imagination.

Follows a confession. I have been holding out on you on one item. There is another play,[3] practically in final shape, about which I have never said a word to you or anyone. I have wanted the script to hit you as a complete surprise, as this opus is entirely different from anything I've ever written— nothing of the "O'Neill play" about it. And I've got it all framed up to force you to read it when you're down here, be it cruelty to guests or not! So grit your teeth to grin and bear it! Seriously, I'm in great need of your judgment here—for it's so out of my line that I hesitate to place any reliance on my own opinion of what I've done or haven't done in it. I wrote it on a sudden impulse—woke up one morning with the whole play clear in my mind. (I had never had even the glimmer of an idea about it before)—and finished it in a month. I've just been over it and done some cutting but found no rewriting necessary. I like it—because I have a real affection for its characters and its period—but, for this reason, all the more do I distrust my opinion on its value as a play. Hence, I look forward to your judgment.

All of which, no doubt, rings very vague and mysterious. Well, it *is* a great secret. No one except Carlotta and Commins, who typed it, has seen it. And whether I will ever want it produced for the general view is something I haven't attempted to decide yet.

See you soon!

As ever,
Gene.

---

1. *Days Without End.*
2. Probably H. T. Parker, critic of the *Boston Transcript.*

3. *Ah, Wilderness!* was copyrighted 8 August 1933; published by Random House, October 1933; presented at the Nixon Theatre, Pittsburgh, 25 September 1933; by the Theatre Guild, Guild Theatre, 2 October 1933.

PREFATORY REMARKS: Handwritten note of dedication of *Ah, Wilderness!*

Bertram Weal                                              Cable Address
Managing Director                                          Madisotel

The Madison
Hotel and Restaurant
Fifteen East Fifty Eighth Street
New York
Telephone Volunteer 5-5000

[August 1933]

To George Jean Nathan
Who also, once upon a time
in peg-top trousers went the
pace that kills along the
road to ruin.

Wurzburg Camp,
Faust, N.Y.[1]
[August 1933]

Dear George:
I have just wired the Guild to call *Ah, Wilderness!* in their official announcement "An American Folk Play" with no mention of comedy. This, I think you'll agree, *does* describe it accurately enough and will help to stop all this comedy talk which, if harped on, will get everyone in a now-make-me-laugh mood for the first night. Funny, all this gabble starting from Winchell's[2] shot in the dark—for he couldn't possibly have heard a thing—and it's an old trick which this time just happened to hit the spot.
I also told the Guild to describe *Days Without End* with the subtitle I have now put on it: "A Modern Miracle Play." It seems to me that this, too, is

O'Neill spent part of the summers of 1933 and 1934 in the Adirondacks at Wolf Lake, near Faust, New York. *(Courtesy of Cornell University Library.)*

accurate and sets the right mood in which the play should be approached. What do you think?

I have been working like hell on it since arrival here and have finished the change back to Catholicism and the priest-uncle. It certainly gives it its proper quality. I was a damned fool ever to change it to a vague Christianity. My reaction on going over it was to confirm a remark you made when you first started to discuss it that night—that more than any play of mine, it needs production to enable one to really see it, that as a script to read it is hard to visualize. So much depends on the atmosphere the mask creates when it is seen and heard—to take its realism to a plane beyond realism, if you get me. A job for the director—and for me! I'll have to be there every minute. Another obvious thing: It's much too long. I'll have to take twenty minutes to a half hour out during rehearsals. Can do—and it will be a big improvement.

Fine up here—beautiful country and lake. Have been fishing but the fish didn't seem to know it—no cooperation whatever.

Love from us to Lillian and you!

As ever,
Gene.

1. To escape the Georgia heat, the O'Neills spent the summer here.
2. Walter Winchell (1897–1972), Broadway reporter and columnist for the New York tabloid *Graphic* and later for the *Mirror*. In September of 1930, Winchell's false report that Eugene and Carlotta were expecting a child had caused them some consternation. Now, apparently, Winchell had printed misinformation about *Ah, Wilderness!*

[postcard postmarked "Sea Island Beach, Ga."]
Oct. 16,[1] 1933

Dear George:

Your condolences on my declining years tearfully accepted. Thank you for remembering the "aged, aged man." In one's sere and senile days those little touches of recollection come to mean such a poignant much!

Gene

1. O'Neill's birthdate.

CASA GENOTTA
SEA ISLAND
GEORGIA

Dear George,

Yes, we weakened on our plan to come up for the bike race.[1] A change to your New York weather didn't look so good. And now we are put at home again, it's so comfortable we sure hate to move until either of us have to. There is really nothing much to call me up there except the dentist, and it's a pleasure to postpone that. So we are making no plans. I am not even planning any work at present—just contentedly loafing.[2] After two productions, one right after the other this season, I am a bit stale on the theatre and don't want to think of plays or writing at all for some time. *The Life of Bessie Bowen* might be the next—or it might be something entirely different. I don't know—and, for the nonce, don't care.

I'm glad to hear the favorable prospect for *Within the Gates*.[3] Hope it comes to something. But you would not want it produced until next season in any event, would you? I had a fine note from O'Casey[4] soon after our arrival here. He was busy rehearsing when he wrote.

Glad you liked the book.[5] Random House sure does a fine job. The play in its ordinary edition has already sold close to as many copies as *Ah, Wilderness*. Not bad, considering, what?

And you will like the play, too—you know, when you at last grow that soul! Yes, this is another of them I'll always think you were dumb about— same like *Lazarus Laughed!*[6]

Are you still bent on Europe this Spring? We hope you'll change your mind and come here. Or why not work both in?

Carlotta joins [in] all affectionate best.

As ever,
Gene

March 3rd 1934.

---

1. O'Neill was an avid fan of bicycle races.
2. After O'Neill's labor over *Days Without End* and his disappointment over its poor reception, Dr. George Draper, his physician, had warned him that he was near nervous collapse and must rest.
3. Play by Sean O'Casey (1934).
4. Sean O'Casey, whom O'Neill was finally to meet that autumn.
5. Random House (New York) had published *Days Without End* in a limited edition, bound in leather and autographed, in January and February.
6. O'Neill always felt that Nathan's atheism prevented him from appreciating the religious themes of his plays.

CASA GENOTTA
SEA ISLAND
GEORGIA

Dear George,
So you've framed that Southern Hospitality privy page[1] and are telling everyone I wrote it, eh? What are you guys trying to do—win me the Nobel Prize?

All best,
Gene

April 29th 1934.

---

1. Unidentifiable now, but the letter suggests the humor the two men shared.

CASA GENOTTA
SEA ISLAND
GEORGIA

March 6th 1935

Dear George:
The *Spectator* announcement was a stunning surprise to me.[1] What I mean is, it isn't so long since I saw you and you seemed still very enthusiastic then. Has anything in particular cropped up in the interval beyond what the statement says? Not that I can't see how you could become very fed up with all that work when you have so many other things to do on top of it. Well, in any case, it's a grand thing to quit on the crest and no one can ever say the *Spectator* ever went back on its original ideals or ever failed to hew to its line—which makes its career an enviable and unique record, as far as my knowledge of such things goes.
I've been, and am, working like hell and full of the old enthusiasm stuff over this new scheme.[2] All the details aren't fully worked out yet but ought to be soon. When they are I'll write you the dope—although if (as we sure hope!), you're visiting us this spring or early summer, I'll wait to tell you about it—for it's a long, long story. I expect to make some announcement through Russel Crouse[3] and the Guild in April, but you know that sort of thing, it won't give away much.

I haven't written before because I knew Carlotta was giving you whatever there was of news. I was damned sorry to hear you'd been suffering again from the old neuralgia around your eyes.[4] That must certainly be hell!

Crouse has just been here for a couple of days—came down dead tired but we sent him back full of renewed pep and sunburn. I don't know how well you know him but, take it from me, he's a fine guy and you'd like him. I thought I knew a lot of the old songs but he has me outclassed. We sang for hours one night—beginning with the mechanical piano[5] accompanying— drove Carlotta to bed with her hands over her ears, and performed, with no liquor aboard, as raucously as if we were blotto. It was beautiful—but you know my voice, I needn't tell you.

Carlotta joins in love to you. Be sure and come down, now! If you do, I'll sing for you!

As ever,
Gene.

---

1. In the first issue, an editorial (probably by Nathan) promised that "the moment the editors feel that the *American Spectator* is becoming a routine job, is getting dull and is similarly continuing merely as a matter of habit, they will call it a day and will retire to their estates." Now, in the March 1935 issue, the *Spectator* announced it would cease publication with these words: "Well, we are tired of the job, although it has been a lot of fun. . . . So we are merrily concluding our performance" (3). But for any new periodical to last more than two years during the Depression was no small achievement.

2. The Cycle (*A Tale of Possessors Self-Dispossessed*).

3. Crouse (1893–1966), playwright and publicity agent for the Theatre Guild, was one of the first to learn about O'Neill's plans for his multi-play Cycle.

4. Nathan suffered chronically from neuralgia in the left side of his face.

5. Shortly after the première of *Ah, Wilderness!*, Carlotta had given him the player-piano for his forty-fifth birthday. He dubbed it Rosie.

CASA GENOTTA
SEA ISLAND
GEORGIA

Dear George,

I've just finished reading the script.[1] It certainly works out most amusingly! The jump from Romeo and Juliet seemed to me to come off remarkably well although I felt a little at sea on the Othello ending. The gap to the Shrew was harder to leap. I think you may find that additional small cuts in the first part of this third act, which would tone down the too-essentially Shrewish quality of the dialogue in the beginning, might help your cause. You see what I mean. If you could possibly insinuate an audience into the Shrew without their being too aware of it until they had accepted it, it would work all to the benefit of the rest of the act, and also be more amusing, I think. I may be all wrong. It's just the feeling that hit me that I could believe in Romeo-Othello and Juliet-Desdemona changing into Petruchio and Katherine if their too-Shrewish dialogue was toned down a bit when I first met them so the jolt of changed character wouldn't be so abrupt.

Thank you for sending the script. I had a lot of fun reading it. It's a grand stunt and the reactions to a production I am grinning at in advance. But, for God's sake, my dear Elizabethan confrere, do everything to keep your end of it dark until after the official unveiling!

Carlotta joins in love,
Gene

July 14th 1935


P.S
The script is being returned to you under separate cover.

---

1. Reversing their usual practice, O'Neill was now reading a draft of a Nathan play, *The Avon Flows* (New York: Random House, 1937). The play was a modern-day Shakespearean pastiche drawing on *Romeo and Juliet*, *The Taming of the Shrew*, and *Othello*.


## CASA GENOTTA
## SEA ISLAND
## GEORGIA

Dear George,

I think I like *The Theatre of the Moment*[1] better than any other of your last three or four books. What do you feel yourself? It seems to me to have more of your old quality in it. Is it that you are growing younger and more full of zip? Or is it that I am growing childish? And, mind you, I like this book so well *not* because it has a chapter about a Recluse.[2] That's the one part of it I haven't read, because you told me it was the same as the *Redbook* article.[3] Anyway, my congratulations!

I have my second play[4] in pretty final shape—my first[5] in first draft and two-plays long, damn it! Whether there shall be nine plays or eight depends on whether I can condense to one play or must make two of it—same old problem that started when you were here. I'll do my best to condense. I don't want nine if I can help it. I groan enough already.

O'Neill and Nathan at Sea Island, Georgia, 1936. *(Courtesy of Thomas Yoseloff.)*

Nathan and O'Neill at Sea Island, Georgia, 1936. *(Courtesy of Thomas Yoseloff.)*

Rosie[6] asks me to ask you if you remember that night you sat on her in Kid McCoy's Rathskellar? "He was such a nice boy," she says, "and so drunk I couldn't help loving him."

As ever,
Gene

August 18th 1936

---

1. Published by Alfred A. Knopf, New York, 1936.
2. Chapter Eleven, "The Recluse of Sea Island," offered intimate details of O'Neill's daily life.
3. The original magazine article was also titled "The Recluse of Sea Island" (*Redbook* 65 [August 1935]: 34).
4. The second play of the Cycle, *More Stately Mansions*. It was completed in a "final draft" version in 1941, but not copyrighted until 1964, when it was published by Yale University Press. Presented in Stockholm by the Royal Dramatic Theatre on 9 November 1962.
5. *A Touch of the Poet* was copyrighted 4 January 1946; published by Yale University Press in September 1957. Presented in Stockholm by the Royal Dramatic Theatre in March 1958.
6. A reference to his player-piano Rosie, which accompanied the late-night singing of O'Neill and such close friends as Nathan.

4701 West Ruffuer St.
Seattle, Wash.[1]
[November 1936]

Dear George:

The past few days have been damned hectic, as you may imagine, what with ducking interviews of all sorts, radio & newsreel men, etc. But things appear now to have calmed down a bit. I'm still in a daze and don't know what to make of it all. The Nobel caught me with my pants down, so to speak. I had absolutely no thought of it this year and did not believe the rumors—had it all doped out a Frenchman was due, Gide or Valéry.

A million thanks for your congrats—and let me take this opportunity to again thank you for all your friendship and encouragement has meant to me and my work. But I guess you know how I feel about that!

Still feeling all shot physically—no chance to rest yet and all this excitement is hell on the nerves. No definite plans, except that I can't possibly get to Sweden in time for the festival (don't feel physically up to it, anyway)—and am waiting now for a letter from the Swedish Academy with whatever suggestions they have to make.

Again, all gratitude, Friend!

Gene

P.S.

As you know, I don't have any U.S. press clippings now, so if you hear of anything interesting outside of the usual crap, let me know of it.

---

1. Craving a change of climate, and also because he hoped to soak up some of the Northwest for *A Touch of the Poet*, O'Neill moved to Seattle in November 1936. He and Carlotta rented a house on Magnolia Bluff, overlooking Puget Sound.

[Seattle]
December 3rd 1936

Dear George,

Your report on the generally favorable reception of the Nobel award pleases me immensely. It confirms what I have heard from other sources—Russel Crouse, etc. Beyond a few editorials, I have seen hardly any actual clippings. It is good, I think, that a smattering of scoffers should protest. If the praise were unanimous, I should feel very, very Eminent and dead. But who in hell is de Voto?[1] I've never heard of him.

A letter from the Secretary of the Swedish Academy informed me the award has been enthusiastically received over there. He also informs me that I need deliver no discourse to the Academy unless I want to—thank God!—that few of the literary winners have ever done so.

But I have sent over a speech, limited to a few minutes, to be read at the official Nobel banquet by the Chargé d'Affaires of the American Embassy in my stead. Most of it is devoted to coming right out in open meeting and proclaiming with grateful pride my debt to the influence of Strindberg.[2] As you know me, I need not say this is no sudden graceful gesture to please the Swedes. It gave me real pleasure to have the opportunity to put it on record. And I thought it might be a refreshing spectacle to have one successful writer come out and acknowledge his literary father, and not act as if he was a miraculous Topsy among scribblers, immaculately conceived by his own genius.

So watch out for the speech. (The banquet is on the 10th.) Not that it's any great shakes, you understand, but the Strindberg angle may interest you.

I've had fine letters from Lewis[3] and Dreiser,[4] which certainly pleased me—cables from Pirandello,[5] Hauptmann,[6] Lenormand[7] and others—in fact, a whole lot of goodwill messages from all over the world which makes me feel pretty humble—a few *even* from my U.S. colleagues, Behrman,[8] Sheldon,[9] Sid Howard,[10] etc.

But—and this is very much for your private ear alone!—there is one guy, a colleague, who ought, if he had any sporting sense of decency or courtesy, to have sent a message, no matter how much he hated the award and choked with envy. I mean, Anderson.[11] You will remember what I wrote for the Critics' Circle last spring when I went out of my way to pass him all possible kudos, even tho' I have by no means such a high opinion of his stuff as I pretended.[12] Well, I don't know what this proves to you, but it sure indicates to me that, personally, that guy is just another cheaply-envious shitheel. Maybe I was reared wrong, but under my code I don't see how even a playwright can be such a lousy sport.

What magazines we get, you ask. None out here. The Sunday *Times*[13] we see. That's all. Seattle papers for news.

Thanks for your warning about the Japanese invasion on the 20th.[14] I am already in an advanced state of preparedness. I have bought a Japanese flag and you can hear my Banzai! a mile away.

Carlotta joins me in love to you,

Gene

P.S.

For once you were right! Seattle *does* seem damp. But the inhabitants claim this was the driest November in history! I toured to a town, last week, where they usually have 180 inches of rain a year and the milkman frequently makes his rounds in a canoe. Well, there's a lot to be said for milkmen in canoes. Maybe they give them noiseless rubber cans, too.

December 3rd 1936

1. Bernard De Voto (1897–1955), American novelist and critic, who was among the minority opposing the awarding of the Nobel Prize to O'Neill. In the *Saturday Review of Literature*, De Voto wrote, "Whatever his international importance, he can hardly be called an artist of the first rank; he is hardly even one of the first-rate figures of his generation in America" ("Minority Report," 15 [21 November 1936]: 3).
2. August Strindberg (1849–1912), Swedish dramatist.
3. Sinclair Lewis, who had received the Nobel six years before.
4. Theodore Dreiser, whom O'Neill had considered the likeliest American Nobel laureate.
5. Luigi Pirandello (1867–1936), considered the greatest Italian playwright of his lifetime.
6. Gerhart Hauptmann (1862–1946), German dramatist.
7. Henri-René Lenormand, French novelist and dramatist.
8. Samuel Nathaniel Behrman (1893–1973), American dramatist who, like O'Neill, had once taken George Pierce Baker's playwrighting course at Harvard.
9. Edward Brewster Sheldon (1886–1946), American dramatist and alumnus of George Pierce Baker's famous Harvard drama course.
10. Sidney Howard (1891–1939), American dramatist who studied under George Pierce Baker at Harvard.
11. Maxwell Anderson (1888–1959), American dramatist and poet.

12. In April 1936, O'Neill had been invited to speak before the New York Drama Critics Circle. Then, he had praised that year's recipient of the Circle's award, Maxwell Anderson (for *Winterset*).

13. *New York Times*.

14. It is impossible to be certain, but perhaps Nathan had made a wisecrack about the imperialistic designs of the Japanese, who had recently invaded China.

PART IV
# The Masterworks

# INTRODUCTORY ESSAY

The final period of O'Neill's friendship with Nathan is bounded on one end by the peak of his critical regard, as symbolized by the Nobel Prize—and at the other, by the nadir, as new critics eagerly sought to discredit the old gods, chief among them O'Neill. In this last phase of his correspondence to the critic, O'Neill reveals a stoic resignation to circumstances over which he has little control: critical caviling, his own poor health, and family discord, all silhouetted against the dark backdrop of World War II. In the foreground stands the dramatist. No character he ever created arouses such pathos as O'Neill himself during these years.

At the summit of the Nobel award, O'Neill paused briefly to enjoy the accolades given his work. Beyond his satisfaction over such honor, he welcomed the chance to acknowledge two great sources of his inspiration. Strindberg and Nietzsche. To this end he began writing his acceptance speech. But the Nobel laureate eschewed the customary trip to Sweden. Feeling an overall malaise, he decided not to travel. Instead the speech was read for him while he continued his work.

As attention focused on O'Neill, he sought the sanctuary of an ever-elusive home. From Provincetown to Bermuda to France to Georgia, he had embraced each new residence with enthusiastic certainty that it would provide the sense of belonging he craved. But before long, when the shortcomings of each place became apparent, whether climate, location, or upkeep, he was on the move again. Thus, sick of Sea Island's heat, humidity, and mosquitoes, the O'Neills had left Casa Genotta for Seattle in November 1936. By December, they were in California.

Several ailments soon plagued him. Shortly after arriving in California, in December 1936, he underwent an appendectomy. Then a prostate-kidney infection dragged out his recovery. In a bedside ceremony at O'Neill's Oakland hospital in February 1937, the Swedish attaché quietly presented the Nobel Prize medallion.

As he recuperated, the playwright recharted his Cycle. *Greed of the Meek*, set in the years 1776–93, would occupy the new lead position. During the second half of 1937, he wrote the first draft at a rented estate near Lafayette, California, while Carlotta supervised the building of their new home, another mansion—this one on a ridge in the Las Trampas hills above

Danville. It was to be called Tao House, after the Chinese "tao," meaning "the right way of life." Eugene and Carlotta moved in during December 1937.

O'Neill's was a mind endlessly fertile. New play ideas constantly burgeoned from its depths. As he outlined them, he resolved to withhold from production whatever he wrote, pending completion of the Cycle. Political unrest abroad strengthened his resolve. In Europe, fascist Germany and Italy conducted foreign policy by threat and tested their armaments in the Spanish Civil War. And given chronic Sino-Japanese strife as well, the world seemed to be spinning into chaos. In such a milieu, O'Neill believed his audience to be weary of gloom and therefore unreceptive to the somber message of his tragedies. Thus, only three major productions would be staged from 1937 to 1945, all revivals. In 1944, he bluntly told Nathan of his pessimism about the future of the theater, nostalgically recalling "how much new life and ambition for a real theatre was rising from beneath the surface of Showshop during World War I, and that it persisted, war or no war." He added, "If anything like that exists now, I haven't heard of it."[1]

The Nobel recognition soon stimulated a number of articles on O'Neill. While most praised his work, some dissented. There was nothing new in this, for O'Neill had always had his detractors. Now, their voices occasionally rose above the Nobel Prize acclaim. No great admirer of the playwright's, Lionel Trilling in the *New Republic* saw him as an example of genius limited, one whose "energy, scope, and courage" had placed him with the best of the ancient tragedians but who plummeted from their ranks whenever he tried to answer the great imponderable questions. Citing the "religious nature of all his effort," Trilling centered his argument on *Days Without End* (then O'Neill's last produced), calling it "O'Neill's weakest play." *Days'* Christian religious ending with its promise of eternal happiness, he reflected, was O'Neill's admission that the naturalistic universe was "too heavy a burden for him." In effect, said Trilling, O'Neill had "crept into the dark womb of Mother Church and pulled the universe in with him." While Trilling admitted that from out of the "dark" limitations of his philosophic position O'Neill might produce lasting works, he thought that more likely the opposite would occur. If any of O'Neill's works were to live on, their longevity would be the result of their dramatic power, not their message.[2] Trilling's essay gave de facto recognition that O'Neill was worthy of criticism, but this was faint praise for one then being awarded the Nobel.

Two months later Bernard De Voto, American novelist and critic, sharply questioned not only the Nobel award but the recognition of O'Neill as a dramatist of stature. De Voto argued that O'Neill had never produced great drama, only great theater.[3]

Now as succeeding months brought no new O'Neill play to production,

voices hostile to him continued while general critical interest waned. Looking back a year later, Leon Edel saw the Nobel as a reward for past
achievements, since O'Neill's "genius [has] ceased to function." The "early
flowering" of his talent had given way to "a premature fading," his "dynamic
force . . . [had] spent itself."[4] That year another critic declared that "unless
[O'Neill] grows out of emotions we associate with adolescence, . . . his
work will not attain permanence."[5] In 1938, still another criticized O'Neill's
inclination toward melodrama as well as "the inadquacy and intermittent
appearance of his sense of humor."[6]

And in 1940, Mordecai Gorelik judged the "inherited weakness of the
will" of O'Neill's characters insufficient for tragedy in the modern age.
O'Neill's "ability to create character and situation in general far transcends
the ready-made pattern of his philosophy." Furthermore, Gorelik charged
that the dramatist's vision was vague, motivated more by the "vivid emotion"
than by the necessity to make "a clear statement." And he agreed with
George Bernard Shaw that O'Neill was only "banshee Shakespeare."[7] Alan
Reynolds Thompson took issue with those "Americans [who] have developed a sort of patriotic touchiness about the greatest American dramatist." He disparaged O'Neill as a romanticist, excessively fond of
"psychopathology."[8] Still another critic saw his characters as often "mas-
ochistic products of modern rationalistic probing."[9] Here is at least a grain
of truth. Many have recognized O'Neill's apparent need to punish himself
through his characters.

Many more voices favored the dramatist, however; among them some of
the most respected. In the absence of new plays from O'Neill, Brooks
Atkinson spoke out for more revivals.[10] Philip Rahv avowed that only
O'Neill, among creative writers of first rank, had "found in the drama his
natural means of expression."[11] And Joseph Wood Krutch in *The American
Drama Since 1918* put considerable emphasis on O'Neill and his art. Krutch
included detailed analyses of all O'Neill's major works as he praised the
playwright's continuing efforts to achieve "a form conveying a tragic view of
life at once valid and unmistakably of our own time."[12] Such praise had been
characteristic of a host of supporters in the past, but now, as O'Neill's
professional silence lengthened, the number of articles on him diminished.

The decline of O'Neill's reputation was paralleled by the deterioration of
his health, yet he continued to write. He had had his first onset of neuritis
early in 1938, but by mid-April he was able to begin work on *More Stately
Mansions,* set in the period 1837–41. By September he had completed a first
draft which was as long as the massive *Strange Interlude,* an exhausting
achievement since in it O'Neill was probing his relationships to both his wife
and his mother. In spite of his low spirits over Hitler's advance in Europe, he
compiled a second draft of *More Stately Mansions* that fall. In early 1939, he

had intended to begin *The Calms of Capricorn*, set on a clipper ship bound around Cape Horn for the California gold fields in 1857. Instead, feeling less spontaneous, he revised *A Touch of the Poet*.

In retrospect his revision of *A Touch of the Poet* was a slackening of his activity, a respite before he would begin the most important creative period of his life. Feeling a mighty compulsion, much stronger than that which brought forth *Ah, Wilderness!*, he stopped work on the Cycle and began to write one of his finest plays, *The Iceman Cometh*. It was 8 June. *Iceman*, warm and humorous in its first two acts, is a saloon play peopled with forlorn outcasts modeled on those O'Neill knew during his early drinking days before he became a playwright. Its message is stark: humanity's only escape from the sorry truth about itself lies in the fantasy world of daydreams.

The events of 1939 seemed to echo his theme. When war broke out on 1 September he was too distraught to continue work. But the hiatus was temporary: the playwright's great impetus to finish *Iceman* was enhanced by its personal nature, its compatibility with his own dark view of humankind. He was able to finish *Iceman*'s first draft on 26 November 1939. Quickly he produced his second and final version of the play.

Having completed one masterpiece he was ready, at last, to begin yet another, the play he most needed to write, *Long Day's Journey into Night*. He had dealt with aspects of his family's story in several earlier plays, among them, *All God's Chillun Got Wings*, *Desire Under the Elms*, *The Great God Brown*, and *Dynamo*. *Iceman* examined his relationship with his mother, but *Long Day's Journey Into Night*, probably O'Neill's supreme work, focuses directly on his whole family and the forces that tormented and molded him into the haunted soul his genius sought to express. It is a play with little stage business and no theatrical techniques other than sharp dialogue. By the end of August 1940, ignoring illness and depression, he had finished three acts. A month later he had finished the fourth and final act and began immediately to revise the whole.

Not until 1956, three years after his death, would *Long Day's Journey* be produced, to considerable critical acclaim. But as O'Neill put the finishing touches on the playscript in the autumn of 1940, in the seventh year of a professional silence that would stretch to twelve, the prospect of such recognition must have seemed remote.

Ill during the rest of that winter and further depressed by the war in Europe, O'Neill still managed to write through much of 1941. He finished detailed outlines of six projects, claiming that all would make fine plays. One was for several short plays spanning the period from 1910 to 1928. These would be largely monologues. Only the play *Hughie* survives. Another project was a full-length work about Satan entitled *The Thirteenth Apostle*. In addition to the six outlines, he jotted down fresh ideas for the

Cycle and resolved to expand *Greed of the Meek* and *And Give Me Death* each to two plays, thus enlarging the number in the Cycle to an imposing eleven. That summer he wrote *A Moon for the Misbegotten*, a play motivated by his feeling that he had not dealt compassionately enough with his brother Jamie in *Long Day's Journey Into Night*. He finished his first draft in January 1942 after a brief, dejected pause when the United States, reacting to the Pearl Harbor attack, entered the war on 8 December. This was the last play he ever completed.

O'Neill's spirits sank when he was told he had Parkinson's disease in February 1942. By autumn, Carlotta would confess to Nathan that she "did not find it so easy to keep Gene happy. Any little mental shock, or any emotional upset, puts him in a shocking state and it takes four or five days careful nursing to get him back to what is now normal for him." She found it heartbreaking to watch him suffer from the tremor, that "insidious disease that creeps in so slowly but so surely & destroys."[13] Yet in 1942 he revised *A Touch of the Poet* and worked on *The Thirteenth Apostle* (now renamed *The Last Conquest*). As his illness and the war continued, O'Neill's general pessimism grew stronger. He burned *Greed of the Meek* and *And Give Me Death*, after a change of plans for the Cycle, although he saved his outlines and the notes for other projected plays, intending still to complete it.

About this time, publicity about Oona, his daughter by Agnes Boulton, was very distressing to O'Neill. Oona, still in her teens, was photographed in night clubs. There were rumors that she aspired to an acting career. Her father thought her behavior highly inappropriate for the times. Her marriage in 1943 to Charlie Chaplin, a man of her father's generation, precipitated O'Neill's final break with her. He cooled towards her brother Shane more gradually. Shane quit school, then redeemed himself for a while during the war through maritime service, only to take to drugs later and eventually lose a child of his own through what O'Neill viewed as neglect. Eventually he disinherited both Oona and Shane, as well as all their children.

Through all his troubles, the dramatist's sense of comic irony helped to sustain him. Occasionally it surfaced in his letters to Nathan. "My 53rd [birthday] found me enjoying a liver attack and hating practically everything," he wrote in October 1944.[14] During World War II, he joked about his Victory Garden, "which we seem to be raising exclusively for hungry deer and rabbits."[15] Later, he dreamed of exchanging his dull San Francisco apartment for "a short stretch at Alcatraz, just to enjoy the sea breezes, a change of view, and the interesting company."[16] And he enjoyed teasing his friend with the fiction that they were once convent school boys together (actually, it was their mothers who had been schoolmates): "Remember how Sister Mary used to paddle your behind to the chime of the Angelus and never miss a beat? Life was so simple them."[17]

But it was not always easy for O'Neill to maintain a bantering mood.

Once again, he had become disillusioned with his home. The crushing upkeep of Tao House, the wartime difficulties of keeping servants, and his need to be closer to medical facilities prompted the O'Neills to move to San Francisco. There he wrote Nathan, "It's a relief to be free of possessions."[18] He and Carlotta took a small apartment at the Fairmont Hotel, then moved to a larger one at the Huntington. They stayed in San Francisco until late 1945.

This was a difficult time, for the all-absorbing activity of writing was over for O'Neill. His tremor had become so pronounced that, even holding one hand with the other, he could not get much down on paper. Although he tried, he could not compose except in longhand, and dictation proved impossible. The dramatist envied a little the critic's unchanging ability to "write—and as well as ever." He guessed that was "the secret" of contentment.[19] For Eugene and, hence, Carlotta, his work had always been the focal point of their life together. Now without the direction that his work provided, the couple began to quarrel as he endured long hours with little to do.

What O'Neill needed was an activity to replace writing as his *raison d'être*. On his hands were five unproduced plays ready for staging and the time and opportunity to produce them. He had long thought that his plays stood their best chance for success if produced in peace time when audiences were more receptive to their bleak themes. The war over, O'Neill moved back to New York where at last he gave the delighted Theatre Guild permission to produce *The Iceman Cometh*. He and Carlotta took a Manhattan penthouse, and he began to attend the daily casting tryouts. His frail appearance gave pause to his old friends, but they found him still the polite, congenial and arresting figure of old.

Nathan marked the prospect of O'Neill's reemergence by concocting an interview piece that played up the human side of his friend. Seeking to present the playwright as the waggish fellow that O'Neill could on occasion be, he had him using Nathanesque phrases. O'Neill asserted that what the American stage "needs more than anything else . . . is another Lotta Faust. There, my boy, was a love-apple, and who said anything about acting."

So the "interview" continued, with O'Neill saying that the presence of Lulu Glaser, "another slice off the top of the pot-roast," and "some fruit-jellies" like Irene Bentley and Bonnie Maginn would revitalize the stage. Insiders might chuckle at Nathan's whimsy, but later in the article they could recognize O'Neill's true voice as he discussed the play:

> I've tried to cut *The Iceman Cometh* about three-quarters of an hour, but all I feel justified in doing is cutting it about 15 minutes. . . . If there are repetitions, they'll have to remain in, because I feel they are absolutely necessary to what I am trying to get over.[20]

When *Iceman* opened on 9 October 1946, the audience saw a poor performance that brought mixed reviews. Writing earlier, Eric Bentley, who had read an advance copy, was not impressed, concluding that "possibly Mr. O'Neill has damaged his drama to save his melodrama." And now he charged that *Strange Interlude* and *Mourning Becomes Electra*, both several hours long, had "seemed contrived, labored, overloaded, and at times false."[21] Bentley was one of a new generation eager to establish their critical stature by toppling such a giant as O'Neill.

A more forceful blow came from Mary McCarthy. In an article entitled "Dry Ice," McCarthy called O'Neill "a playwright who—to be frank—cannot write." She classified him with Farrell and Dreiser, none of whom "possessed the slightest ear for the word, the sentence, the speech. . . . What they produce is hard to praise or to condemn; how is one to judge the great, logical symphony of a tone-deaf musician?" And O'Neill, she added, "is probably the only man in the world who is still laughing at the iceman joke or pondering its implications."[22]

At the opposite pole was Nathan. He wrote an extravagant review in his weekly *New York Journal-American* column on 14 October. "Hallelujah, hosanna, hail, heil, hurrah, huzza, banzai, and gesundheit!" he began, heralding O'Neill's return to Broadway. Nathan thought that *Iceman* made most of the plays of O'Neill's "fellow American playwrights produced during the twelve year period of his absence look like so much wet tissue paper." "One of the best of its author's works," *Iceman* revealed O'Neill "not only as the first of American dramatists but, with Shaw and O'Casey, one of the three really distinguished among the world's living."[23]

When Bentley's remarks, written earlier, appeared in November, Nathan wrote a stinging rebuttal. Discussing all of O'Neill's plays to that date, Nathan placed the criticism of the Oxford-educated Bentley in context. It was typical of the generally tepid British reception, characterized by a "lofty derision."[24]

But the poor production of *Iceman* seemed to support those who attacked the playwright. Though O'Neill always had his champions, Nathan first among them, his standing became diminished as many questioned the lasting importance of his work and turned to new voices such as Tennessee Williams and Arthur Miller.

The following year, *A Moon for the Misbegotten* closed after off-Broadway tryouts in Columbus, Detroit, and St. Louis.

O'Neill moved to Boston to be near its excellent medical facilities, and in the spring of 1948 bought a home on the coast at Marblehead Neck, twenty miles north of the city. At last, the son of the sea had returned to his home. There the ailing playwright received a devastating blow. Eugene O'Neill, Jr., the child of his first marriage, had given up a brilliant scholarly career at Yale to pursue a bohemian life in New York. Troubled for several years, he finally committed suicide in 1950. His death brought profound sorrow, for the two had once been relatively close.

From Marblehead, Carlotta wrote Nathan that "life follows the same pattern here. I am still on 16 hrs. duty."[25] For a short time, O'Neill still faintly hoped that he might be able to resume his writing. But that hope quickly died. "As for writing, that is out of the question," O'Neill told Nathan in August 1949. "It is not only a matter of hand, but of mind—I just feel there is nothing more I want to say."[26] "Alas," Carlotta wrote the critic three years later, "the theatre is no more for him. As he says, 'I have retired.' It is all very sad—& very worrying."[27]

Revivals had drawn little attention as critical interest continued to wane in the early 1950s. Eugene and Carlotta burned most of the Cycle, scenarios and rough drafts, in the winter of 1952–53. After the playwright's death the following November, the decline of his reputation continued. Then, early in 1956 came, at last, a grand resurgence, expected and acclaimed by Nathan.

## NOTES

1. 19 October 1944.

2. Lionel Trilling, "Eugene O'Neill," *New Republic* 88 (23 September 1936): 176, 179, 178, 179.

3. Bernard De Voto, "Minority Report," *Saturday Review of Literature* 15 (21 November 1936): 3.

4. Leon Edel, "Eugene O'Neill: The Face and the Mask," *University of Toronto Quarterly* 7 (October 1937): 33, 18.

5. Bonamy Dobrée, "The Plays of Eugene O'Neill," *Southern Review* 2 (Winter 1937): 444.

6. Homer Woodbridge, "Eugene O'Neill," *South Atlantic Quarterly* 37 (January 1938): 25, 34.

7. Mordecai Gorelik, *New Theatres for Old* (New York: Samuel French, 1940), 231, 232, 235.

8. Alan Reynolds Thompson, *The Anatomy of Drama* (Berkeley: University of California Press, 1942), 299–300.

9. Harry Slochower, *No Voice Is Wholly Lost . . . Writers and Thinkers in War and Peace* (New York: Creative Age Press, 1945), 252.

10. Brooks Atkinson, "After All These Years," *New York Times,* 12 October 1941, sec. 9.

11. Philip Rahv, "The Men Who Write Our Plays," *American Mercury* 50 (August 1940): 463.

12. Joseph Wood Krutch, *The American Drama Since 1918: An Informal History* (New York: Random House, 1939), 301.

13. Letter from Carlotta Monterey O'Neill to George Jean Nathan, 3 November 1942, Cornell University Library.

14. 17 October 1941.

15. 4 June 1943.

16. 16 September 1945.

17. 13 May 1939.

18. 6 March 1944.

19. 20 March 1949.

20. George Jean Nathan, "Eugene O'Neill Discourses on Dramatic Art," *New York Journal-American,* 26 August 1946.

21. Eric Bentley, "The Return of Eugene O'Neill," *Atlantic Monthly* 178 (November 1946): 66.

22. Mary McCarthy, "Dry Ice," *Partisan Review* 13 (November–December 1946): 577, 579.

23. George Jean Nathan, "The Iceman Cometh, Seeth, Conquereth," *New York Journal-American*, 14 October 1946.

24. George Jean Nathan, "O'Neill: A Critical Summation," *American Mercury* 63 (December 1946): 714.

25. Letter from Carlotta Monterey O'Neill to George Jean Nathan, 17 December 1952, Cornell University Library.

26. 27 August 1949.

27. Letter from Carlotta Monterey O'Neill to George Jean Nathan, 17 December 1952, Cornell University Library.

# LETTERS: JANUARY 1937–AUGUST 1949

PREFATORY REMARKS: Seeking to settle on the West Coast, Eugene and Carlotta traveled to Seattle, then to San Francisco. Suffering abdominal pains on 26 December 1936, O'Neill entered Samuel Merritt Hospital in Oakland, California, where an appendectomy was performed. Although the operation went well, a prostate-kidney infection ailed him in mid-January 1937. He was finally recovering when he wrote this letter.

SAMUEL MERRITT HOSPITAL
OAKLAND, CALIFORNIA

Jan. *27th*, '37

Dearest George Jean——
    At last we got a *Cosmopolitan*——& loved your article.[1] It was really charming. The only thing I heard against it was in a line from Blemie.[2] He was a little hurt that his name had not been mentioned!——
    All goes on in a good way here. Gene getting better every day——but the doctor thinks he is safer here than in an hotel or rented house——as the weather is so unsettled.
    We have heard of good prospects of selling Casa Genotta. Let's hope it's true. Because Gene & I feel that we would like to *try Northern* California.
    I hope you haven't caught the flu. Do be careful.——
    Are the Cuties cute this Winter?
    Do keep out of mischief——
    Gene wants to write a line——

Love——
——Carlotta——

Dear George:
    Forgive pencil but I'm too jittery for pen & ink yet. I was getting over this operation in great shape when some kidney complications came up to put me

178

down again. Nothing serious but damned annoying, and could get serious if let go. Anyway, it means I'll have to stay in hospital for another month to get all clear, and I better do it.

I liked your article in the *Cosmopolitan* immensely—better than anything you've ever done on me personally, I think. Much appreciation for it, George! It was damned fine of you.

Let me know your news when you have time. It's a damned bore, this being jailed in a hospital so long.

As ever,
Gene

---

1. "The Cosmopolite of the Month," *Cosmopolitan* 102 (February 1937): 8.
2. The O'Neills' pet Dalmatian, now about eight years old.

SAMUEL MERRITT HOSPITAL
OAKLAND, CALIFORNIA

Feb. 3rd, '37

Dear George:

Your letter arrived yesterday. Carlotta left last night via Overland Limited, for N.Y. Arrives Sat. a.m. for two days—then to Sea Island to get stuff out of house.[1] She will call you up. She will be at Madison.[2] So I won't give you any news stories. You'll learn all from her. Suffice it George Boll[3] did well by us—that and my inexorable refusal to listen to a lower price—and the fact that the people concerned have enough savvy to appreciate Carlotta's work in the Casa and its worth. Anyway, we will get out at a slight profit—and that's practically a miracle where houses are concerned.

This one thing I want to take up with you. There may be nothing to it, but if there is, it's urgent from my standpoint. It occurs to me the Critics' Circle[4] might take it into [their] heads to ask me to write another speech or something, particularly after the Nobel Prize. Now I would have to refuse this, no matter who wins prize. For one thing, I said my all last year. For another more important reason, I feel it's very punk stuff for me to appear as the Dean of the Drama who lays on the hands and contributes the official blessing on the prize-giving. You know what I mean—the venerable Stuffed-Shirt, whom the mobs get to assume is dead because venerated. I can't tell you all the stuff of that kind I've been adamant about since Nobel. I've refused everything of any sort that could possibly add to Eminence either here or abroad.

Now, all I'd like you to do is, if you have any such asinine suggestions arriving among your confreres, please talk them out of it, so it won't come to a showdown which would be equally unfair to the Critics Circle, of which my approval is on record, or to me, who may be in a hospital but am by no means dead yet.

All best, George
Gene.

---

1. The O'Neills had sold Casa Genotta, their home in Sea Island, Georgia.
2. Hotel Madison, East Fifty-Eighth Street, New York, New York.
3. Real estate agent of the Sea Island Company, who had sold the O'Neills their land there. Boll had become a good friend of O'Neill's.
4. The New York Drama Critics Circle, a professional organization founded in October 1935, partly out of dissatisfaction with the drama selections of the Pulitzer Prize committee. Nathan served as its president, 1937–39.

SAMUEL MERRITT HOSPITAL
OAKLAND, CALIFORNIA

Feb. 10*th*, 1937

Dear George:

Much gratitude for your letter! I am so glad you agree with me on that matter. Let's hope it will not come up. I don't think it will either. My letter was just in case.

I'm feeling better but have some treatments still to go through and my reaction to them will decide how soon I'll be released.

I'm glad you saw Carlotta. It is a tough break she has to see to this now but I was flat on my back, and this sale is too lucky a break to miss. If she will only sit by and direct—she will have help enough available down there,[1] God knows!—she won't get too tired—and she has promised to.

*The Avon Flows*[2] arrived. Well gotten out by R.H., don't you think? It strikes me as a very good-looking job. I'm so damned glad to know it has had such a good press. I expected a lot would take this chance to give you a jealous and revengeful boot. I won't attempt to reread it just now. My brains are about equal to the San Francisco papers these days. Even detective stories seem much too highbrow!

As ever,
Gene.

1. At Casa Genotta, Sea Island, Georgia.
2. Nathan's play, a Shakespearean composite, published in 1937 by Random House, New York.

PREFATORY REMARKS: While Carlotta was in Sea Island, Georgia, supervising their move to California, O'Neill received the Nobel gold medallion and diploma of award from the Swedish consul general in a bedside ceremony. Upon discharge from the hospital, he returned to his suite in the Fairmont Hotel in San Francisco. Then he and Carlotta rented an estate near Lafayette in Contra Costa County for the rest of the year.

LAFAYETTE
CONTRA COSTA COUNTY
CALIFORNIA

Dear George,

We were delighted to get your letter. We have been wondering lately if you had done the Mexican air trip as you planned, or gone to England, and were about to write and discover if you had returned to New York. The trip sounds to me more like a hardship than a vacation jaunt. Did you get air sick at all? It's the fear of that which will keep me true to the railroads. But, since you were able to finish your book,[1] I guess it couldn't have bothered you much.

Thanks much, George, for the John Francis[2] clipping. I had had no other word of his death. I feel a genuine sorrow. He was a fine person—and a unique character. I am glad the article speaks of him as my friend. He was all of that, and I know he knew my gratitude, for I often expressed it. The article gives a good idea of him. There is nothing exaggerated about it.

Your last letter mentioned your *Scribner['s]* article on the Critics Prize.[3] I read it and agree with you in theory. But in practice, wouldn't it work out that there might be few years in which an award could be made? Whenever there was much difference of opinion, you'd be stymied. There is one great improvement, though, that I think should be made in your rules. Give the award to the best play of the season by *any living dramatist.* Stop being Pulitzer Prizish and coddling the American playwright. American drama can stand comparison with any other. Prove you critics believe it can. What do you think? It seems to me it would make your prize a great deal more important and adult.

Carlotta is in a frenzy of creative ability over the new house.[4] I needn't tell you, who know her capability in this regard, that this means it is going to be some house! And the site has the most beautiful view I have ever come across. Wait and see if you don't agree when you visit us next year—as you certainly must. We expect to be able to move in by the first of the year—barring delay thro' strikes.

My health has been improving steadily. I have low spells still, now and again, but in general I'm beginning to feel pretty fit. Have been flirting with the Cycle[5] each morning lately but am not going to risk hard work on it for a while to come—perhaps not until we are settled in our new home.

We listened to the Louis-Farr fight to-night.[6] Did you see it? What another laugh that one was on the expert sport writers! Those boys had better give up predicting!

Our love to you, George—and let's hear some details of plane travel as you found it. And is it true what they say about Mexican gals?

As ever,
Gene

August 30th 1937
Love to you, dearest George Jean——
I'll write soon. Am going 'round in circles trying to keep house here, look after Gene, & build & furnish a new house. Blemie[7] sends love.——And so do I——

Carlotta

---

1. Probably *The Morning After the First Night,* published by Alfred A. Knopf (New York) in 1938.

2. John A. Francis of Provincetown, a businessman who had befriended O'Neill and the Provincetown Players during their early days.

3. Nathan had praised the Critics Circle, but had also regretted that it, "like the lamentably doltish Pulitzer Prize committee, is . . . on the arbitrary way to favoring—if not insisting upon—plays with an American scene, an American theme, and American characters." And he had urged that the individual opinions of the critics not be "influenced waywardly . . . into largely meaningless group opinion." Nathan demanded "a clearly and forthrightly chosen best play for award or no award at all" (George Jean Nathan, "Theater," *Scribner's* 101 [June 1937]: 65).

4. The O'Neills purchased land on an isolated ridge above Danville, California, where they would build their new oriental-inspired home. They named it Tao House, after the Chinese "tao," which means "right way of life."

5. His envisioned great cycle of plays, eventually planned to number eleven.

6. Heavily favored Joe Louis, world heavyweight boxing champion, fought Tommy Farr, heavyweight champion of England. Louis won by a decision but only after fifteen hard-fought rounds.

7. Their dog, a Dalmatian.

LAFAYETTE
CONTRA COSTA COUNTY
CALIFORNIA

Dear George,

Taking up where we left off, I still persist that if your prize[1] were thrown open to all comers it would give it added weight. All the better if, as you say, there are no playwrights but the Irish to challenge seriously. Just what I would like the prize to impress upon everyone!

There is not much news with us except that the building of the new house is proceeding on schedule. We haven't been bothered by strikes yet—business of knocking on wood!—but there are constant threats and alarms. The unions sure tell you where you get off these days, and you can like it or else—

How is New York reacting to the Stock Market slump? We see only the *San Francisco Chronicle* which, being Republican, is full of dire forebodings.

My health continues to improve, work a bit every day now and will soon be hard at it again. I'm also becoming a football fan in fact as well as fancy. Carlotta and I go to the University of California games at Berkeley. They have a grand team this year—as good as any in the country, I imagine.

Speaking of work, aren't you taking on too much? I'm wondering where you find the time—and the energy—for all you do now. Better watch it that your health doesn't take revenge and crack-up on you. Nothing is worth that, I've decided after my recent experience. And we are at the age when it pays to be a bit wary.

I note what you tell me concerning the passionate, play-loving Puerto Rican. Sounds to me like *the* Coon of the Caribbees.

Carlotta joins in love to you,

Gene

October 11th 1937

---

1. The Critics Circle Award.

LAFAYETTE
CONTRA COSTA COUNTY
CALIFORNIA

Dear George,

Much gratitude for the birthday greeting![1] It was damned kind of you to think of it. The day passed without undue repining about Time's relentless chiseling. In fact, I can say candidly that I felt younger in health on this birthday than I have for two or three years. So what ho!

Thank you for the clipping of your criticism on the Anderson play.[2] Well, he was about due to pull a very punk one. He must be going out for a writing endurance record these days—doing originals for the radio as well as his legit stuff, I hear.

No new news with us. We're looking forward to that long letter you promise.

Love from us both,

As ever,
Gene

October 18th 1937

Dearest George Jean,

I miss your letters. Particularly those telling me of your soul's welfare! And the gals. (Our Chinese boy[3] was always telling Freeman[4] about his "delicious girl"!)

Genie is getting better every day, please God, and the new road leading to the house (our new one) was oiled to-day. So that proves things really are getting on. But, *what* is going to happen to the stock market?[5] What reports do you hear?

Blemie[6] sends his love and a sweet kiss—

As always,
Carlotta

---

1. O'Neill's birthday was 16 October.
2. In his *Newsweek* column of 11 October 1937, Nathan had called Maxwell Anderson's *The Star-Wagon* "an exhibit so muddled, so fruity with sentimental wham, so bogusly metaphysical, and generally so amateurish in thought and execution that even a critic for *St. Nicholas, The Youth's Companion,* or a London newspaper should be able to appreciate its childish hollowness" (10:27).
3. Probably a servant.
4. Herbert Freeman, long-time chauffeur and utility man who had been with the O'Neills at Casa Genotta on Sea Island, Georgia.
5. The United States suffered a major recession in 1937.
6. The O'Neills' pet Dalmatian.

Lafayette, Contra Costa Co.,
Cal.
Dec. 23rd 1937

Dear George:

Your book just arrived,[1] and I hasten to send you our gratitude. I don't suppose, what with the Christmas bustle piled on top of our trying to get moved into the new home on the 28th, that either of us will get a chance to read it for a while, but meantime we want you to know how much we appreciate this gift.

If the wholly unexpected is news, then I have Big News for you. The critical reception of *Mourning Becomes Electra* in London was quite extraordinary—almost as good as it received in New York, and you will remember how good that was.[2] When you consider what it must have taken to keep those superior Limeys in a theatre four hours and more at a stretch—they run it through without any dinner break—for a Yank's play, it seems incredible. I expected the most indignant, snooty, condescending sort of a reaction. But not at all. The only really unfavorable piece I've seen, and the International Bureau has sent me all, was Ivor Brown's in the *Observer*.[3] He seemed to find psychology in an American play not only an impudent impertinence but also inherently humorous—like throwing custard pies. Of course, a few of the other lads took exception to this or that, but ended up by being all on the praise side. And some of them were so high in their praise—Desmond MacCarthy in the *New Statesman*,[4] for one—that I couldn't believe my eyes. Agate in the *Times* went off the deep end, etc., etc.[5]

But I'll show you all of them when you visit. I'm giving you so much of this because I know you will be astonished, too. It's surely one time when a Yank gets the breaks. They are all in praise of the acting, too. Evidently Beatrix Lehmann[6] as Lavinia did a fine job.

As for the public flocking in hordes in response to the critical ballyhoo, I haven't heard much on that yet, but I imagine I'll get little from it beyond my advance. The Westminster[7] is a tiny theatre, I know, and I doubt if moving it to a larger West End[8] one would do anything but kill the production in two weeks. This is just too bad, because I could do with a production bringing in something these days.

*Mourning Becomes Electra* is also soon to be given at the Burg Theatre in Vienna. My Central European agent seems to think this is quite an honor. I hope it is. I know damned well it won't be anything else.

I go on so much about *Electra*, George, because it really strikes me as amazing that this trilogy, so difficult to produce, demanding so much of critics and audience, challenging such crushing comparisons, should be the one play of mine which has been proclaimed as a work of art *everywhere* it has been done in Europe. Every other play of mine has gotten the bird in at least one country. And outside of the Fascist countries,[9] where it is barred, and France, which has no theatre above contempt, *Electra* has now been done almost everywhere (including Finland!). It makes me feel proud of myself. It must have something.

How about this production of *Julius Caesar* in N.Y. I hear so much of?[10] Didn't see your criticism of that, although we keep up with you nearly every week via *News Week* and usually see *Esquire*. It sounds damned interesting. I'm glad *Mice And Men*[11] is so good. I liked the book a lot—so much so that I found myself deeply regretting it was not a bit better, if you get me. It wasn't geared to penetrate deeply enough and acquire the profounder significance it should have had. But it was a fine piece of work, anyway.

My working has been held up a bit lately by the confusion of getting ready for the trek to the new house, and by rheumatism in my writing arm—not so good, to pick that arm!—but I hope to get hard at it as soon as we're put in the new place.

> Love from us both & Happy New Year!
> As ever,
> Gene

---

1. Probably *The Morning After the First Night* (published in 1938).
2. Michael MacOwen produced the revival of *Mourning Becomes Electra*, which opened 19 November 1937. It had 106 performances.
3. Ivor John Carnegie Brown (1891–1974), English author and dramatic critic for the *London Observer*, had criticized O'Neill's "too heavy Freudian emphasis" in *Mourning Becomes Electra* (*London Observer*, 21 November 1937).
4. Desmond MacCarthy, "A Tremendous Play and Great Acting," *New Statesman and Nation* (London) 14 (27 November 1937): 875–77.
5. James Agate (1877–1947), dramatic critic for the London *Sunday Times*, and a major English critic of his day. His reviews of *Mourning Becomes Electra*: *London Times*, 20 November 1937 and 22 November 1937, third and fourth editions only.
6. Beatrice Lehmann (1903–1979) played Lavinia in the London production of *Mourning Becomes Electra*.
7. The Westminster Theatre, London, in Palace Street, near Victoria Station.
8. London's theater district.
9. Italy and Germany.
10. Directed by Orson Welles (who also played Brutus), *Julius Caesar* had opened its run of nearly five months at the Mercury 11 November 1937.
11. John Steinbeck's novel, published in 1937.

Tao House, O'Neill's home from December 1937 to February 1944. Part of a 158-acre estate, the Chinese-style mansion offered the dramatist the seclusion necessary to complete his last plays: *The Iceman Cometh, Long Day's Journey into Night, A Moon for the Misbegotten, A Touch of the Poet,* and parts of his great Cycle of plays. *(Courtesy of Cornell University Library.)*

TAO HOUSE
DANVILLE
CONTRA COSTA COUNTY
CALIFORNIA

Dear George,

Well, we are almost settled in the new home.[1] I say almost because we've been living amidst carpenters, painters, electricians, ever since I last wrote you and it seems too good to be true that we are at last to have a little peace. But all discomforts will be justified in the final result. Carlotta has done a wonderful job in the interior—better than Casa Genotta—as you will agree when you visit.

I've just finished *The Morning After The First Night.*[2] I like it better, I think, than any book of yours in years. Or, if that is because I see this one clearer, having just read it, than I remember the others, then I like it as well, and that means liking it a hell of a lot! The amazing thing, looking back over all your critical books, is that you never let yourself let down; each book has the same vital integrity, wit, clear vision, zest and love of the theatre. When I consider the twenty or more boring evenings in the Showshop Racket you have to pay for one interesting one in the Theatre—season after season for so many years—well, my hat is off to you! It seems miraculous that just the wear and tear of the job doesn't weary your spirit into a let-down year now and then. I don't mean in the integrity of your criticism, of course. You couldn't do that. I mean in the vitality of your writing, in general quality— that that never becomes overtrained or stale. I guess we better begin to call you Iron Man![3]

What's new with you? We haven't heard from you in ages.

We had a letter from O'Casey[4] a few weeks ago. He seemed as pleased about the *Electra* London lauds[5] as if it were his own play. A grand guy, Sean, if there ever was one! As you probably know, *Electra* has moved to the West End[6] after packing them in at the Westminster.[7] The joker in this record Westminster business is that capacity gross there is a little above the old Provincetown Playhouse. Even at the West End theatre it has moved to, three hundred pounds a performance is S.R.O.[8] So I'm not liable to grow rich on royalties—British Income Tax taking 25% and agents' cut further reducing them. The last report I had, business was steadily building at the new theatre but by no means capacity yet.

Neuritis[9] has been giving me hell. The diagnosis as to cause seems to be teeth. So I go to the dentist this week-five more teeth must come out. This dentist gag is getting to be so monotonous it's almost a laugh. What I've contributed to dentistry in the past ten years is plenty! But the end is in sight because I soon will have few left for the boys to work on!

Love from us,
Gene

Feb. 7th '38

---

1. The O'Neills had moved into Tao House in December of 1937.
2. Published by Alfred A. Knopf (New York) in 1938.
3. Reminiscent of "Iron Horse," the nickname of the popular New York Yankees player, Lou Gehrig.
4. Sean O'Casey, the Irish dramatist.
5. Especially James Agate in the *London Times* and Desmond MacCarthy in the *New Statesman and Nation*.
6. London theater district.
7. Westminster Theatre, London, in Palace Street, near Victoria Station.
8. Standing room only.
9. This was a new ailment for O'Neill.

TAO HOUSE
DANVILLE
CONTRA COSTA COUNTY
CALIFORNIA

Dear George,

Progress on the Cycle wasn't mentioned in my letter because since Christmas there hasn't been any. The irritating delays and noise and discomfort of our trying to get settled here while work on the house was being finished (in the midst of a record-breaking deluge when it rained every day for eighteen days at one period), combined with the pangs of neuritis, which the weather intensified, stopped me in my tracks. But before I stopped I did manage to finish the 1st draft of the new play of the nine, which means I now have the first three plays in first draft.[1] This sounds more progressive than it really is, because only the third play is any way near what I want it to be yet. The other two have a lot of work still to be done on them before they can take final shape. And I feel so utterly lousy at present writing—after a wisdom tooth extraction which made my neuritis worse than ever, as they claim it always does for a while—that I'd hate to prophecy when I'll begin to take interest in the Drama again.

*Electra* isn't building in the West End as the too-optimistic producer hoped it would. Due in part to bad weather, I believe. But I also believe it wouldn't build, anyway, weather or no weather. To have it a box office success, too, is a bit too miraculous to ask of London.

It will be grand to see you this Spring. I am looking forward to long talks on things theatrical and to hear of the interesting developments you mention. And I have a lot to confide in you—mainly in the nature of misgivings, for the developments this season that I've heard most about are, as you can imagine, neither interesting nor such as to inspire an enthusiasm for production!

We promise you there will be real sunshine by then and that the last hammering carpenter will long since have gone his noisy way—and that the swimming pool will be functioning.

Love from us both,
Gene

February 22nd 1938

---

1. *The Greed of the Meek* was the new first play of the Cycle. The other two were *And Give Me Death* and *A Touch of the Poet*. The latter, drafted in 1936 and finished in 1942, was the first of the Cycle to be completed.

TAO HOUSE
DANVILLE
CONTRA COSTA COUNTY
CALIFORNIA

Dear George,

I certainly sympathize with you on the neuritis siege.[1] And by sympathize I mean sympathize, because I now know from experience what it's like, although I imagine it's much harder to bear in the face than in the arm. My arm, thank God, is almost rid of it now.

We suggest the first thing you do when you feel well enough is hop a plane out to us. It's beautiful now and we can promise you, without any California-climate-lying, all the sunshine you can absorb. We have a fine, if not gaudy, pool. You can swim. You can rest. Frisco is less than an hour's drive away, if you get that city yen. In short, all we have to offer is everything!

That newspaper stuff about my breaking with the Guild is cockeyed.[2] Outside of my son, Shane,[3] who is at school in Colorado, and spent spring vacation with us, we haven't had a single guest who stayed overnight. Cerf[4] spent a day with us some months back. Russel Crouse[5] a day about a month ago. Except these two, no one. So you see. I suspect the basis for the rumor—if it has any—may have been something Cerf said casually at some party or other. I did pan the Guild, talking with him—as I have to their faces—for this stupid Movie star casting system, and I said I was just as well pleased they had nothing of mine to do in their present state of jitters. What makes me sorest about the story isn't the fact that it's not true, but that it came out at this time. Even if I hated the Guild, instead of feeling nothing but friendship for them, I would not be such a louse as to break with them just when everyone is jumping them, and they've had a disastrous season. I wired their publicity department to quote me in emphatic denial, as I trust you saw. I hope that kills the rumor for good.

Lots to tell you about the Cycle when you visit. Suffice it for this, I'm hard at it again and the old bean is functioning better than it has in years. I'm encouraged to hope that my particular allotment of the fatal-forties period of physical bog-down and mental meandering is about over and I can take up where I left off when I finished *Mourning Becomes Electra*. Of a certainty, those who look for any wishful answers or doddering benignity are going to be bitterly disappointed in the Cycle.

We came near losing Blemie last week, and there was much sadness in the Hacienda O'Neill. An intestinal complaint due, I fear, to his lack of will power regarding horse turds, the old rake! Teams have been up here cutting the hay. Enough said. A good Vet pulled him through and he's fairly fit again. He says he can't understand it, that something he drank must have disagreed with him.

Here's hoping the damned neuritis has gone.
Love from us both, George, and let us welcome you here soon.

As ever,
Gene

May 29th 1938

---

1. For many years, Nathan suffered chronically from neuralgia in the left side of his face.
2. On 7 May 1938, the *New York World-Telegram* had reported that, according to a recent visitor at the O'Neills', the playwright had outlined his production plans for the Cycle, in such a way that might require him to break with the Theatre Guild and to start his own theater.
3. Shane, born of O'Neill's marriage to Agnes Boulton, was eighteen and a student at a prep school in California. He had just spent his spring vacation at Tao House.
4. Bennett Cerf, O'Neill's publisher.
5. Playwright; publicity agent for the Theatre Guild in the early 1930s.

TAO HOUSE
DANVILLE
CONTRA COSTA COUNTY
CALIFORNIA

Dear George,
    The Family O'Neill is mediumly in the pink, thank you kindly, con-valescent not so much from the Hitler jitters as from a rash of servant trouble. It is probably just as well for your comfort that you couldn't visit in August, although things were not as dire then as they later became. We had a couple composed of an Irish lady cook married to a Greek,—a sour com-bination!—and believe me, toward the end of their period of strictly faithless service, we never knew what we would get for dinner, if any, or how. The Greek believed—and said out loud—that all men are brothers, and why shouldn't his brothers support him. His wife believed that all the Irish are descended from kings—except the O'Neills—and how could a Princess be expected to know much of vulgar matters like cooking. We stood them as long as we could take it, on the theory that bad is better than none, for it isn't so easy to get anyone to work in the country here. Finally Carlotta fired them. And now we have a Japanese couple, who are splendid so far, just what we want—business of knocking on wood.
    The Cycle, like Ol' Man River, rolls on. I finished the first draft of the fourth play[1] about a month ago and since then have been going over it, doing considerable revision. When I have that done, I'll rewrite one scene in the

third play.[2] Then I'll have these two plays pretty well set and finished, and shall give myself a brief rest before starting the fifth play.[3] I'll have earned it because by that time I'll have been working every day—and I mean every day—for seven or eight months. The first drafts of the first two plays[4] can't be revised and finished until I am much farther along with the Cycle. It's hard to explain, but the aspects of the theme shown in them tie in with the recurrence of the same aspects in later plays. It's a question of just how much do I need in the first two, and how must I save for the last part of the Cycle. And I find I can't really figure this out until I write the later plays. Of course, I have outlines of these, but I never know how closely the characters, when they begin to live, will follow my plans for them.

From your description of *Hellzapoppin*[5]—a grand title, eh?—that would be one evening in the theatre I'd enjoy spending. As for your new Hawaiian passion, if it takes you to Waikiki next Spring, all the better. You can stop off for a visit here. You mustn't miss us next year. Think of the fair in Frisco! Anyone not attending the Frisco Fair will be simply not alive. They are to have the greatest collection of Japanese art ever gathered together under one tent, for one thing—and that must mean geishas, don't you think?

Hawaii I could never acquire a yen for—even with a palm tree and a dill pickle thrown in. That revolting old primitive rite of the Islands in which a publicity agent from the Chamber of Commerce drapes a welcoming lei around your neck has me stopped.

Love from us both, George—and keep us posted on the hula hula lessons.

As ever,
Gene

October the fifth 1938

---

1. *More Stately Mansions.*
2. *A Touch of the Poet.*
3. The fifth was to be called *The Calms of Capricorn.* In 1951, realizing he could not finish the Cycle in his lifetime, O'Neill destroyed many of his notes for the unfinished plays. However, he left a detailed scenario for *The Calms of Capricorn* (which by that time had moved from fifth to seventh place in the eleven-play Cycle). From O'Neill's scenario, Donald Gallup developed the play into publishable form (New Haven: Ticknor & Fields, 1982).
4. *The Greed of the Meek* and *And Give Me Death,* respectively.
5. *Hellzapoppin,* a hilarious revue in two acts, had opened 22 September 1938, at the Forty-sixth Street Theatre. It was enormously popular, due in part to persistent publicity from the columnist Walter Winchell.

TAO HOUSE
DANVILLE
CONTRA COSTA COUNTY
CALIFORNIA

Feb. 27th 1939

Dear George:

I have meant to write you before this but we have been passing through an extremely anxious period. You will probably remember how Carlotta has always joked about how badly her eyes focused at times. She laughed it off, but it really bothered her a lot more than she would ever admit. The condition was due to the blundering work of an eye surgeon who operated on her when she was ten years old, or around that. Well, to make a long story short, during the past six months this trouble has become very serious and almost driven her nuts. Constant headaches, etc. She finally went to the best eye man in San Francisco and he decided that the only chance of relieving it was to operate again. It was only a chance, he admitted, because he could not tell until he cut into it what he would find, not knowing to what extent the mistake made in the operation when she was a girl had damaged the muscles. He operated a week ago in the Stanford Hospital in San Francisco, and so far, thank God, it seems to be a great success. But he cannot tell finally until she begins really to use the eye and puts a strain on it. Not for a month or so yet. At present she is home again with a nurse, wearing an arrangement of bandages and goggle which only permits her to see straight ahead through a tiny peep hole of dark glass over the sound eye. Not very pleasant for her but she is taking it in a brave spirit and never complains. The worst is that unless the operation turns out as successful as he hopes, he will have to operate again later on—on the other eye to try and bring it into alignment with the position of this one.

A damned uneasy time! Carlotta has been grand about it, but you can imagine how worried and scared she has been underneath. And how worried I have been.

I will let you know how things develop. Meanwhile, Carlotta joins in love to you.

Overlook this lousy typing. I am all out of practice, but I figured it would be more merciful on your eyes than my longhand.

As ever,
Gene

TAO HOUSE
DANVILLE
CONTRA COSTA COUNTY
CALIFORNIA

Dear George,

Many thanks for the clipping. Ah, Wilderness, those dear old days when you and I were little convent boys together! Remember how Sister Mary used to paddle your behind to the chime of the Angelus and never miss a beat? Life was so simple then.[1]

I was sorry to read your report on the new O'Casey play.[2] I suppose these lousy times make it inevitable that many authors get caught in the sociological propaganda mill. With most of them it doesn't matter. They have nothing much to lose and the sociological attack helps them by giving a lot of shallow stuff a phoney partisan importance. But O'Casey is an artist and the soap box no place for his great talent. The hell of it seems to be, when an artist starts saving the world, he starts losing himself. I know, having been bitten by the salvationist bug myself at times. But only momentarily, so to speak, my true conviction being that the one reform worth cheering for is the Second Flood, and that the interesting thing about people is the obvious fact that they don't really want to be saved—the tragic idiotic ambition for self-destruction in them.

However, O'Casey, I'm betting, will soon get a sick bellyful of the Comrade Church after he's seen through the power-greed of a sufficient number of its communicants.

The only important news with us is that Carlotta's operation was a complete success. Her eyes are in better shape now than they ever have been. I've been working steadily, without yet taking the rest I'd promised myself. Going back over the third play lately to make some changes that will hook it up more closely with the fourth.[3] That's the devil with this job, the amount of time spent on such revision. It's a sort of special, additional task for a playwright. No one who confined himself to writing single plays could ever imagine how much extra thought and labor are involved. Sometimes, I feel sick about it—the constant driving on while seeming, in the light of final completion, to be making no progress. Still and all, I do keep pretty damned interested, for it is an arousing challenge, and the stuff is there, if I have the stuff to make it mine.

How about your plans for Europe? Have you decided yet? We are still hoping you may come here.

Love from us, George. It will be grand to see you again, whenever it is.

Always yours,
Gene.

May the 13th 1939

---

1. O'Neill is indulging here in some creative banter with his friend. Actually, it was not they who were in convent school together but their mothers, at St. Mary's Academy in Notre Dame, Indiana.
2. *The Star Turns Red* (1940). In his *Encyclopedia of the Theatre* (1940), Nathan expressed his regrets that O'Casey had been adversely influenced by Communism in the writing of this play. (The critic tended to disdain any play he felt was too leftist.)
3. *A Touch of the Poet* and *More Stately Mansions*, respectively.

TAO HOUSE
DANVILLE
CONTRA COSTA COUNTY
CALIFORNIA

Dear George,

Many thanks for the copy of your broadcast.[1] Anna Held[2] having forgotten somehow to give me that pink garter you mention, I shall treasure your essay side by side with a picture of Bonnie Maginn in tights which I once clipped from the *Police Gazette*[3] in an aspiring prep school moment.

As for the dedication of *Encyclopedia Of The Theatre*[4] to me, my deep gratitude, George. I am honored and delighted.

I note in a recent *Newsweek* article[5] you speak of my having finished the fifth play of the Cycle. I wish I had! The truth is I haven't even started the fifth[6] yet. Madden,[7] I know, is responsible for handing you this bum steer. He wrote me some time ago he had spoken to you of the great progress I had made on the Cycle. I explained at great lenth, when he was here, just how I stood, that the fifth play was the one I would tackle next, but he evidently got it balled up.

Just between us, I haven't done a lick on the Cycle in several months. It had me worn to a frazzle and stale as hell. I'd been working on it continuously, practically every day, since I recovered from my stretch of illness two years ago. So I decided to forget it for awhile and do one play, or maybe two, that had nothing to do with it.[8] Which I've done, and I expect to finish a first draft of one[9] in about two weeks. I will then go over it and get it in final shape. So it's on the cards that you will be getting a script for your valued judgement before many moons have passed. It looks good to me. At any rate, it has been an interesting time writing it. I'm not going to tell you a word about it, not even the title. I want you to read it without any advance information as to what kind of a play it is, or anything.

Keep this very much under the hat. All I've let out to Cerf[10] for the Guild or Madden, is that I had several ideas for plays outside the Cycle which I *might* do later *if* I could forget the Cycle for a while. And that's as far as I wish any authorized rumor to go. The reason is, I don't know when I will want to publish or produce this play, or any additional separate plays I may write. I may want to keep them to myself for years[11]—until financial pinch forces my hand. Every time I think of making that trip East to face casting, rehearsals and all the rest of the game, I feel a great bored weariness and reluctance, as if I'd had quite enough of that for one life. Anyway, my point about secrecy is that if my publishers, producers, and agent knew I had anything finished, they would be on my neck all the time with this or that persuasive argument, and I want to duck that.

After this play is finished, I may go back to the Cycle and start the fifth play. Or I may do a separate second play.[12] I have a fine idea for one that is much on my mind. But it's no good prophesying now. It all depends how the spirit moves then.

I suppose, with all the rest of us, this European mess[13] has given you the jitters. It has certainly convinced me that only pessimists are not morons, and that only a blithering near-sighted idiot could desire to live very long in the future.

Carlotta joins me in love and Blemie, now a patriarch of twelve but still going strong, sends you a Dalmatian Heil!

As ever,
Gene

October the 1st 1939

---

1. Probably the 23 April 1939 NBC broadcast of the New York Drama Critics Circle award proceedings, at which Nathan spoke.

2. Anna Held (1873–1918), coquettish actress in many musical comedies and vaudeville. One of the songs she popularized was "Won't You Come and Play with Me?"

3. *National Police Gazette* was a barbershop crime, confession, and pinup magazine, whose trademark was its pale pink paper.

4. Published by Alfred A. Knopf (New York) in 1940. Nathan dedicated the book with these words: "To Eugene O'Neill, After Many Years."

5. George Jean Nathan, "Prodigals' Return" (his Theater Week column), 14 (18 September 1939): 38.

6. The fifth play would be *The Calms of Capricorn*.

7. Richard Madden, O'Neill's agent.

8. *The Iceman Cometh* (completed in November 1939), and, probably, *Long Day's Journey Into Night*, which he began in the early spring of 1940, and the idea for which he had developed at least a year before.

9. *The Iceman Cometh* was copyrighted 12 February 1940; published by Random House in October 1946. It was presented by The Theatre Guild on 9 October 1946, at the Martin Beck Theatre.

10. Bennett Cerf, O'Neill's publisher.

11. *The Iceman Cometh* did not receive production until seven years later; *A Moon for the Misbegotten*, in 1947. *Long Day's Journey Into Night* was produced posthumously in 1956.

12. He did—*Long Day's Journey Into Night*, completed in 1940.

13. Hitler's army had invaded Poland on 1 September 1939, and shortly thereafter England and France had declared war on Germany, launching World War II.

TAO HOUSE
DANVILLE
CONTRA COSTA COUNTY
CALIFORNIA

Dear George,

*Encyclopedia of The Theatre*[1] arrived several days ago while I was on the last lap of going over the typed script of the new non-Cycle play[2] and getting it into final form. I waited until this job was finished before reading *Encyclopedia*.

I like it as much as I liked all the others. You know how much that is. The encyclopedia idea is a darned good angle, it seems to me, and has real value beyond its use for this one book. What I'm thinking of now is that you might find it the right form if later on you should ever want to publish a comprehensive opus—in two or more volumes, say—that would collect whatever you felt was most significant and representative in all the books—a record of everything that has appeared to you, as it happened, of genuine importance in the growth of the American theatre in your time. It would be, also, a sort of biography of your criticism. Outside of the other values of such an encyclopedia, from a practical standpoint it would make a grand reference work for all future students of the development of the modern American theatre.

How does this notion strike you? It is just my immediate reaction to the form of the new book. I like it. It appeals to me as convenient to the reader, without sacrificing any of its values to achieve the convenience.

But, of course, it is the dedication of *Encyclopedia Of The Theatre* that impresses me most! I am immensely pleased and grateful for that, George.

I'll send you the new play as soon as Carlotta gets a chance to type copies of the final edition. I did a pot of pruning on the first draft. How soon she will be able to get this done, I don't know. She's just recovering from a bout with flu and has to do her typing in her time out from housekeeping. So it may be some time.

I like this one a lot. Unless I am badly mistaken, you will like it, too.

All the good old seasonal greetings—and much gratitude again for the book and the dedication.

As ever,
Gene

December the 18th '39

---

1. Published by Alfred A. Knopf (New York) in 1940.
2. *The Iceman Cometh.*

TAO HOUSE
DANVILLE
CONTRA COSTA COUNTY
CALIFORNIA

Dear George,

If you recall various of my reminiscences, you will recognize in this play[1] a lot of material I have talked about using ever since you've known me. But never until a year or so ago did it take definite line and form as a play in my mind, its many life histories interwoven around a central theme.

All of the characters are drawn from life, more or less, although not one of them is an exact portrait of an actual person. And the scene, Harry Hope's dump, is a composite of three places.[2]

The plot, if you can call it that, is my imaginative creation, of course, but it has a basis in reality. There was a periodical drunk salesman, who was a damned amusing likable guy. And he did make that typical drummer crack about the iceman,[3] and wept maudlinly over his wife's photograph, and in other moods, boozily harped on the slogan that honesty is the best policy.

The story of Parritt has a background of fact, too.[4] The suicide really happened pretty much as shown in the play. But it was not the man the character of Parritt is derived from who bumped himself off that way. It was another person and for another reason.[5]

The script probably still needs pruning in stage directions and tightening here and there. Not much, however, and I don't feel like doing it now. The play will always have to be too long, I think, from the ordinary production standpoint. But to hell with that angle. I'm not giving a thought to production. In fact, I hate to think of it being produced—of having to watch a lot of actors muscle in their personalities to make strange for me these characters of the play that interest me so much—now, as *I* have made them live!

Again, for God's sake, keep this play under your hat. No one but you and Cerf[6] and Saxe Commins[7] know it exists. Saxe is the only one who has read it. He typed the revised first draft during his visit with us. As for Bennett, I told him when he was here, but only after he had pledged absolute secrecy, and on the strict understanding that he should not mention publication until I did, if he had to wait ten years. One reason I told Cerf was because I want him to have one script buried in his safe, in case of accident—and in case I need the advance on the book.

You know if Madden and the Guild got wise I had finished this play what pressure arguments and pleadings would put me on a spot. The trouble is, they are personal friends as well as agents and producers. Otherwise, a go-to-hell rebuttal would be simple.

Besides the fact that I want to keep on now doing the only work that interests me in the theatre—writing—and that a production always throws me off work, sometimes for six months, there is a physical reason why I now dread the New York casting, rehearsal strain. Although my health is good, I am not the same as I was before my long illness, and never will be again. Even here, in the most peaceful healthy environment, I get sudden set-backs of complete exhaustion when I have to stay in bed for several days. (I'm enjoying one right now—am writing this in bed). I'm honestly afraid of what such an attack would do if it caught me in New York at the ragged end of production strain. I might come out of it an invalid for years, or even the rest of my life. This is no kidding. And what the hell production, no matter how successful, would be worth that, particularly in these times when nothing seems of less importance than whether another play is produced or not produced—or written, or not written, for that matter!⁹

Well, I hope you like *The Iceman Cometh*. Including the title, which I love, because it characteristically expresses so much of the outer and inner spirit of the play. I really admire this opus, George. I think it's about as successful an attempt at accomplishing a thing comprehensively and completely in all aspects as I've ever made. And I feel there are moments in it that hit as deeply and truly into the farce and humor and pity and ironic tragedy of life as anything in modern drama.

What ho! There's nothing like being one's own severest critic, eh?

Carlotta joins in love to you.

As ever,
Gene

February the 8th 1940.

P.S. Play is written in exact lingo of place and 1912, as I remember it—with only the filth expletives omitted. If you catch any slang you think doesn't belong in that time, let me know.

---

1. *The Iceman Cometh*.
2. All New York bars he had once frequented: Jimmy the Priest's (James J. Condon's saloon at 252 Fulton Street); the Hell Hole (actually the Golden Swan on Sixth Avenue in Greenwich

Village); and the Garden Hotel taproom on Madison Avenue (near the old Madison Square Garden).

3. The title of the play contains a double meaning: first, it is a reference to the old bawdy story about the man who calls to his wife, "Has the iceman come yet?" to which she replies, "No, but he's breathing fast." The more sinister meaning of "iceman" in the play is death.

4. In the play, Don Parritt is the son of Rosa Parritt, an anarchist (modeled on Emma Goldman) who has just been given a life sentence for a bombing on the West Coast. (This background is based on the famous MacNamara bombing case in Los Angeles during the 1910s, of which O'Neill was aware.)

5. In *The Iceman Cometh*, Parritt, tortured by a guilty conscience (for he has turned in his own mother to the authorities), leaps from a top-floor fire escape at Harry Hope's bar. His death recalls the fatal leap of O'Neill's friend James Findlater Byth in 1913 at Jimmy the Priest's.

6. Bennett Cerf.

7. O'Neill's editor at Random House and trusted friend.

8. Not until 1946 would *Iceman* be produced—the last of his plays that were presented in New York during O'Neill's lifetime.

**PREFATORY REMARKS:** O'Neill wrote the following note on the outside of an envelope, probably that used to mail the previous letter.

Dear George:

*Important!* Don't read this letter until *after* you have read play.[1] It contains some comments and explanations that may interest you, but I want you to read the play without any advance info. from the author whatever.

Gene

---

1. Probably *The Iceman Cometh*.

## TAO HOUSE
## DANVILLE
## CONTRA COSTA COUNTY
## CALIFORNIA

Dear George,

I needn't tell you how delighted I was to get your letter about the play.[1] I have been eagerly awaiting your critical judgement. I was sure you would like it, but still—Well, you know how it is, you write a thing with growing confidence and elation, and you finish it in an exultant mood of accomplishment. Then suddenly the reaction comes and you become tired and empty, and what you have done grows blurred in your mind, and all you remember is a lot of dialogue and some characters that seem to have gone dead on you. Although I was certain you would like it, if it was what I had thought it to be, I had reached the stage where I was no longer sure it was that. So your letter is a grand boost and I feel gratefully revived.

You are undoubtedly right about the flow of unnecessary reiterations here and there. I have never been over this script. I went over the first draft, which Carlotta had typed, cutting and pruning, but I also added a lot of insertions and rewritten sections. Saxe[2] typed this second script and there wasn't time to go over it before he left, even if I had not felt too stale to tackle the job. I was anxious to have him take it back with him, for safety sake, and to have you read it as soon as possible. I knew whatever might still have to be done on the script would be editing stuff and not affect the real values of the play as a whole.

Well, I sure am pleased you think so well of this opus, George! And equally pleased that you write about coming out here this year as if you had definitely decided on it. That's grand. There is a lot to talk over. And I know you will love Tao House and the old rancho.

A bit of good news is that I've just sold the film rights to the four one-act *Glencairn* series plays. It's more than financial luck, too, because the people who bought it are John Ford, who directed *The Informer, Grapes of Wrath*, etc. and his partner, and it is to be done as an independent production. Ford and Dudley Nicholas, who is to write the film version, and whom you will remember as the man on the old *World* who wrote the *Strange Interlude* criticism in Woollcott's place, were up here to talk over their ideas with me. Two fine guys, whom you would like. I am convinced that the intention is to make a picture like *The Informer* with real integrity and no concession to Boy-Meets-Girl, and I believe Ford has enough control over this production so that no one can interfere with his plans. So a really fine film may come out of it, and while I am not much interested in films, as you know, it would please me a lot to have the old *Glencairn* one-acters decently handled in an honest story of the crew on a tramp-steamer voyage. The one big change they had in mind when they were here was to make this voyage present day stuff with the *In The Zone* part [of] this war instead of the last—which is something I would have suggested myself, if Ford hadn't.

Sounds too good to be true, eh? Well, I am keeping my fingers crossed, but if Ford can work with a free hand, I think it will be something. Bob Sisk has an extremely high opinion of Ford as a director. It was through Sisk, by the way, that this *Glencairn* deal came about.

Anyway, whatever happens, the sale is a lucky break for me financially.[3]

Carlotta joins in love to you—and, again, here's much grateful appreciation for your appreciation of *The Iceman Cometh*.

As ever,
Gene

February the 28th 1940

---

1. *The Iceman Cometh.*
2. Saxe Commins.
3. O'Neill sold the film rights for twenty thousand dollars. The film was entitled *The Long Voyage Home* after one of the four one-acters. Artistically well done, the film did not enjoy commercial success probably because it was too somber for contemporary tastes.

TAO HOUSE
DANVILLE
CONTRA COSTA COUNTY
CALIFORNIA

Dear George,

It's too bad the jury duty stuff has upset your plans for a visit out here, but Carlotta and I will keep hoping you can make it at a later date. Any time you like will be all right for us, so do your damnedest to fit it in. We would sure love to have you here. There is so much to talk over, before all the world we've lived in vanishes in this debacle. And there isn't much time left.

You ask about my health. Well, now that swimming time is here again, and thanks to a series of shots I have been taking for low blood pressure, I am pretty fit again—physically. But mentally, spiritually, and creatively I feel like a dead clam—a nerve-ridden, dead clam, if you can imagine such a paradoxical bivalve. Haven't been able to write a line for the past couple of months, or take the slightest interest in work. After I finished *The Iceman Cometh* I started another non-Cycle play, [*Long*] *Day's Journey Into Night*—not concerned with the present world's crisis, as the title might indicate, but the story of one day, 8 A.M. to midnight, in the life of a family of four—father, mother, and two sons—back in 1912,—a day in which things occur which evoke the whole past of the family and reveal every aspect of its interrelationships. A deeply tragic play, but without any violent dramatic action. At the final curtain, there they still are, trapped within each other by the past, each guilty and at the same time innocent, scorning, loving, pitying each other, understanding and yet not understanding at all, forgiving but still doomed never to be able to forget.

But hell, I'll tell you about it when I see you. What I started to say was, I finished the first draft of Act One (five acts in it) and then got physically washed up. On top of that, the debacle in Europe, and I became totally demoralized and have been unable to concentrate on anyting but war news ever since. So there the play rests, and God knows when I'll go back to it. Hardly now, when Paris has fallen and we may soon hear they are fighting for Tours,[1] which is like an old home town to us, as you know. Perhaps Le Plessis will be blown to pieces! This war is hitting us where we belong, so to speak.

And yet, what can one do as a person, remembering the United States first, beyond subscribing to Red Cross and Relief Funds, and what is that? And what can one do as an author who tries to remain an artist? Forget history, forget philosophy, forget the last war and what it did to this country, forget that it was the stupid, double-crossing greed and fear of democratic politicians (particularly the swinish British Tories whom the O'Neill in me loathes, anyway)—that conspired with Hitler to create Nazi Germany, forget all this and everything else a free intelligence should remember because one loves France in spite of its politicians? And then feel it one's duty to devote one's work to a hymn of hate? Well, although I hate Nazism as bitterly as anyone, I can never do that to my work.

But I envy authors who can honestly voice in work of genuine integrity, a belief in salvation through any sociological idealism. Or through Holy Wars. But such faiths are not for me. Or any other faith, I'm afraid, except a profound pessimism, convinced of the futility of all faiths, men being what they are. All I know is, if we must reinvent a God here in America, it had better be a God infinitely more noble than the State, democratic or otherwise. Or else!

My main selfish worry is that now the Cycle recedes farther and farther away, until I cannot imagine myself ever going back to it. It isn't that anything which is happening or may happen can affect the truth of the main theme of the Cycle. Quite the reverse! It proves it! It is I who am lacking, who have been affected to the point where I cannot believe the Cycle matters a damn, or could mean anything to any future I can foresee. And if I become finally convinced it is not in me to go on with it, I shall destroy all I have done so far, the completed plays and everything else down to the last note. If it cannot exist as the unique whole I conceived, then I don't want it to exist at all.

Well, it isn't considerate of me to be wishing this load of woe on you. I know you have enough troubles of your own right now. But the jury duty is a blessing in disguise, isn't it?—I mean, it compels you to forget war news for a while.

Love from us and here's hoping again we will have you here later on.

As ever,<br>Gene

June the 15th 1940

---

1. The O'Neills had lived in their chateau, Le Plessis, only eleven kilometers from Tours, from 1929 to 1931.

TAO HOUSE
DANVILLE
CONTRA COSTA COUNTY
CALIFORNIA

Dear George,

Both Madden and Saxe had already sent me the thing from the *Times*.[1] And before that, I knew Sam Zolotow[2] had nosed out something because he wired me a questionnaire and gave the title. I evaded his questions, telling him the matter was of no importance in this time of crisis, particularly since I regarded no play of mine as ready for production or publication yet. I wouldn't lie to Zolotow, who has always been damned decent to me. Of course, my evasion was as good as an admission the play[3] existed, but there wasn't any other way I could handle it.

I have no idea where the leak came from. Madden didn't know about the play. He knew I had planned to do something outside the Cycle, that's all. Langner[4] and Helburn[5] of the Guild knew that much, too, but no more. Of course, as soon as I saw the *Times* notice, I wrote these three confirming the report and explaining why I hadn't let them see it yet—because I don't want it produced now. I told them they could read it, provided they agree not to talk production afterwards.

The leak is irritating but not important. It will soon be forgotten, if it isn't already.

I will remember what you say about Dowling[6]—when the time comes. I feel he would be the right man, judging from what he has done. But remember this is a Guild play. It automatically comes under my contract with them, and I wouldn't break that contract if I could. The Guild has always dealt honorably with me, and most of its members are friends of mine. But perhaps some kind of hook-up might be arranged by the Guild with Dowling, as was done with the Saroyan play.[7]

However, that's all future stuff-when and if.

We will look forward to *The Bachelor Life*[8]—and meanwhile keep hoping you will have a chance to pay that visit.

Love from us,
As ever,
Gene

July the 19th 1940

---

1. On 14 July 1940, the *New York Times* had announced O'Neill's completion of *The Iceman Cometh*, a new drama that might be part of his nine-play Cycle ("Rialto Gossip: News of the Plans and Some of the Hopes of the Broadway Theatre," sec. 9).

2. Drama reporter for the *New York Times*.
3. *The Iceman Cometh*.
4. Lawrence Langner, codirector of the Theatre Guild.
5. Theresa Helburn, codirector of the Theatre Guild.
6. Eddie Dowling (1894–1976), actor, author, and producer who directed the New York première of *The Iceman Cometh* (1946).
7. In 1940, O'Neill had seen Dowling's performance as Joe in *The Time of Your Life* in San Francisco. The Theatre Guild produced the play, in association with Dowling, who directed. It ran for 185 performances and won both the Pulitzer Prize and the New York Drama Critics Circle Award.
8. Published by Reynal & Hitchcock, New York, in 1941.


TAO HOUSE
DANVILLE
CONTRA COSTA COUNTY
CALIFORNIA

Dear George,

I would be extremely grateful for a mention of *The Iceman Cometh* in your October article.[1] As you say, the leaking is bound to continue now, and it will probably be accompanied by the usual misrepresentation and distortion of the true content of the play through gossip about its sordid surface. A word from you will be regarded as authoritative and will stop a lot of this misleading stuff. I judge from your letter you don't intend to go into details of plot but just to speak of the quality of the play. That's exactly what I'd like. There are certain things about it, though, it might be good to mention, if you have the space—and agree with me: That the play is not "timely" and has no sociological significance, as such significance is defined nowadays. (I mention this because Zolotow had a Communist in it[2]—which, of course, isn't true because there is a world of difference—and hatred—between a Communist and a Communist-Anarchist. The latter is shot on sight in Russia). That it marks a return to the character and spirit of my earlier work, but with a big difference in scope. That a travelling salesman is the character around which the play develops, but there is no "lead" in the usual sense. That it is *Iceman* in the title and not *Ice Man* (which spoils it).

If any of these suggestions strike you as bum stuff, forget it. You know I'm the last one to attempt wishing anything on you. It's merely that, from my angle, it seems desirable people shouldn't get the idea I've jumped the Cycle to do a timely pro or anti anything play—except a pro-drama one; and that they shouldn't expect, because my last known play was *Days Without End*, my next must be pro-Catholic and use masks!

Even though you give us the bad news that it looks doubtful if you can get out here, we are still hoping.

Love from us.
As ever,
Gene

August the 2nd 1940.

---

1. George Jean Nathan, "Coming Plays of the Prizewinners," *Liberty*, 12 October 1940: 29–30.
2. The *New York Times* article of 14 July had listed among the characters of *The Iceman Cometh* "a former leader in the Communist movement" ("Rialto Gossip: News of the Plans and Some of the Hopes of the Broadway Theatre," sec. 9).

TAO HOUSE
DANVILLE
CONTRA COSTA COUNTRY
CALIFORNIA

Dear George,

About the *Iceman* leak, I believe with you that Cerf[1] had nothing to do with it. Nor, of course, did Saxe.[2] But I have a good idea how the amount of dope Zolotow had could have been obtained without coming from anyone who had read the play. Three people besides you, Saxe, and Cerf knew the title and its death double meaning. Everyting else Zolotow printed could come from a glance at the list of characters and scenes, and I know how he could have got that easily. I'll tell you when I see you.

The way I feel about it now, my secrecy precautions were not justified. Both Terry Helburn and Langner understand my attitude about production, and have done no urging. Terry was here last week for a day, and we hardly spoke of that side of it. I suggested to her that I release my titles for the Cycle and two other plays through the Guild publicity department, and she is going to do this. Quite a few people know the Cycle titles—the one for the whole thing and those for the separate plays. Zolotow has wired me several times asking that information. It's bound to leak so I might as well give it out. It may help Guild prestige a little, too, even tho' they know there is no chance of the Cycle being completed for a long, long time, and spike the rumours that keep cropping up that I have had a fight with them. As for the danger of anyone stealing a title or two, I can always dig up another as good or better, if I have to.

Madden's reaction to the *Iceman* is amusing. Reading between the lines of the letter he wrote me after reading it, I know he was deeply shocked and outraged, and ashamed of me for writing about such degenerate scum—especially at a time when our country is in danger. However, I can't help taking this philosophically, because I know in his heart Dick has disapproved of a great number of my plays, and only the fact that we have been friends ever since he became my agent back in 1919 has kept him silent on the matter. He's so damned honest in his omissions. I accused him of not liking *The Iceman Cometh*. He didn't answer that. Then in his last letter he tells me how much you and Langner like it, but he won't say he does!

I've been working hard. Have four-fifths of the first draft of *Long Day's Journey Into Night* finished. And am getting several good new ideas for plays. I think my putting the Cycle on the shelf indefinitely will prove to be a damned good thing. Particularly for the Cycle. When I do take it up again, I hope to be not only somewhat older but somewhat wiser. It can do with a bit more wisdom, and it needs a new orientation inspired by the fresh insight the present world revolution should give its author—if he can be wise!

Much love from us. We've about given up hope of seeing you this year, darn you!

As ever,<br>Gene

August the 30th 1940.

---

1. Bennett Cerf.
2. Saxe Commins.

TAO HOUSE
DANVILLE
CONTRA COSTA COUNTY
CALIFORNIA

Dear George,

Many thanks for the Liberty article.[1] Speaking for the author of *The Iceman Cometh*, it does him proud and hits the exact spot. There won't be so much irresponsible gabble about that play now.

I'm just putting the finishing touches of revision on the first draft of *Long*

*Day's Journey Into Night.* I'm pleased with it, but pretty exhausted because it has taken a lot out of me. So this is just a line from a fagged out guy.

Again, much gratitude, George—and love from us both.

As ever,
Gene

October the 6th 1940

---

1. Nathan, "Coming Plays of the Prizewinners," *Liberty,* 12 October 1940: 29–30.

[postcard, Tao House, California]
Oct. 20*th* '40

Dear George:

Many thanks for the birthday[1] wire! I spent the day singing that dear old New England hymn: "My thoughts on awful subjects dwell, Damnation and the dead."

Love from us
Gene

---

1. His birthdate was 16 October.

## TAO HOUSE
## DANVILLE
## CONTRA COSTA COUNTY
## CALIFORNIA

Dear George,

I can't remember any Mahan. Probably he is one of those barroom drinking acquaintances who knew me when—that is, if we ever met at all. Where and when does he claim the "close crony" stuff happened?

Don't let such guys pester you, George. Why did you bother to see him? You know I would never stand for anyone using me to crash the gate to you, even if I did know him well.

I suspect this Mahan may have a touch in view—as soon as he feels you've become pals!

The past five or six weeks have been an ordeal—flu, followed by bronchitis, and the outside world made me no cheerier by the fact that it has rained nearly every day. All I've done is fiddle around with notes on various ideas—no real work—and I still feel way below par. Blemie's death was a blow. I knew I would miss him badly when he went, but I had no idea how badly.[1]

We are looking forward to *The Bachelor Life*[2] and the *Mercury* article.[3]

I will write you a real letter about work when I pull out of this physical slump. As a matter of fact, the spirits are high as far as work is concerned. *The Iceman Cometh* and *Long Day's Journey Into Night* are, I know, among the best plays I've ever done, and I wrote both within a year and a half. Also I'm full of fresh ideas and enthusiasm for the Cycle, which will come in handy when I return to it, and new ideas for plays outside it. It's these damned physical sinking spells that slow me up. You can't work when you're sick—or, at least, I can't. It's hard enough in these damned days—damned is right!—to think playwrighting important even when I'm feeling fine.

I'm damned sorry to hear you have been ill, too. Be sure and come out this year, and we will do a grand job of groaning in chorus. Tell you all about *Long Day's Journey Into Night* then. It isn't typed yet—I haven't gone over it—but should be by that time. There are good reasons in the play itself why I'm keeping this one very much to myself, as you will appreciate when you read it. It isn't a case of secrecy about a new play merely for this or that practical reason, as with *The Iceman Cometh*.

Much love from us, George.

As ever,

Gene

January 30th 1941

---

1. The O'Neills' Dalmatian had been like a child to them, sleeping in his own four-poster and enjoying his own bathtub. Half-blind, deaf and lame, he lingered, then died on 17 December 1940. O'Neill wrote a sentimental will for the dog and buried him in the garden with an inscribed headstone.

2. Published by Reynal & Hitchcock, New York, 1941.

3. George Jean Nathan, "The Theatre: The Decline of the Playwrights," *American Mercury* 52 (March 1941): 355–60. In this article, Nathan's theme was the general deterioration of the work of contemporary American playwrights (excepting O'Neill).

Tao House

Dear George,

*The Bachelor Life* is grand stuff! I've just finished it. It's a book one should be enormously grateful for these days, I think. I approached it with misgiving—about myself, I mean, reflecting that it wasn't fair to you to tackle it when I felt so mentally low and rotten physically. But it soon had me chuckling delightedly. One of the biggest laughs for me was the bit on air conditioning in summer. I remembered a red hot stifling night when Carlotta and I took an air conditioned train from Georgia. In five minutes both of us had a chill. We had to get extra blankets from the porter to survive the arctic blast. It was a hundred times harder to take than the heat outside.

A great many people ought to welcome this book, George. It *is* nepenthe—and God, how many of us need a bit of nepenthe right now! Let me know how it is received, will you? I'm curious to see if people are already so stupid in war neurosis that they resent wit and charm as unpatriotic frivolities.

Don't you worry about your mention of *Long Day's Journey Into Night* in your *Mercury* article[1] (which I haven't seen yet, being tied down to the house). No secret about my having written a play with that title. I've told a lot of people. The point is, that's all they know, or are going to know, and no fooling about it. I'm not even having it copyrighted so it won't be on record anywhere.[2]

The Mahan guy is pure phoney. Neither Carlotta nor I remember ever meeting anyone from Glendale. I wonder what his game was.

Carlotta is just recovering from intestinal flu. She had a tough time of it for several days and is still woozy. This has been a most unhealthy winter for the O'Neills.

It's fine to hear you hope to come out this year, but we won't believe it until we see you.

Love from us,
As ever,
Gene

February 13th 1941

---

1. In the March 1941 *American Mercury*, Nathan had mentioned the title and that the play was completed (356).

2. Copyrighted in 1955 as an unpublished work by Carlotta O'Neill; published by Yale University Press in 1956. Presented in Sweden in February 1956; in New York, 7 November 1956, Helen Hayes Theatre.

TAO HOUSE
DANVILLE
CONTRA COSTA COUNTY
CALIFORNIA

Dear George,

I have been meaning to write ever since your last letter arrived, but Eugene Jr. came out for a visit and I postponed it until he left. Speaking of him, he is a fine guy and I am extremely fond of him. Also proud. He works hard, keeps his enthusiasm about his job, and is steadily moving ahead at Yale.[1]

My daughter, too, was with us in July, and I can make the same favorable report on her.[2] She is sixteen now, quite pretty and charming and intelligent. So as a parent, I am getting a good break.

It was a big disappointment when you failed to arrive but, of course, I understand why it was not possible. It will not be long, I'm afraid, before none of us will have much to say about what we do, or be able to keep any of the money we earn. I will be especially hard hit by the new taxes, being one of those Forgotten Men, the Alimony Victims. You have no idea what non-deductible alimony on top of these taxes can do to you. For example, if I earn $30,000 I really get only a thousand more than if I'd earned $18,000. So what's the use? It makes me more indifferent than ever about the production of new plays.

You ask about work? Well, in a way I'm suffering from an embarrassment of riches. Since the first of the year, I've written detailed outlines of six new non-Cycle ideas. All of these will make fine plays, I think. One of them is for a series of seven short plays, practically monologues, more to be read than staged, although they can be staged, too, if any producer ever dares do them. I've finished one of them[3] and will send it to you when it is typed. Then you will see better than I can tell you just what I'm trying to do in each and how. Title for all, *By Way Of Obit*, with a separate sub-title for each, the name or nickname of the recently deceased.

I've also written the first scene of one of the other plays. Title, *The Thirteenth Apostle*.[4] But for the most part—where the embarrassment of riches comes in—I have been unable to decide just which one I ought to do first. One day I think this one, the next, that one. There's one entitled *Time Grandfather Was Dead*[5] I've been keen about lately—but I still haven't decided.

Undoubtedly this indecision has a lot to do with the general mental unrest and uncertainty and insecurity everywhere. You can't escape it even in this California valley. It's hard to make your mind stay put. However, if it hasn't been a period of great dialogue labor, it has been one of varied creative activity in ideas. So I am not too depressed by myself, particularly as I have had the very real excuse that my health has had all kinds of bad fluctuations which make hard labor impossible.

What do you think the chances are for the Guild *Ah, Wilderness!* revival?[6] They tell me Carey[7] has the right personality and will do a grand job. I hope so. Later on, they plan to do *Desire Under The Elms*—if they can get the right actress for the woman and Walter Huston[8] for his original part. Who, among present actresses with a following, would you suggest? You know I don't want stars in my stuff for first productions but revivals need "name" casting to overcome New York's apathy to anything but this year's model in cars, plays—and models.

And that, as Elmer Davis, the commentator, says, is the news to this moment.

Love from us, and let us hear from you when the spirit moves.

As ever,
Gene

September the 19th 1941

---

1. By this time, Eugene O'Neill, Jr. was recognized as a brilliant professor of classics at Yale University. He had recently coedited the definitive two-volume work, *The Complete Greek Drama* (New York: Random House, 1937).

2. This was Oona's second visit with her father in eight years.

3. Completed in 1941, *Hughie* was not copyrighted until February 1959, when it was published by Yale University Press. It had its première in Stockholm in 1958, but not until 22 December 1964 was it produced in the United States, at the Royale Theatre.

4. Later called *The Last Conquest*, this was to be a full-length play with a prologue and eight scenes. O'Neill never finished it.

5. This was never developed beyond a scenario.

6. The Theatre Guild had recently decided to revive several of his plays, of which *Ah, Wilderness!* would be first. As it turned out, *Ah, Wilderness!* was the sole play the Guild revived.

7. Harry Carey (1878–1947), a film actor, played the role of Nat Miller.

8. Walter Huston (1884–1950) had played the role of Ephraim Cabot in the original 1924 production.

O'Neill's letter dated 17 October 1941, showing his characteristic closing. By this date the effects of his tremor on his handwriting were more pronounced. (*Courtesy of Cornell University Library.*)

Tao House
Danville
Contra Costa County
California

Oct. 17*th* '41

Dear George:

Just a word of gratitude for your birthday wire. My 53rd found me enjoying a liver attack and hating practically everything. Your message did much to lighten my jaundiced spirits.

I'll be writing you soon. Carlotta joins in love to you.

As ever,
Gene

PREFATORY REMARKS: The following, a handwritten card, appears to be written on holiday stationery. The reverse side reads: "Greetings."

[Tao House, California]
[Dec. 1941]

Dear George:

We are enjoying blackouts each night in our valley—not half as disrupting as I thought they would be. I'm working right along and Carlotta is fine.

Love from us,
Gene

Carlotta

January 17th 1942

TAO HOUSE
DANVILLE
CONTRA COSTA COUNTY
CALIFORNIA

Dear George,

Much gratitude for the inscribed, *The Entertainment Of A Nation*,[1] which I finished reading last night. Again, as for all those that have gone before, my admiring felicitations! It is as keenly alive and stimulating and amusing as all its predecessors. In brief, I like it immensely.

What hit me with particular satisfaction this time, is your chapter on current Irish drama. I agree with you enthusiastically. During the past two years, the Guild has wished two Irish scripts on me they were considering, asking my opinion. My opinion was, Nuts! I honestly could hardly finish the damned things. I love Irish poetical speech where it belongs, but when a poor playwright is playing it up and pumping it out of the mouths of characters, who are dismal garrulous bores you would avoid like the itch in real life, the result is the most irritating brand of tripe I know of.

Many thanks for the Elsa Maxwell[2] thesis! After reading it, I took a hopeful look in the mirror but regretfully decided the original script of her article must have been written in braille.

How is everything with you these chaotic days? From all I hear of New York, I'd say the war is being taken much more seriously on the Coast. There have been several blackouts even in our valley and people obey orders. Although we are thirty miles from San Francisco, this valley and others paralleling it, would, if the houses were lighted, look from the air like lanes leading toward the Bay. So it is important. I am not one of the jackasses who think Frisco can't be bombed. I think, sooner or later, it will be. The Japs hate California more than all the rest of the U.S.A. and it would be a big boost for their morale to sneak a carrier within range to do the job—worth the risk of losing the carrier, I should say. All I hope is, it doesn't happen before they get civilian defense well organized in Frisco—or there will be a terrible mess.

My health has been poor lately and I've had to take daily shots—and give them to myself—to keep the old blood pressure pressuring. So I've done little work. Too sunk. Even if I were fit, I couldn't concentrate now. Or kid myself that plays matter a damn. The mind is in Pearl Harbor, the Philippines, Singapore, etc. I can't take anything else seriously. As far as I'm concerned, the drama is dead for the duration, and what of it?

Much love from us—and again, thank you for *The Entertainment of A Nation.*

As ever,
Gene

---

1. Published by Alfred A. Knopf (New York) in 1942.
2. (1883–1963); New York socialite and internationally known hostess of lavish parties; also an actress and songwriter.

TAO HOUSE
DANVILLE
CONTRA COSTA COUNTY
CALIFORNIA

Dear George:

There is little to report from Tao House except the war-begotten worries that are hitting everyone. Our worst one at present is that Freeman[1] may be drafted any day. You can imagine what that will do to our household. We depend on him so much as a man of all work, who is more like a member of the family than a servant, who can be absolutely trusted and is able to take care of almost any job that comes up. When you live in the country this means a lot. It is practically impossible to hire anyone now to do anything.

They are all in ship yards or in the service. It's a tough time to own a farm, believe me! All the farmers in this valley are rapidly going nuts wondering how they can work and harvest their crops—including the man who farms our place. And we couldn't afford to hire more help, if we could get them. We have had to cut down—have only a cook now—Carlotta has to do a lot of housework. The combination of alimony plus new taxes will take all of any income I earn.

All this—and I haven't mentioned half of the complications—could be borne more cheerfully if we were both in good health. Neither of us are. My tooth trouble would be easy if it was just [a] tooth, but any infection I get now immediately spreads to the weak spots left by my '36–'37 collapse, and I become really ill and good for nothing at all. I needn't say that war nerves do not improve this chronic condition of susceptibility.

I haven't done any work since January and, from the way I've felt lately, never will be able to again. If Saxe[2] reported to you I was active, he only meant what I had reported to you before—that I was full of ideas but found it hard to write any of them. Since then, even that form of activity has run dry. I'm too sick in mind and body. As I wrote you before, I managed to finish a first draft of *A Moon For The Misbegotten*[3] in January but even as a first draft it won't do. After Pearl Harbor I had to drive my mind to keep on being interested—and, of course, that means bad work.

I'm damned sorry to hear your verdict on O'Casey's latest play.[4] I suppose the war has got him, too.

I don't understand Whit Burnett calling you up about the *Anthology*.[5] I wrote him to count me out of it.

There's an idea for a propaganda play I'd like to write—not the usual obvious stuff either in theme or technique, but something which hits at what is behind all this chaos, the realistic attitude which has lost the knowledge of the opposites of Good and Evil within Man and their struggle for possession of Man's soul. I know you regard the word "soul" with scepticism, but I don't mean it in any specific orthodox religious sense. Perhaps if I said Man's spirit it would be as close, but "spirit" is another word that has been worn thin and meaningless by stupid misuse. Anyway, I like the idea for this play, which could be subtitled *An Outmoded Prophetic Fantasy for the Blind and the Deaf*. Its title is *The Last Conquest*.

My daughter, Oona, let herself in for a fine splurge of silliness at the very worst time, didn't she?[6] As you can imagine, I was thoroughly disgusted. Which does me no good, because I have no veto or legal control, and the real influence behind her is shallow and stupid. I expect any day to hear she's caught in the Hollywood racket. Well, as my father often pointedly remarked, "God deliver me from my children." However, I have one compensation. I am justly proud of Eugene, who has gone ahead quietly on his own, shunning all publicity as my son, and is a damned fine guy as well as a brilliant classical scholar.

Look out for that May wine! As I remember it (yum-yum, them dear departed days!) it packed a hangover inferior only to the aftermath of mulled Italian Red Ink taken on top of Jamaica Rum-ginger ale highballs!

Love from us!<br>
As ever,<br>
Gene

May the 21st 1942.

---

1. Herbert Freeman, the O'Neills' chauffeur and utility man.
2. Saxe Commins.
3. Completed in 1942, but not copyrighted until 1945; published by Random House (New York) in 1952. Presented 20 February 1947, by the Theatre Guild at the Hartman Theatre, Columbus, Ohio.
4. Sean O'Casey's *Red Roses for Me* (1942). On 2 June 1942, Nathan wrote O'Casey that he had found "much that is fine" in *Red Roses for Me* but that O'Casey's *Purple Dust* (1940) "remains the superior play, by far" (Robert G. Lowery and Patricia Angelin, eds., *My Very Dear Sean: George Jean Nathan to Sean O'Casey, Letters and Articles* [Cranbury, N. J.: Associated University Presses, 1985], 60).
5. Whit Burnett, ed., *This Is My Best*, an anthology of the work of "America's 93 Greatest Living Authors" (New York: Dial Press, 1942). It included an excerpt from O'Neill's *The Great God Brown*. Nathan was represented by his essay "Aesthetic Jurisprudence" (from *The Critic and the Drama*).
6. The previous month, Oona, not quite seventeen, had been chosen "Debutante No. 1" of the year at the glamorous Stork Club in New York. Aspiring to a theatrical career, she had found such publicity not unwelcome, but her father was outraged at the frivolity of such an event during wartime.

TAO HOUSE<br>
DANVILLE<br>
CONTRA COSTA COUNTY<br>
CALIFORNIA

Dear George:

Under separate cover, I am sending you a script of the one-act *Hughie*— the only one of the series titled *By Way Of Obit* I have so far completed. You will remember I threatened to send you this soon after I finished it a little over a year ago, but I didn't have it typed for a long time, and then didn't go over it for months after that. It is really only recently that I've had a clean typed copy.

I've forgotten how much or little I explained about this series—there will be seven or eight of them if I ever manage to get them all done. *Hughie* is a good example of the technique. In each the main character talks about a person who has died to a person who does little but listen. Via this monologue you get a complete picture of the person who has died—his or her whole life story—but just as complete a picture of the life and character of the narrator. And you also get, by another means—a use of stage directions, mostly—an insight into the whole life of the person who does little but listen.

These plays are written more to be read than staged, although they could be played. But to hell with more explanation. You'll get it all reading *Hughie*.

Some of them will be based on actual characters I've known—some not. *Hughie* isn't. The Night Clerk character is an essence of all the night clerks I've known in bum hotels—quite a few! "Erie" is a type of Broadway sport I and my brother used to know by the dozen in far-off days. I didn't know many at the time the play is laid, 1928, but they never change. Only their lingo does. As for "Erie's" slang, I've tried, generally speaking, to stick to the type's enduring lingo, and not use stuff current only in 1928 but soon discarded. Being too meticulously timely is not worth the trouble and defeats its purpose, anyway.

I'm fond of *Hughie* myself. I'll bet Ring Lardner would have liked it. And here's hoping you do.

Love from us.
Gene

June the 19th 1942

P.S.—*Hughie* is the last in time of all. They range from 1910–1928.

TAO HOUSE
DANVILLE
CONTRA COSTA COUNTY
CALIFORNIA

Dear George,

I am delighted you liked *Hughie*. It has its own quality, I think, which makes it a bit different from anything else of that kind—at least, as far as my knowledge goes. And it gives you an idea of how the others in the series will be done. Of course, they won't all be humorous. Here's hoping I'll get around to writing them. They are clearly mapped out in my mind, and in notes.

You can give the script to Saxe Commins. I'm writing him to get in touch with you. This will save you the trouble of mailing or expressing it back. I want a script kept in New York, anyway—just in case.

Harry Weinberger,[1] with or without shorts, hasn't run up our hill yet. It all depends on whether a big case he has takes him to the Coast or not. We have the oxygen tent and the pulmotor ready to receive him.

Love from us!
As ever,
Gene

July the 7th 1942.

---

1. O'Neill's personal lawyer and long-time friend.

TAO HOUSE
DANVILLE
CONTRA COSTA COUNTY
CALIFORNIA

Dear George:

Much gratitude for your birthday wire. I sure appreciated your remembering. The reason I delayed is that I wanted to do a letter, not just a grateful note, and things have happened in the past week which upset me and kept me on the nervous jump.

"Nervous jump" is no mere expression these days. My "Parkinson's disease" stuff[1] has become progressively worse in the past few years, as it was bound to do, with war strain an added inducement later, until now there are days when it is physically impossible to write at all. This infuriates me, as you can imagine, and that doesn't help. I've never mentioned "Parkinson" to you before. If you know anything about it, you will appreciate my annoyance. It is certainly not the right affliction for war time. No cure, and the remedies to counteract it have such a bad effect on me, I prefer the Parkinson's.

However, I continue to get some work done. Not on new stuff. I feel stopped on that most of the time. Have done a little on *The Last Conquest*[2]—about which I wrote you—but not much. What I have been doing lately is revising one of the Cycle plays, *A Touch of the Poet*—the one which takes place in 1928. I would like to get this one, at least, in final shape. It needs only revising, while the other three that are written need a fairly complete rewriting of their first draft versions.

It seems a bit ridiculous to be bothering about all this, or telling you about it as if it had the slightest importance. The world drama you hear over the radio every day, or read in the papers, is the one important drama of the moment, and one can't write anything significant about that because it's too close and the best one could do wouldn't be half as effective as a good war correspondent's story of the front line. Real Marines in the Solomons, grand and heroic! Stage marines posed by a director against a bum palm tree and a phoney backdrop lagoon, nuts! And what are the real ones dying for? Because it is a plain case for them, and for this country, of kill or be killed. All right, there could not be a better reason, as far as it goes. But beyond that, what for? Who knows now? My own prediction is, for the same kind of peace treaty which has followed all wars, because the same kind of greedy politicians and monkey diplomats will make it. Those boys' trade is never to learn anything, and they are much stupider now than in the days when foxes like Talleyrand, Metternich, and Castlereagh cooked up the relatively intel- ligent Vienna treaty. I cannot understand how anyone who has read history can waste time in sentimental wishful thinking about the next peace. I have no doubt of our final victory in the war, but I have nothing but doubt about our even wanting to force a just peace on Europe—even if that were possible. People have one attitude now, "it must never happen again," but the minute an armistice is signed they will change and be fed up and say "for Christ's sake let's forget the war. We won, didn't we? To hell with it."

Well, well! I didn't mean this letter to play that blues!

What would you think of the idea of publishing *The Iceman Cometh* next year?[3] I've been toying with that notion—just toying, haven't mentioned it to Cerf.[4] Am inclined to think it's a bum hunch, but I would like to know your reaction.

Carlotta joins in love to you. Give our affectionate best to the Dowlings[5] and Julie.[6] And write when you have leisure and give us all the dirt. We need something to cheer us up. This valley is in the depths these days, with all the small tradesmen, etc. being forced to the wall, and the farmers about to cut their throats—all caused by the beautiful bungling of Washington bu- reaucracy!

Yours, Comrade, for any old kind of post-war revolution,

As ever,
Gene

October the 24th 1942.

1. O'Neill had been diagnosed as suffering from Parkinson's disease in February 1942.
2. Earlier called *The Thirteenth Apostle*.
3. The play was published by Random House (New York) in October 1946.
4. Bennett Cerf.
5. Eddie and Rae Dooley Dowling. Eddie directed the 1946 première of *The Iceman Cometh.*
6. Julie Haydon (born 1910), actress, whom Nathan married on 19 June 1955.

PREFATORY REMARKS: This is likely a Christmas card. On one side is the printed message: "The Season's Greetings," with an illustration of the American eagle and flag, patriotic symbols that may date the card to World War II.

[Tao House, California]
[December 1940s]

Much love to you from us both!

Gene

Carlotta

P.S. I'll be writing you a letter soon.

Gene

TAO HOUSE
DANVILLE
CONTRA COSTA COUNTY
CALIFORNIA

Dear George:

Ungrateful of me not to have thanked you for the Luchow[1] memento before this. I was touched by it—but not tempted. The way my nerves are now, one glass of beer would have me weeping on the nearest stranger's shoulder. Or worse, singing a little ditty in his ear.

The reason you haven't heard from me is that there has been much unrest in the O'Neill house. Carlotta was laid up with flu, and we've been suffering with cook trouble. They come—and they go. The precedessor of our present one turned out to be a real looney—and I mean, real! Which is exciting in a wrong way. We were delighted to see the last of her—and when you're delighted to see the cook leave these days, that means something!

Other than the domestic disturbance, there's little news since I last wrote you. I'm rewriting *A Moon For The Misbegotten*, the play Pearl Harbor blew apart, and it's going well. (I knock on wood.) But slowly. It can be something—simple and unusual, comic and tragic. Not easy, technically speaking, because only four characters, and one of them only appears for a short scene at the opening of the play. If I ever get it finished to my satisfaction and typed (which is hard now because Carlotta has little time out from housekeeping for secretarial labors), you shall see it.

It sure would be grand if we could get together and I could tell you about this play, and *The Last Conquest* on which I have done some work, and *Long Day's Journey Into Night,* which I like better than any play I've ever written, and all the new and revised ideas I have about the Cycle, which I will probably never live to get done but which I cannot abandon because it won't abandon me. But I guess we cannot hope for such a session until postwar days.

Love from us and our best to Julie[2] and the Dowlings.[3]

As ever,
Gene

Feb. 24th '43

---

1. One of Nathan's favorite New York restaurants.
2. Julie Haydon.
3. Eddie and Rae Dooley Dowling.

TAO HOUSE
DANVILLE
CONTRA COSTA COUNTY
CALIFORNIA

Dear George:

I should have written long ago but kept putting it off. My only excuse is that affairs in the O'Neill household, under pressure of war conditions, and bouts of illness, have steadily become more complicated and restrictive. You have no idea how much time is absorbed in the mere business of keeping this place from going entirely to pot, and doing the necessary bit of daily eating. Impossible to get help. Carlotta finally decided that the only solution to the cook problem was to do the cooking herself. So now we have no servant at all. It is terribly hard on her. Her health is poor. She has had no experience—has to study cook books—but within a few days of taking on the job she was doing it better than any of the alleged cooks we have had in the past couple of years. A remarkably capable and gallant lady, my spouse! She just goes ahead and laughs it off. But at the end of each day she is utterly exhausted. All this at a time when the doctor tells her she must rest all she can to give her bad arthritic back a chance not to get worse. I feel like hell having to watch her do so much hard work she shouldn't do. Lately, to make matters worse, she contracted a bad dose of poison oak—and that, Brother, is no one's idea of fun! It spread all over her body and she went through hell. But she kept right on the job all through it.

I dry dishes—and this and that. Outside, help the farmer at this and that—taking care of chickens, etc.—in the garden, cut hedges, etc.—but have to watch my step. A little too much of it and bang I suddenly fade out, and my latent ills begin to act up. It happened once already this spring—worked too long on a hot day cultivating around young almond trees, and for a week after I was entirely washed up. This puts an added burden on Carlotta. So I have to be careful, not only for my own sake. This house can't afford anyone laid up in bed.

This is all by way of explanation, not complaint. It's the common lot these days. And there are so many others with greater worries that it would be ungrateful to kick. All I wish is, we were both a bit younger and more physically fit to take it.

Needless to add, Carlotta has little leisure for secretarial duties. One good reason I haven't written. You couldn't read my handwriting now. Parkinson's is worse—and I can't even typewrite without a million mistakes—fingers too aimless plus fact I haven't touched one in twenty years or more and was always bad at it when I did.

Also, needless to add, I'm not writing much.

We were so damned sorry to hear you've been laid up with the old neuralgia. We know what hell you go through with that. Here's hoping it has all disappeared by this. You'd better come out and join us and we'll all compare symptoms and moan low together—that is, of course, if you can make beds, cook, hoe in the Victory garden (which we seem to be raising exclusively for hungry deer and rabbits) and are handy with chickens (with feathers).

Russel Crouse[1] was in Frisco recently. We managed to get in to see him for lunch on our A gasoline ration, with the hardware man in Danville doing the driving for us, and Russel and Lindsay[2] drove out here later for a few hours (but no meals!) with us. It was fine to be able to relax and laugh a bit at one's worries. We enjoyed this break in the old routine a lot.

Love from us and our affectionate best to Julie and the Dowlings.

As ever,
Gene

June the 4th 1943.

---

1. Playwright; had been press agent of the Theatre Guild in the early 1930s.
2. Howard Lindsay (1889–1968), who had coauthored a dramatization of Clarence Day's *Life with Father* in 1939 with Russel Crouse.

TAO HOUSE
DANVILLE
CONTRA COSTA COUNTY
CALIFORNIA

Dear George:

The long silence was due to a tough time I have been through for the past six weeks or more. Started with an abscessed tooth. Before I was over that, I got bronchitis and took to bed. Then, the infection spread to my chronic ailments and they kicked up in great shape and a trained nurse joined the household for awhile. Of course, all this didn't improve the nerves, and the old Parkinson's went wild and woolly.

Well, I'm better now but still not where I was before these incidents occurred. The Park. is still hectic and I have little hope of that doing anything but get still worse. The men you know who have it and take it in their stride evidently are helped by atropin or stramonium or similar drugs. I'm not, and have had to cut out trying them because I react so badly. And probably the men you know were not as nerve-ridden before they acquired the Park. as I was.

The Docs have also discovered I have an adrenal deficiency and I have to drink large tumblers of a mixture of sodium citrate, plain table salt and water with a bit of lemon juice to take the curse off. You can have no idea what a loathsome beverage this is, George. It would never, never become a favorite tipple at Luchow's.

I'm sorry this has to be such a clinical letter, but what the hell, it's the only news I have to report. Also you may get a grin from the picture of me absorbing salt water highballs.

Work? I have not written a line lately, not even a note.

Your *Theatre Book Of The Year*[1] arrived two days ago. Much gratitude for it and for the inscription enclosed in your note. I've read most of the book and will finish it to-night. Again, as year after year, my enthusiastic congratulations! It belongs with the others that have gone before. I can't think of higher praise than that. I get a great feeling of stimulation from it, of renewed interest in the theatre—and, believe me, in my present jaded, dejected state of mind and body, it takes something to do that!

Carlotta joins me in love to you and Julie. I hope my next letter will contain a more favorable report about work.

As ever,
Gene

September the 25th 1943.

---

1. Published by Alfred A. Knopf (New York) in 1943.

TAO HOUSE
DANVILLE
CONTRA COSTA COUNTY
CALIFORNIA

Dear George:

Much gratitude for the birthday note! It did a lot toward making me feel reconciled. And it arrived right on the dot, the morning of the 16th. Wartime mail service being what it is, that was surely luck.

There is nothing much of news to report. Carlotta is again suffering from her bad back, but keeps on with the job in spite of it. I'm feeling a bit better and hope to start work again soon. If and when, I'll let you know what I'm at.

Again, my gratitude, George—and our love to you and Julie.

As ever,
Gene

October the 20th 1943.

TAO HOUSE
DANVILLE
CONTRA COSTA COUNTY
CALIFORNIA

Dec. 1943

Dear George:

Here's wishing you the merriest possible—and much love from us!
Will be writing you soon. Have news—but nothing to do with plays.

As ever,
Gene

PREFATORY REMARKS: Following the sale of Tao House in February 1944, the O'Neills had moved to an apartment at the Hotel Fairmont on Nob Hill in San Francisco, then to a larger apartment at the Huntington Hotel. Tao House had cost about one hundred thousand dollars when built in 1937. The realty tax stamps put the 1944 sale price at sixty thousand dollars, about a forty percent loss.

1075 California Street,
San Francisco
(Apart. 1006)
[Date mark on envelope: March 6, 1944]

Dear George:

This is not the letter I promised you—or, at least, not in the detail it should be. It is mainly to give you our present address. The "news" I was going to write you was that our place was for sale. Well, we had luck—found a buyer quickly—got out at a good price—what we put into it, which is saying a lot.

It had become a case of this place owning us, and it was crushing both of us. Carlotta, particularly, since most of the burden fell on her. We had loved it but we were getting to hate it because we were slaves to it—always living in daily uncertainty and insecurity. Well, I'll go into details about all this later.

We left a week ago—were fortunate to find this apartment here. Intend to stay here until at least the German part of the war is over. Carlotta, worn out, started relaxing by catching some infection. Now she's in bed. Taking sulphur. Her condition was serious last night—trained nurse here, etc.—temp. 104! She's better tonight, thank God!

All is sold, automobiles, furniture, everything except books! It's a relief to be free of possessions.

More anon. I hope you can read this. I loaded up with bromide & chloral to get my hand steady enough to give you a break. Carlotta won't be able to type for some time.

Much love from us, George—and please forgive my not writing you sooner. The hell of wanting to write a long letter is that you keep putting it off.

As ever,
Gene

P.S.

I'm all shot nervously—but otherwise holding up. This part from rush of selling, packing, moving, etc. has been a great upheaval and strain.

P.S. II

Just got a wire telling me of Harry Weinberger's[1] death. It hits me hard. Twenty-eight years of friendship. It started with him doing work for me for nothing—as he did for so many. There was a lot of extraordinary fineness in Harry that few people ever gave him due credit for. I shall miss his ever loyal and generous friendship. I only hope he knew the depth of my affection for him—and I feel sure he did.

---

1. O'Neill's personal attorney and old friend.

[San Francisco]
July 11th 1944

Dear George:

The photograph of your portrait arrived yesterday and we have had much debate over it. We like it—and we don't like it. I suppose that is the usual reaction to any portrait of a friend. What do you think of it, yourself? Of course, photographs of a portrait almost always fail to do justice to the original, because the colour is lost. We'd like to see the portrait itself before going on record with any final opinion. And then it is so long since we've seen you, we don't know how you look now.—I mean, how much the intervening years have changed you. We do know they sure have changed us a lot.

Well, it won't be long now before we can be together again. As I guess I wrote before, we expect to come East before the first of the year. That's definite—if we can get a place on a train. But just when before year's end we will be able to leave here depends a lot on personal affairs. For one thing, Carlotta has been continuously ill during the past four months since we sold the place. All kinds of doctors—the best—and they have cleared up some of her ailments, but don't seem able to get at the root of all her afflictions yet. She has gone through a lot of pain and still has to. We have a nurse here, week days, and damned lucky to get one. So you see, our departure date depends a lot on Carlotta's getting on her feet again.

As for me, well you know what being cooped up in a city apartment does to me. The old Parkinson's has spells now worse than ever before, accompanied by fits of the direst depression, as I believe is symptomatic. Anyway, it's hell. I don't bother going to doctors anymore about it. It's futile. If they're honest, they confess there's nothing they can do about it. My only medical calls are for treatments on other matters that can be helped.

We shall be glad to see the last of the Coast. For the past four years or more—leaving the war and its effect out of it—we seem to have lived under a jinx here—sickness—upsetting family matters from both sides of the family, etc. I agree with the W. C. Fields gag when he tells the stooge his aunt has just died and the stooge remarks sympathetically, "It must be hard to lose a close relative" and Fields retorts, "Hard? It's practically impossible!"

No news about work. I can't do any. And our return East will not mean I have made any plans for a production of *The Iceman*. I haven't. That has nothing to do with it. We are just eager to get away from here and change our luck.

Love from us to you and Julie.
As ever,
Gene

October the 9th 1944

Dear George:

Alas, this letter has sad tidings. Our coming to New York in November is out. The doctors have said no, decidedly precarious to jump from seven years of Coast weather smack into a New York winter—in the present state of both our healths. And although we are bitterly disappointed—we had transportation arranged and everything—we have to admit there is sense in what they say. After all, it will be only a few months and we are comfortably situated here (as far as apartments go). We can leave around the first of April.

And the one thing we don't want is to arrive in New York and have one or both of us go into a nose dive and be laid up. We have had our fill of that during the past year and a half.

All the same, I'm not as reconciled as the above sounds. I want to be East again. Ever since we sold our house—or even before that, when it became such a worry and a burden—I've felt that life out here had become meaningless.

The copy of your *Theatre Book of the Year*[1] arrived two days ago. I've read it. It's the same you—and for the nth time, my congratulations! But what a dull season!

Much love from us to you and Julie. Don't give us up as hopeless. We'll make it yet!

As ever,
Gene

1075 California Street
San Francisco
California

---

1. Published by Alfred A. Knopf (New York) in 1944.

October the 19th 1944

Dear George:

Your hunch that the *Theatre Book* did not fetch me is honestly all wrong. As a matter of fact, it was exactly the humour which came as a particular God send this time. I got many and many a laugh from it—and it's pretty hard for me even to chuckle at anything these days. For example, I've always been able to witness political campaigns with a sardonic grin at their abject buffoonery & hypocrisy. But this one simply wearies and disgusts me.

What I think caused your feeling about my letter was that you sensed the mood of bitter despondency in which it was written. I really should not have mentioned your book while the blues were on my neck, but I wanted you to know I had received it, and when I wrote "It's the same you" I considered it as the highest compliment. Also, you know I agree that the best way to slap down bad plays is with humour. But the season you describe did make me blue because I remembered how much new life and ambition for a real theatre was rising from beneath the surface of Showshop during World War I, and that it persisted, war or no war. If anything like that exists now, I haven't heard of it. Let's hope a similar spirit springs up after this war. I doubt it, though. There will be too much against it, too many financially tempting mob-entertainment mediums—radio, television, the movies (as powerful as they are now and were *not* in '14–'18).

Well, better not get on that subject or I'll never stop! Much gratitude for your birthday greeting and love from us to you and Julie.

As ever,
Gene

1075 California Street
San Francisco

P.S.

No, the San Francisco winter is mild—plenty of rain but no real cold, snow, freezing or anything like that—temperature rarely below fifty.

[San Francisco]
Sept. 16th 1945

Dear George:

Many thanks for the clipping. I sure hope your prophecy about *The Iceman Cometh* will prove correct.[1] That, however, will not be put to proof this coming season. The time now all depends on when Eddie wears out his present big success.[2] (How happy we were when we heard he had struck gold at last!) As you know from the letters of the past, I made it an absolute *"must"* that whenever I did release *The Iceman Cometh*, Eddie *must* play the part and also direct the play *if he* felt able to direct in addition to the long and tough job of playing Hickey.[3]

What I really started this letter to tell you was, that the last play I half wrote in '41 before Pearl Harbor, and then finished in '43 is at last typed and I am sending you a copy as soon as I can find a cover for it—not so easy to get now.

I'll say nothing about this play except that I like it a lot—and I hope you do. The title is *A Moon For the Misbegotten*. Please keep this under your hat for the present. It cannot be produced until the '46–'47 season, and the least said about it now the better.

Carlotta and I continue to suffer from ill health spells and I'm so sick of this apartment I wish they'd give me a short stretch at Alcatraz just to enjoy the sea breezes, a change of view, and the interesting company. We are longing to get East and will surely make it by the end of March.

Yes, a long talk with you is long overdue and will, I know, do me a lot of good. I have become so apathetic about the theatre that I really don't give a damn whether any play of mine is ever produced again or not. I have to fake an interest.

Carlotta joins me in love to you and Julie—

As ever,
Gene

---

1. In the August 1945 *American Mercury*, Nathan had predicted: "If Eugene O'Neill saw fit at last to permit the production of his play, *The Iceman Cometh*, . . . it would win both the Pulitzer and Critics Circle prizes hands down and would be a great box-office success to boot" ("Predictions and Reflections," *American Mercury* 61 [August 1945]: 175).
2. Eddie Dowling was directing *The Glass Menagerie* (in which he also played the role of Tom). The play had opened in New York on 1 April 1945.
3. Ultimately, Dowling did direct *The Iceman Cometh;* but it was James Barton who played the role of Hickey.

PREFATORY REMARKS. A three year gap occurs in the letters because of the O'Neills' return in October 1945 to New York, where the playwright and the critic could see each other again. In generally declining health, his tremor worse, O'Neill nevertheless enjoyed a more active social life as he took part in the production of *The Iceman Cometh*, which opened on Broadway in October 1946.

In mid-January 1948, the O'Neills briefly separated. Shortly thereafter the playwright fell and fractured his shoulder. In April, during his hospital stay, he and Carlotta were reconciled. Then they moved to Boston to take advantage of its excellent medical facilities. Within a month of their arrival, they bought land on a far point by the sea, at the tip of Marblehead Neck, which had a view of the coast and the harbor.

## POINT O'ROCKS LANE    MARBLEHEAD NECK, MASSACHUSETTS

Dec. 3rd, 1948

Dear George:

I have postponed writing to you until we were really settled here a while, and the last disturbing plumber had flown. What I could have given you before this, by way of news, would have bored you to tears—the tale of anyone who builds or rebuilds a house at this time. You've heard all about it, I know, from friends who are doing, or have done it. The one thing that really matters is that we had to have a home and now we have it—a delightful little place—interior as simple and charming and comfortable as only Carlotta could make it—as I am writing I glance out the window and see nothing but ocean. And the house is dry and warm! We had it completely insulated when rebuilding. We are not isolated, either. The home right behind us is occupied the year round, although most of the places here are for summer only. More and more people are deciding to stay here all winter because it is warmer than Boston.

I hope to return to my old occupation of playwrighting before too long. God knows I have plenty of ideas, and the tremor which had me stopped for so long—along with war, critics, hotels, and apartments—seems now to affect my hands less—while in my legs it is much worse! Some eminent Docs in Boston are really going after tremors, it being recognized at last, so I believe, that there are more than one kind celebrated by Parkinson. At any rate, there is hope in what appeared to be hopeless—as this letter, written without aid of medicine or psyschiatry (spelling?) proves.

Well, enough of me. I just wanted you to know how things are with me. When the mood strikes you, drop me a line and let me know what's new on the Rialto & what you and Menck.[1] last devoured at Luchow's.

As ever, love to you and Julie—in which Carlotta joins!

Gene

P.S.

I need not tell you, no truth in rumors (Bobby J.[2] sent me a clipping) of my rewriting *A Moon For The Misbegotten* or *A Touch of the Poet* for current production. I don't want production now and I've done no work on the scripts at all.

There is a chance of musical version of *Desire Under the Elms*—not lighter stuff but serious play—opera so to speak—(Jo Mielziner[3] had the idea and is handling it)—but no contract yet—Take year or two to do it, anyway.

Other news: I am owed 36000 reich marks royalties. What shall I do about it? And the lire they have for me in Italy. Stupendous! But I guess I better not do anything about that, either!

---

1. H. L. Mencken.
2. Robert ("Bobby") Edmond Jones.
3. (1901–76); renowned Broadway set designer.

George Jean Nathan and H. L. Mencken. *(Courtesy of Cornell University Library.)*

## POINT O'ROCKS LANE    MARBLEHEAD NECK, MASSACHUSETTS

Dear George:

I should have dictated a reply to your letter of March 6th long before this but I have been feeling so lousy since almost the day after I wrote you that cheerful, hopeful letter, that I haven't felt up to anything. If there have been gloomy reports in the papers, as you say, they are the truth. The damned tremor has been giving me hell. As for writing a new play, that pipe-dream seems as remote and unattainable as memorizing the *Encyclopedia Britannica*.

So much for the gloomy reports you have seen. What bothers me much more are those well meant but false reports saying my tremor has been completely cured. I *know* about these reports because of the flood of letters from the sufferers who write asking for what medicine cured me, who my doctor is, etc. They all saw the report in a newspaper, and they believed it. They have tried everything. I can only answer that there is no truth in such reports, that I have tried everything, too, with only bad results. Most of these letters are extremely sad and anything but a boost to my morale—or to Carlotta's. She is crippled and in pain[1] practically all the time, and yet has to answer them for me.

Lately, I have even received letters of this kind from England, Belgium, Holland and Germany! So you see how a little well meant ballyhoo can kick back. If I only had some hope to offer these people it would be wonderful, but I have nothing.

Yes, I can well imagine you have your full share of ailments. The wonder to me is, how you can keep up and not collapse under a heap of bad plays before the rare good one turns up. You can still write—and as well as ever. I guess that is the secret.

Carlotta joins me in all best to you and Julie.

As ever,<br>Gene

March 20th 1949

---

1. From arthritis.

All his life, O'Neill was irresistibly drawn to the sea. From Provincetown to Bermuda to Sea Island, Georgia, and finally to Marblehead Neck, Massachusetts, he made his home nearby. *(Courtesy of Thomas Yoseloff.)*

POINT O'ROCKS LANE
MARBLEHEAD NECK
MASSACHUSETTS

Dear George:

You have not heard from us because all our news has been monotonous and dolorous—that is, Carlotta's arthritis has continued to plague her, and so has my tremor.

Since I wrote you last I tried out one more experimental nostrum—enormous white pills increasing per diem. The result was very bad and only left me a little more hopeless.

As for writing, that is out of the question. It is not only a matter of hand, but of mind—I just feel there is nothing more I want to say.

I know from your letter that you are feeling in a brighter state than this, so sometime, when the Muse hits you, drop me a line about this, and that, and the other.

Love from us—
Gene

August the 27th 1949

# AFTERWORD

When Eugene O'Neill was trying to market his plays in 1917, George Jean Nathan, already well established, gave him important recognition. Publishing O'Neill's one-acts in *Smart Set,* he and his coeditor H. L. Mencken introduced the young playwright to an audience far beyond the stage of the Provincetown Players. Nathan's subsequent urging of producers to back O'Neill helped persuade John D. Williams to risk bringing *Beyond the Horizon* to Broadway. *Beyond,* in 1920, made O'Neill a rising star.

It is likely that a dramatist of O'Neill's magnitude would have realized success without Nathan's support. But certainly the critic speeded his acceptance. Nathan, sensing a waiting audience for serious drama and recognizing the premier talent of the playwright, had acted boldly. O'Neill's gratitude set the tone as the friendship began.

O'Neill was too independent to settle easily into a protégé-mentor relationship. Rather, he shared with Nathan a growing camaraderie. Over the years together they would enjoy eating peanuts at baseball games, singing bawdy ballads around O'Neill's player piano, and contemplating a Mediterranean cruise. But beyond the good times, the common touchstone of playwright and critic was excellence in drama. The O'Neill-Nathan friendship lasted for decades because they shared a passionate commitment to establishing in America a drama that was significant and honest.

Eugene O'Neill and George Jean Nathan regarded one another as equals, each pursuing this ideal in his respective domain. Theirs were contrasting sensibilities. While Nathan had chosen the Grand Tour, the rite of passage of the well-bred young man, O'Neill had shipped out with sailors to South America. He was at home in the waterfront saloons and flophouses, with the outcasts he later immortalized in drama. Nathan was not, but he could appreciate O'Neill's celebration of those people of the slums.[1] Perhaps most compelling were the playwright's authentic characterizations and dialogue, bearing the imprint of his spiritual kinship with the destitute, the lonely, the forgotten. The critic recognized the truths that O'Neill's uncommon empathy with the less privileged moved him to expound in his art. In his own writing, Nathan rarely delved beneath the surface of things. He depended upon his sparkling wit to dazzle his readers as he exposed dramatic sham. Yet he could appreciate O'Neill's exploration of the profound.

When Eugene O'Neill died on 27 November 1953, he was buried as he had wished, in a simple private ceremony, attended only by his wife and his nurse. The following Sunday Carlotta wrote: "Dearest George Jean: The Master is gone. I am alone . . . It has been a long hard pull, as you know, but now it is over———. . . the Master always loved you———&, so do I!"[2]

After O'Neill's death, his reputation waned for a while. Though occasional articles about him appeared, no major production of his work was staged in 1954 or 1955. Then, in 1956, his widow was persuaded to allow a production of *Long Day's Journey into Night* by the Royal Dramatic Theatre in Stockholm. Although O'Neill had indicated the play was not to be released until twenty-five years after his death, she understood that he had expected it might be released earlier and had wanted the Swedish company to undertake it. *Long Day's Journey's* success abroad prompted a demand for a New York production. Meanwhile, that May a highly successful revival of *The Iceman Cometh* took place in a small Greenwich Village theater. The play was presented in the round, giving the audience a feeling of intimacy with the long play's large cast. Starring as Hickey was Jason Robards, Jr., whose superb performance was instrumental in establishing this production as far superior to the 1946 original. It ran for 565 performances. Carlotta O'Neill was so pleased she asked that director José Quintero also stage *Long Day's Journey*, which opened on 7 November 1956, running for 390 performances. It starred Fredric March, Florence Eldridge, Robards, and Bradford Dillman, as, respectively, the characters based on James, Ella, Jamie, and Eugene O'Neill.

The now elderly critic called the play "a grinding study in recrimination and bitterness, . . . permeated with the mercy and understanding that has always been the mark of the O'Neill drama. There is in it all the underlying charity of a big heart's big feeling." The result was "an impressiveness and depth of feeling not even remotely matched in his contemporaries' writings."[3] Critics everywhere echoed his judgment, and the play easily won both the Pulitzer and the New York Drama Critics Circle prizes. As *Long Day's Journey* was O'Neill's eulogy for his family, so too was its critical veneration a eulogy for the playwright, marking the start of his posthumous ascendancy.

Decades later, audiences are still moved by O'Neill revivals. His stature as the foremost American dramatist is secure. And at least a part of George Jean Nathan's place in the pantheon of drama rests upon his early recognition of the talent of Eugene Gladstone O'Neill.

## NOTES

1. Charles Angoff, "George Jean Nathan," *Altantic* (December 1962): 45–46.
2. Letter from Carlotta Monterey O'Neill to George Jean Nathan, 6 December 1953, Cornell University Library.
3. George Jean Nathan, "George Jean Nathan on Eugene O'Neill," *Esquire* 47 (June 1957): 101.

# INDEX

Page numbers in bold type refer to illustrations.